D1530436

Zanzabuku

ZANZABUKU

[*dangerous safari*]

LEWIS COTLOW

RINEHART & COMPANY, INC.,   NEW YORK • TORONTO

PUBLISHED SIMULTANEOUSLY IN CANADA BY

CLARKE, IRWIN & COMPANY, LTD., TORONTO

Acknowledgments

No African expedition that leaves the centers of civilization can succeed without the active help of scores of people. When the purpose of the trip is to take authentic and meaningful motion pictures of African tribes and wild animals, such assistance is all the more essential. Every time I encountered an obstacle—and they were legion—there was someone who took time and expended effort to help me overcome it. On my three African expeditions I have received such help in abundance from officials high and low, military leaders, businessmen, corporations, missionaries, doctors, naturalists, hunters, African chiefs and their tribesmen. I owe much of whatever I have accomplished to these people, and I can only express my deep gratitude and humble thanks to them all, naming here but a few of those to whom I feel particularly indebted:

Sir Frederick Crawford, Deputy Governor of Kenya, who during my third expedition went beyond the ordinary call of courtesy to help salvage my project when it was seriously threatened. Other officials in East Africa, notably Col. Merwyn Cowie, Head of National Game Parks, Kenya; Gerald H. Swynnerton, Head of Game Department, Tanganyika; G. W. M. Holmes, Warden, Queen Elizabeth Park, Uganda; William H. Hale, Game Warden, Kenya; Leslie E. Whitehouse, District Commissioner, Lodwar, N.F.D., Kenya; District Officer Riley, Monduli, Tanganyika; Kenneth Cowley, Native Commissioner, Kenya; Eric White, East African Information Service. And the chiefs of two other British Information Offices, Major E. B. Omerod in New York and Harold Evans in London.

Pierre Ryckmanns, Governor General of the Belgian Congo during my first African expedition and now head of the Belgian delegation to the United Nations; Eugene Jungers, Governor of

Ruanda during my first expedition, now honorary Governor General of Belgian Congo, and many other Belgian officials in the Congo, notably Commandant Ernst Hubert of the Albert National Park; Phillippe Veys, Territorial Administrator, Mambasa, Belgian Congo; Alfred Synave, Territorial Administrator, Kisenyi, Belgian Congo. And also two outstanding Belgian representatives in America, Baron Dhanis, Attaché for Belgian Congo Affairs, Washington, D.C.; and Dr. Jan-Albert Goris, Commissioner of Information for Belgium and the Belgian Congo, New York City.

General Matthew Ridgway, former Chief of Staff, U.S. Army, who on my third African expedition, as on my last venture into the Upper Amazon, opened many doors and smoothed my path. Lt. General Sir Dudley Ward, Deputy Chief of the Imperial Army, whose words to the British Colonial Office served to add even greater energy to the active co-operation I always received from East African officials. Sir Geoffrey de Havilland, whose letters to East Africa unrolled several red carpets on that rough terrain.

K. T. Keller and the Chrysler Corporation, who contributed the remarkable Dodge trucks which carried me and my men and equipment over thousands of miles of mountain, desert and veldt.

Many missionaries of numerous denominations, especially Father Albert J. Nevins, of Maryknoll, N.Y.; Father Joseph A. Reinhart, of Rosana Mission, Tarime, Tanganyika; J. A. Schoeman, of the Seventh Day Adventist Mission at Tarime, Tanganyika; F. G. Reid, Seventh Day Adventist Mission, Musoma, Tanganyika; Dr. George W. Allen, former medical missionary in Nigeria, later of Nairobi, Kenya, and now of Portland, Oregon.

Robert Buell, American Consul General in Leopoldville, Belgian Congo, during my second expedition, the kind of public servant of whom Americans can be most proud.

Mrs. Margot Rydon, Arusha, Tanganyika, whose sincere and unselfish interest in what I was trying to accomplish prompted her to bring me together with August Kuenzler, who by permitting us to accompany his wild animal capturing ventures, made possible the filming of several exciting action sequences.

Herbert J. Yates, President of Republic Pictures, whose interest and confidence made my third African expedition possible; Harry C. Mills of New York City, a valued friend who first envisaged my association with Republic for the production of "Zanzabuku"; Reginald Armour, Vice President of Republic Pictures of Great Britain.

Dr. James P. Chapin, American Museum of Natural History, who has for many years given me invaluable encouragement and inspired me for all of my expeditions.

Maxwell A. Kriendler, whose never-failing interest in my projects has been on a number of occasions a great help.

Dr. Emory Ross, former Executive Secretary Africa Committee, Division of Foreign Missions, and his successor, George W. Carpenter, for suggestions and advice; and Kenneth Brett-Surman, of California Texas Oil Co., Ltd., for more of the same, since no author can have too many good suggestions.

RKO Radio Pictures for permission to reproduce some still pictures from "Savage Splendor," the film made in the course of the Armand Denis-Lewis Cotlow African Expedition.

Republic Pictures of Great Britain for permission to reproduce some of the still pictures from "Zanzabuku," the film made on my Third African Expedition.

Marshall McClintock, for editorial help in preparing this book.

LEWIS COTLOW

New York City, April 20, 1956

Contents

Zanzabuku

I

In Search of the Primitive

IT was late afternoon, and the sun's rays which had been so bright and hot during the day were now subdued and pleasantly warm in the cool breeze that began to tell us how cold the night would be. I felt tired but satisfied, for after hours of jouncing over the rock-strewn plains in a hard-riding truck I had filmed the lion shots I wanted. My spine tingled when I recalled the baleful look of the lioness as she raised her blood-smeared head from the zebra carcass and stared at me. It was a good camera shot from fifteen yards.

Now we relaxed—the two white hunters, native gun-bearer, and I—and enjoyed the cups of tea that welcomed us back to our camp. It stood at the edge of an acacia grove and looked out over broad grass-covered veldt, with thick forest off to our right and some scrub growth along a donga at the left. This dried-up riverbed still held a few waterholes where animals gathered at dusk from miles around.

Mafuta touched my shoulder and said, "*Bwana!*" I followed his pointing finger and saw a strange procession as it crested a slight rise of ground about two hundred feet away and headed for the donga. The central figure was a lion, one of the most majestic lions I have ever seen, huge and black-maned. He walked slowly and deliberately, with the subtle grace and hidden power of all cats—but above all with awe-inspiring dignity.

The lion did not see us—or if he did would not deign to acknowledge our existence with a glance. He did not, indeed, seem to recognize the existence of any other living creature, and this was most difficult because he was surrounded by a throng of jeering animals that usually serve as his tastiest meals.

I say they jeered, although they made no sound. Just in front of the lion cavorted three wildebeests, usually the awkwardest of all antelopes, with their wrinkled skins and grotesque beards and their impression of being assembled from spare parts of other animals. On this occasion they were acting as comical as they looked, kicking their heels clumsily, almost in the lion's face, and leaping as if in imitation of the graceful impala. They were so close to the lion that I wondered if they had forgotten that wildebeests are a lion's favorite food. But this lion did not notice them, even when they kicked up clouds of dust in his eyes.

Bringing up the rear were four or five slope-haunched topis, their reddish-brown skins glistening in the sun. They made mock charges toward the king of beasts, darting swiftly within ten feet of him, taunting him with their lack of fear. Flanking the lion on either side were six or eight Thomson's gazelles, graceful little "Tommies" with long, slightly curved horns and eternally twitching tails. On this occasion their tails were wagging twice as fast as usual and each flick was an insult flung at the haughty lion.

There was only one possible interpretation of this scene and we all agreed on it. The lion had recently awakened from his afternoon siesta beneath a bush on the edge of the forest and found that he wanted a drink. He headed across the plain for the waterhole. Several herds of animals had seen him. They knew either that he had eaten recently or could not, in any event, catch them in broad daylight on the open plain. They seized the opportunity to taunt and humiliate him, with every mocking gesture, with every kick of their heels and flick of their tails.

There was only one recourse for the lion, of course—to ignore completely the mocking actions of these small fry, these fresh and impudent creatures which he could kill with one blow of his paw. They did not exist. Just once, in that long and embarrassing march across to the waterhole, did he stop. Then he looked contemptuously at the topi behind him. All the other animals stopped, too, and stood stock still. Then the lion decided that the topi was too far away for one spring, and he might make himself look silly. He turned his eyes forward again and took up his dignified walk.

We desperately wanted to get pictures of this unbelievable scene, but the light was bad by that time of day and what there was of it streamed directly into the lenses of our cameras. So we rushed to one of the trucks and tried to circle around in position for some shots that might possibly turn out all right. At the sound of the motor, however, all the antelopes took fright and darted away. The lion continued his solitary march until he disappeared in the bush near the waterhole. It was a sad thing to have missed filming this scene but a wonderful thing to have seen it at all and recorded it in memory.

That scene and that memory will tell you just a little bit about why I like Africa and have gone back to it for three long trips. There are hundreds of others, too, such as the lone ostrich we saw one day, sitting in the middle of a hot sandy plain. It was a big male bird, apparently taking its turn at sitting on some eggs while mama was off looking for food. As we approached in the truck, it rose to its feet nervously and took flight—but not the normally swift flight of the ostrich. It let one wing flop uselessly at its side, and its gait was almost a halting limp. The bird was obviously feigning a wound to entice us into pursuit which would lead us away from the precious eggs.

But it was the eggs that interested us—nine of them lying in a slight depression that could not be called a proper nest, scarcely hidden in the sparse grass. One had already been cracked, but the emerging chick had died in its futile efforts to force its way out. This told us that the other eggs were probably just about ready to hatch.

It was too late in the day for pictures even if we had witnessed some action, but we returned to the spot the next morning, this time frightening away the female, who also acted the part of a wounded and easily caught bird. She finally stood some distance away and watched while we set up our cameras and trained them on the cluster of big eggs. Then we just waited. We might have sat there for several days, of course, but this time luck was with us. Within an hour there was a pecking sound in one of the eggs, which rocked slightly from the struggles of its occupant to fight his way to freedom and life.

Our cameras turned as the egg cracked and one small piece fell to the ground. The scrawny head and neck of the ostrich chick emerged, and the little fellow blinked furiously at the blinding sunlight. But his struggles were not over, by any means. He pushed and shoved and strained to force his body up through the jagged little hole, pecking at the sides to chip away another segment of the tough shell. Two more pieces cracked off, but still the chick was held fast, this time by the umbilical cord that bound him and tried to keep him prisoner in the egg. The little chick twisted and turned and tugged, collapsed occasionally with exhaustion, returned each time to the battle.

Finally the baby ostrich burst from the shell. He lay panting on the hot sand for a few seconds, still wet and glistening, then tried to stand on his feet. He pushed himself up, but his spindly legs had no strength, and he fell—beak and eyes plunging into the sand. There was anger as well as determination in the next attempt, but another crash followed. There was no stopping this little fellow, however. He just kept at it as if his life depended on it, as of course it did. Within ten minutes the ostrich stood unsteadily on his own two feet and looked around curiously at the world that was to be his home—a world of jackals and hyenas and wild dogs and other lovers of ostrich eggs and ostrich chicks. The wonder was that the eggs had not been eaten long before, and it was difficult to understand how any ostrich managed to survive to maturity.

We returned again the next morning and once more the female limped away from the nest. But the little ostrich that had fought his way to life the day before was not running away from anything. He cocked his head on one side and stared perkily up into the cameras, full of confidence and the juices of life. He was going to pack a mighty hard wallop in his legs when he grew up, and we wished him luck in a tough career as we drove away.

That's the sort of fascinating thing you can see in Africa just by being there for a short time, traveling off the beaten paths, and looking. You don't need to be a big-game hunter or daring explorer. Africa shows you everything.

It shows plenty of death as well as life, of course. In the same area we encountered the lone sick zebra. We concluded that it must be sick, since only the very old, wounded, or sick are abandoned by a zebra herd. And this fellow looked quite young, about half-grown. He stood still and looked rather wistfully at us as we approached, but we slowed down and stopped for zebras often panic and run at the sound of automobiles and men. This zebra was different. He was lonely, bewildered, lost. We got out of the truck and stood near it, making no sudden motions to frighten the poor animal. Slowly and hesitantly he walked toward us, stopping occasionally because of his natural fear, coming on again because of his desperation. In time he came close enough for us to pet him. He was obviously quite sick and unsteady on his legs, but there was nothing we could do for him so we drove on.

About a mile away we saw a pack of wild dogs loping along in the direction from which we had come. In a few minutes they would catch the scent of the lone zebra and would be on him in a flash, ripping the flesh from his bones, tearing open his belly to get at his entrails. We didn't like the thought, so we turned around and drove back to the zebra who actually seemed happy at our return. Ace Du Preez put a bullet through his head. At least his death was quick this way, without the terror of the wild dogs bearing down on him.

Only human beings—and so-called civilized human beings at that—would feel concern for one lost zebra. Most animals have little sentimentality within them and can be thoroughly cruel to their fellows. But a lioness will baby-sit for another lioness with cubs while mama goes off to get some food. An elephant will help a wounded comrade from the field to safety, will make a long detour to mourn silently at the grave of a lost mate. A male gorilla will sleep at the foot of a tree in which the mother and young ones are safely tucked for the night. I've seen most of these things and photographed many of them in color, and for every incident I've mentioned there are fifty more stored in my memory as a result of three trips to Africa. Is it any wonder that I have returned and stayed longer each time?

Of course there are hordes of mosquitoes that threaten to destroy you, clouds of locusts so thick that you cannot see ten feet ahead, flies that bite as if they carried pincers—some bearing the deadly trypanosome of sleeping sickness—and ants that can strip the flesh from an elephant in a couple of hours. There are chiggers and worms and poisonous snakes by the millions. There are days of rain, rain, rain when no pictures can be taken, no cars can be driven, no clothing can be dried. But all these unpleasant aspects of Africa seem to fade from memory rather quickly.

Still vivid, however, is the recollection of an evening in the heart of the Ituri Forest when the Pygmy hunters came home from their day's labor. They were successful, so the strange barkless hunting dogs were allowed to race ahead, the wooden clappers around their necks beating a happy refrain. The little brown-skinned hunters marched into the village singing, shouting, laughing, waving their tiny bows and arrows, pointing triumphantly at the antelope they had killed. Women and children raced around making a bedlam of joyous sound, and soon there was feasting, gorging and universal gluttony. When the eaters could move again they started dancing, and kept me awake far into the night.

I recall an afternoon's visit with three Watussi princesses—as lovely and aristocratic as the women of any continent. And I still feel, when I look at their pictures, the appeal of the sensuous Mangbetu women. I remember fishing in the roaring rapids of the Congo with the Wagenia fishermen, catching crocodiles along with hundred-pound perch with the Turkana tribe in Lake Rudolf, seeing the deadly charge of the spear-bearing

Masai who had gone beserk as they raced toward our cameras.

I saw snow-capped mountains on the equator, endless desert, grass-carpeted veldt, smoking volcanoes, the loveliest and bluest lakes in the world, literally millions of birds, including flocks of pink flamingoes that virtually obscured the sun's light.

What I am trying to say is that Africa has everything. Africa is a time machine that can carry you back along the world's lifeline as far as you want to go. It will show you modern up-to-date today in its bustling cities, factories, mines and housing projects, or will transport you back just a generation or two into a nation where racial discrimination and talk of the master race fill the air. If you want to go a little further into the past you can find a parallel of American history, when tribesmen were pushed farther and farther off their lands by white settlers establishing farms; and they retaliate with massacre as spirited tribesmen always have.

You can unwind the reel of history five hundred years, a thousand, two thousand—even twenty thousand years. You can see ancient history and pre-history not just through the pottery sherds and stone inscriptions of archaeologists but through living human beings. In Africa you can visit and talk to prehistoric man, old Adam's cousin, and that creature which is perhaps Adam's uncle, the gorilla.

But this primitive world is shrinking fast. Civilization, which has been nibbling at its edges for almost a century, is now biting huge chunks from it, cutting it into smaller pieces with roads, and covering the remainder with scheduled airlines. On three visits over a period of eighteen years I've watched Africa's Neolithic world contract violently. I've seen millions of Adam's cousins begin the mighty leap from the primitive to the modern, trying to accomplish in two or three generations what most of us took a few million years to do. I've seen the animals of the primitive world grow more scarce and retreat into forests, up steep mountains, and into the sanctuary of huge protective game parks and reserves.

Back in the thirties, one-third of the continent still existed as a living museum of natural history, and I made up my mind to visit it before it was demolished by the steam-roller of modernity. I was not an explorer or a scientist—just a man with an insatiable curiosity who had traveled around the world three times with countless detours in order to see strange and wonderful sights—and above all to become acquainted with strange and wonderful people. I had traveled over most of the broad tourist highways of the world and many of the less frequented paths. Now I wanted to cut cross-lots, away from the conventional routes of travel.

That is the point, I suppose, at which I became an explorer, although I didn't realize it until more than a year later, after my first African trip, when someone introduced me at a dinner in New York as "that well-known explorer." The term did not sit quite comfortably on me at first, but now I have behind me encounters with wild animals and almost wild tribes in Africa, three journeys to the head-hunting Jivaros of South America, three feature-length movies, and hundreds of lectures with the first colored film to come out of the primitive areas of two continents.

I have rarely traveled the way a self-respecting explorer is supposed to, however. On most of my trips I've had no elaborate equipment, no retinue of assistants and natives, no subsidies from rich institutions, philanthropists, or industrialists. The financing of most of my trips has come from one Lewis Cotlow, an insurance man who managed to organize his business so he could take off three to six months now and then. I've usually traveled alone or nearly alone, without fanfare and without frills.

On my first African trip I lacked even the essentials, through no fault of my own. I had made careful preparations, reading everything I could lay my hands on about Central Africa, consulting all the experts I could buttonhole, among them Martin Johnson, Dr. James L. Clark, Dr. James Chapin and others from the American Museum of Natural History. I arranged to

have a truck and proper equipment waiting for me at Juba, in
the southern Sudan, in time for me to start for the Belgian
Congo before the rainy season set in. And finally I obtained several thousand feet of some newly improved Kodachrome from
Eastman, in addition to my black-and-white film, hoping that
they had finally licked the problem of color disintegration in
the tropics.

The only trouble was that I couldn't get to Juba, where my
truck and supplies awaited me. Instead I landed on Lake Victoria because British Imperial Airways had put a new flying boat
on the African run, so large that it could not land on the Nile at
Juba during the low-water season. I found myself about seven
hundred miles from my meager though adequate equipment,
with no way to get to it. With more experience I might have
called the whole thing off, but as it was I started my career as
an explorer—my search for the primitive—with two suitcases
and two cameras—and that's all.

But there had already been some compensations. First, a
herd of about a hundred fifty elephants over which our pilot
flew low so I could get some pictures. We could see even the
white egrets on many of the elephants' backs. The roar of the
plane's engines frightened these most imperturbable creatures,
and they took off across the smooth expanse of papyrus and grass
in a frantic rush, trumpeting, bellowing and flapping their ears.
Second, there was the sight of Victoria Nyanza from the air, a
vast blue sheet of water, the largest lake in Africa, second largest
in the world. You could plop Vermont, New Hampshire and
Massachusetts down into it.

The lake was not quite what I had pictured, looking more
like one of our great lakes than a tropical inland sea. Gentle,
rolling slopes led down to its many bays, giving it an air of
placidity and fertility. Only later did I see swampy, papyrus-
filled areas and a mountain or two rising three thousand feet
above the water, which is itself almost four thousand feet
above sea level. And when I saw a log turn into a crocodile,

and experienced one of Victoria's violent electrical storms that lashed the water into frothy waves, I forgot the gentleness of its first impression.

As the plane circled for a landing, I saw villages of beehive huts along the shore and on some of the many islands. A big Arab dhow spread its sails and pointed its prow for the other end of the lake, two hundred fifty miles south. For years after its discovery in 1858, these ships and native canoes were the only transportation on the lake. Then in 1896 the first steamship was carried overland in sections to be assembled on its shores, followed by others that now do a brisk business.

Our plane came to rest, and I looked at the distant horizon where water and sky met almost imperceptibly, and I understood how the first explorers, coming from the east, thought they had traversed all of Africa and reached the Atlantic. Turning, I saw Entebbe, Britain's administrative capital in the Uganda Protectorate. Situated on a promontory jutting out into the lake, it showed smooth, green lawns lined with mango trees and colorful shrubs. Near shore enormous lily pads floated on the water, and across them ran strange-looking birds with enormous feet, apparently searching for food.

Two young Imperial Airways men, very British in spite of their volubility, took me from the plane in a small boat and welcomed me to Africa with an invitation to tea. On the way I saw that Entebbe looked like a lovely country club for British civil service officials, not even very tropical in appearance despite its location almost exactly on the equator except for its scores of brilliantly colored birds. It was somewhat muggy, but not really hot.

I felt far from the primitive world as I sipped tea and listened to the young Englishmen bewail the dullness of social life in Entebbe and, above all, its lack of attractive young women. After listening sympathetically to their tale of woe I retaliated with my own and asked, without much hope, if they knew of a truck, a man, and equipment for a trip into the Congo. They seemed not the least disconcerted by such a request.

"If you're going on to Kampala this evening—and you'll have to, for there's no hotel here," one said, "you will find there a young Belgian named Cézaire. He's been placer-mining in the Congo for several years, but right now he's looking for something interesting to do. I'll notify him to come to your hotel if you like."

That's how I came to meet Cézaire and his old Chevrolet sedan. He was a slender, quiet-spoken fellow in his early thirties who seemed to know his way around this part of the world. The car was equipped with a tent strapped alongside, a rack on top, and room in back for baggage and numerous extra five-gallon tins of gasoline. Within fifteen minutes I realized that a bad predicament had suddenly been switched to a fortunate break. He was, I felt, exactly the man I needed and I found no reason to change that opinion during the following four months.

We quickly came to an agreement, and I went to sleep that night feeling that despite my presence in a comfortable hotel in a busy city, I was not far from the primitive world I had come to see. When I awoke the next morning, however, primitive people and animals still seemed far away. Traffic noises floated up through my window, and I looked out on a city built on seven hills, one of which was dominated by a cathedral, another by a school. When I went downstairs, I found that most of the traffic bustle was caused not by automobiles but by scores of bicycles that darted along the paved main street.

Most of the riders were dark-skinned men wearing European clothes but no shoes. The vehicles had become tremendously popular with the African population when a British bike manufacturer had advertised his wares by showing a black man escaping from a pursuing lion on his speedy bicycle.

The women—Baganda is the name of the tribe—were different. They are erect, poised, dignified, graceful—possibly because they carry everything on top of their heads and gain thereby a flowing ease of motion. Their clothing is at the same time African in feeling and suitable to a city street, colorful and simple. Apparently they wore the same type of dress before the white men came, but made of bark cloth dyed in bright colors. It is a long, slim robe, fitting tight over the breasts, gathered at one side at the hip, and falling straight to the unshod feet. Bare shoulders, smooth and well-formed, gleamed in the sun.

One reason I wanted to go to Africa then was to see it before the invasion of calico and khaki was supreme and all-pervasive. There had been an invasion of non-African cloth in Kampala, all right, but in the form of red silks, blue velvets, and bright cotton prints—all adapted to the African style.

Attractive and pleasing as all this was, it was nothing of the primitive I was searching for. Three British banks and a branch of a drugstore chain, plus hundreds of shops run by Hindus and Sikhs, scarcely suggested the prehistoric world. Kampala was a cosmopolitan commercial center of a productive country—cotton being the outstanding product.

The region had not really been primitive, of course, when the British first came in 1862. They found a well-organized kingdom with a parliament, reasonably complete laws and effective control. Blood drenched the country's history pretty thoroughly, but that seems to be as much a characteristic of modern civilization as it is of the truly primitive. The blood has largely vanished since the British protectorate came into being, around the turn of the century, and in this case the word seems to be a correct one, for the British *have* protected rather than ruled. Uganda is still a black man's country, run primarily by its natives. Significantly, there have been no Mau Mau killings here, as in nearby Kenya.

Even though impatient to get away from civilization, I was grateful to it at the moment, for Kampala had all the supplies we needed. Cézaire suggested waiting until we reached the Congo to buy guns as they were less expensive and we would avoid customs difficulties. For clothing he took me to a shop run by an emigrant from the tiny Portuguese territory of Goa on the western coast of India. There were five hundred Goans in Kampala alone. Years before, a high Uganda official had married a Goanese wife, who had encouraged him to hire her countrymen as clerks. They proved so efficient that soon a good deal of the trade fell into their hands, giving rise to a saying current in Kampala, "God save the King—from the Goans." Being Roman Catholics, they held aloof from the three thousand or more Hindus and Sikhs who handled most of the other business of the city.

All went rapidly and well in the outfitting department. I was supplied with excellent and succinct advice by Captain Roberts, who served as Uganda's chief detective-policeman and showed me some beautiful photographs he had taken of Africa.

"If you observe a few simple rules," he said, "you'll be as safe in Africa as in most places. If you don't wear a sun helmet, you'll have a heat stroke. If you drink any water that isn't bottled or boiled, you'll have dysentery or typhoid. If you don't take a dose of quinine every day you'll come down with malaria and perhaps blackwater fever. If you let a tsetse fly bite you, it may mean sleeping sickness. Bathe your feet every day to keep them clear of ticks, chiggers, and hookworms. Stay away from fleas if you don't want the plague. Don't make yourself bait for lions and leopards by wandering around at night. And last of all, if you want to avoid venereal disease, keep away from Baganda girls—and that probably goes for other girls, too."

On the surface, it sounded somewhat forbidding, as if Africa offered nothing but pests and dangers. Actually, it presented just a different set of problems from those I was accustomed to.

At last we headed west from Kampala, along a red-dirt road pointing into the heart of Africa. The morning was bright and warm, the air clear, and the rolling hills as green as Eire in an Irishman's dream of home. Cars and bicycles moved along the broad smooth highway, as they do on the outskirts of most cities anywhere. Kampala has its suburbs of native huts, then its surrounding farmland of "shambas" large and small. We saw endless fields of cotton, banana groves and, on the higher levels, coffee plantations. We might have been driving through the Carolinas, except for the absence of billboards and filling stations.

The road grew narrow, the shambas smaller and farther apart, the cultivated fields were replaced by a thick growth of grass and papyrus, sometimes ten feet high. The road was a narrow tunnel through the green walls, and we could see nothing but its enticing path ahead, leading around a gentle curve and putting miles and centuries behind us.

An inner excitement began to build up inside me. I took my Bell and Howell movie camera from its case, set my Leica on the seat beside me. But for a long time we saw nothing. The clutch of civilization had not been firmly extended this far, but it was too close for wild life to feel comfortable. We were in a kind of no-man's land between the advancing forces of civilization and retreating world of the primitive. There are always these areas, although sometimes they are very narrow as when the city of Nairobi was so new that a herd of bewildered zebras found themselves racing down the main street.

Usually the process of civilizing follows an established pattern. A beachhead is established, a point of light in the darkness that gradually grows brighter and sends its beams farther. (From another point of view, you can call it a tiny point of infection that gradually spreads.) Next a road is cut through the darkness, and another central lighting station set up. Ten feet on either side of the road, of course, the primitive forces lie in wait, ready to snatch it back quickly when it is not used. They also hover around the growing points of light, but apparently the armies of civilization are inexorable. In Africa, at least, their points of light have been spreading and increasing in number, the thin lines connecting them cutting the big areas of darkness into the tiny pieces of jigsaw puzzle. The airplane has speeded up the whole process tremendously, of course.

We knew that we were coming out of the neutral fringe when we saw a great hornbill blunder awkwardly across the road, wild geese and ducks fly overhead, and brightly colored birds of many kinds unknown to me dart over the tall reeds. Then these gave way to rolling fields of grass growing about knee-high.

We had traveled across this plain a few hours when I saw three enormous black blotches looming high above the grass. I touched Cézaire's arm, and he slowed down. There could be no mistake—they were elephants!

Now, I have seen elephants in zoos, in circuses, in Burma and India, but they were all captive or trained, and that really didn't count. I wanted to see wild animals in their *own* world, not man's. Here were elephants at home, giving me my first unadorned close-up of the primitive. It was an occasion that had to be recorded on film.

By the time we stopped the car, the three elephants were less than a third of a mile away, but they seemed not to have noticed us. To them, cars are perhaps great big powerful animals, too. But when I started to get out of the car, Cézaire cautioned me.

"We haven't any guns yet," he protested. "If they should charge, we can't protect ourselves."

"I don't see any young ones," I said. "I don't think they'll be upset."

I had a feeling, confirmed by the reading I had done, that most wild animals would not charge a human being unless they were cornered, wounded, persistently annoyed, or protecting their young. These elephants were just standing in the grass, placidly eating, their trunks snaking out for bunches of green grass and plopping them into their mouths, their ears flapping idly as they moved their heads. Still, I knew that without a rifle— and a big one at that—I wouldn't have much chance if anything went wrong. Photographing an animal can be much more dangerous than hunting it with a gun, particularly if you are the kind that likes to get as good a close-up as possible. Then too, there are rogue elephants, crazy creatures who attack without provocation; but they are more rare than raving maniacs among humans. The law of averages, which the insurance business had certainly taught me, was against my meeting such a danger.

So I circled around toward the elephants, making sure they would not get my wind. The disapproving Cézaire followed me until we were about a hundred fifty yards from the big creatures. From that point my telephoto lens gave me a good shot, and we returned to the car without incident. I felt quite pleased with myself, but I could see that Cézaire was concerned.

"Don't worry, Cézaire," I said. "I'm not going to take any foolish chances, but on the other hand I'm not going to miss any good bets just to make sure I'm a hundred-per-cent safe. I believe in taking calculated risks to gain worthwhile ends, but not in throwing caution to the winds."

But Cézaire was still unconvinced. He began to cite instances of hunters being killed by elephants and other animals. "You must have heard the story about Carl Akeley," he said reproachfully. "It was only a fluke that he wasn't killed."

I had heard, of course. The great naturalist's almost unbelievable escape from a charging elephant in the bamboo thickets of Mount Kenya was a classic of African adventure. As the huge beast lunged at him, Akeley seized its tusks, one in each hand, and pushed with all his might. They drove deep into the earth instead of into him, but then the elephant toppled, and the huge head came down right above him. He was trapped between the tusks, unable to escape being crushed to death. But then—the tusks struck a rock in the ground, or a big root, and sank no further. Akeley lay on the ground and the elephant fell over him, missing him by an inch or two. He was badly hurt, unconscious on the ground. The elephant righted itself, burning with anger, and turned. But the man seemed dead, so the elephant went off about its business. Akeley's natives rushed to him and took care of him.

"Of course, I know an elephant can charge you," I said to Cézaire. "But I just want pictures. Akeley was looking for specimens. He wanted the elephant itself and kept tracking it, filling it with anger and fear. In this case, as I remember, the elephant was smart and doubled back on its tracks and attacked Akeley from the rear. But I'm not planning on bothering any elephant that much. And anyway, they told me in Kampala that if a man hugs a tree and doesn't move an elephant will pass by without noticing him. Isn't that true?"

"It may be," said Cézaire. "But where are the trees?"

I looked over the grassy plain and knew he had made a point. Then I recalled the story about the cyclist who was coasting down a steep hill and suddenly saw an elephant directly ahead in his path. He couldn't stop, so he just rang his bell for all he was worth and the elephant snorted off into the bush.

"Yes, that's possible," Cézaire said, "but still——"

He left his sentence unfinished to point out an elephant trail, going for a space alongside the road. I was surprised at how narrow it was for such a large animal. In marshy ground, the elephant's prints look like miniature bathtubs, for he has no trouble pulling his feet from deep mud because they are constructed to spread out when his weight is on them, then contract as he lifts them.

Night was approaching when we reached another light in the darkness—Fort Portal, center of an area of coffee plantations. Stopping at the Busirasagama Rest House, we were told not to be disturbed by any strange sounds during the night because the surrounding woods were filled with colubus monkeys who liked nothing better than to jabber at each other and the world in general while they should have been asleep. They kept me awake a good part of the night, and I had just dozed off when the proprietor awoke me to take a look at the highest peak of the Ruwenzori range, Margherita. Since I knew that the mountains were so often blanketed with clouds that they were not visible for weeks at a time, I was willing to cut short my rest for a look.

On this occasion, as on many others, Africa made my head whirl. Here I was, just one-half a degree north of the equator—and the equator meant to me what it means to most people, burning sands or dense tropical jungles. What I saw instead was something from the Alps or the Himalayas, a huge and imposing mass of earth from which peaks of unbelievable grandeur

rose to heights of more than 15,000 feet. Margherita, one of the
twin peaks composing Mt. Stanley (one of six mountains of the
range), shot its glistening spire 16,814 feet into the sky, higher
than any of its neighbors. The top two thousand feet were covered with snow and glaciers, which seemed to be a frosty pink
in the light of the rising sun.

For some time I stood with my glasses looking at the Ruwenzori, the Mountains of the Moon, as ancient Ptolemy called
them without having seem them. Or had he, perhaps? I suspect
that a few thousand years ago people knew a great deal more
than we give them credit for. Just because much of their knowledge was lost and it took us so long to rediscover it, we need
not feel so superior. Ptolemy's maps showed a glacier-covered
mountain range in the heart of Africa, whose streams were the
source of the Nile. Even before him the ancient Greeks had
spoken of the Nile as rising in snow-fed lakes, and Arab geogra-
phers later perpetuated the idea. But for centuries, until less
than seventy-five years ago, this was considered arrant nonsense.
Snow-covered mountains on the equator? Glaciers in the heart
of tropical Africa? Tommyrot. Ancient myth and legend. When
Africans told the first white explorers about snowy peaks in the
center of the continent, their tales were dismissed as fantasy
which illustrated just how ignorant these people were. Stanley
even camped for some weeks on Ruwenzori's foothills without
knowing the peaks were there, for clouds obscured them completely. Later he saw them, and so did others, and they were
finally scaled in 1906.

The Ruwenzori are not volcanic in origin like Kilimanjaro
and Kenya, the only two taller mountains in Africa, or like the
Virunga chain to the south which we were to visit later. They
are instead just a gigantic upthrust of earth and stone from the
surface of this old globe, an upheaval that occurred when the
African rifts were formed. A massive crack in the earth, with
branching crevices, runs from deep in Africa northward into
Asia Minor. The Red Sea is part of it, and probably also the
Gulf of Akaba, the Dead Sea, the Jordan Valley and the Gulf of

Galilee. In Central Africa the rift is split in two—on the east, the Great Rift; on the west, the Albertine Rift. Each is a deep trough, sometimes forty miles wide, between two gigantic escarpments running a thousand feet or more in height. In the trough lie fertile lands, beautiful lakes, volcanoes both active and extinct, and the overpowering mass that is Ruwenzori. Briefly, there are three theories about rift formation: faulting, or the dropping in of a kind of keystone in the arch of the earth's crust; continental drift, or the effort of half a continent to split off from the rest; and pressure, or a jutting up of the surface on two sides of a plain.

Whatever the origin, the rift accounts for some of the most spectacular beauty in the world as well as some perplexing problems for the invading forces of civilization. When the first railroad in East Africa reached the escarpment, it just ended and started the tracks again a thousand feet down on the floor of the trough. Passengers and goods had to be lowered on cable-cars. In time, of course, engineers solved the problem with a series of hairpin bends and the builders of motor roads followed.

Ruwenzori tempted me, for I knew that on its slopes was a rich animal and vegetable life rare indeed. Elephants, buffaloes, chimpanzees, wild pigs, many kinds of antelope and strange monkeys lived there; leopards ranged as high as thirteen thousand feet. In the tropical forests of the mountain sides there were bamboos, palms, ferns of great size; buttercups, daisies, violets, and giant lobelia twenty feet high. And very high, green moss, moss eighteen inches deep on tree trunks, moss the climber had to cut through—almost tunnel through. There are deep caves, rushing mountain torrents from the glaciers, leaping over ledges in lovely cascades.

I was tempted, but I was no mountain climber. A real exploration of Ruwenzori would take a larger party, more equipment, and many weeks. I could not spare the time, for I wanted to see many things on this first trip to the primitive world—pygmies, giants, fishermen, hunters, and even more different animals than I could find on Ruwenzori, and one of the animals I wanted to see most of all did not live there—the gorilla.

So we left Fort Portal, heading for the border of the Belgian Congo, skirting the Ruwenzori by going south as well as west. In a half hour I thought I had my reward, for we encountered along the road a group of Bantu Negroes much smaller than the average height.

"Pygmies?" I asked Cézaire hopefully.

"Baamba," he answered. "Part Pygmy, part Bantu. Their teeth are filed to sharp points, supposedly from the time not very long ago when they were cannibals."

Cézaire told me that there were still cases of cannibalism in central Africa, most of it on bodies that had just been buried. The authorities in some localities still had trouble over it occasionally and there were tales of isolated tribes who practiced it regularly as they always had.

We stopped and talked to the Baamba awhile and I was delighted to find that Cézaire could communicate with them rather easily. Although there are about eight hundred different languages spoken in Africa, natives and whites have found a way of communicating in a kind of *lingua franca* introduced by Stanley. He had brought with him carriers from the east coast who spoke Swahili, and in much of central Africa this had become the dialect called Kingwana. It had almost no grammar and no standard pronunciation, but it served its purpose for transmitting simple ideas and requests. Cézaire handled it well.

A little later, I knew for sure I was in Africa when Cézaire took one hand from the wheel and slapped me on the neck. "Tsetse," he said. I felt uneasy, with a kind of hollow at the pit of my stomach, but this time Cézaire didn't seem overly concerned.

"Just watch out for them," he said. "You can recognize them because the wings overlap like the blades of a scissors."

Only a small percentage of tsetse flies carry the dread trypanosome of sleeping sickness. Osa Johnson had told me that she had been bitten ten thousand times without getting sick, so I knew that the law of averages was with me. The disease can be cured, too, if it is caught early. Most natives won't come to doctors for help until the sickness if far advanced. Later, in Kenya, I heard that there was something about the air or climate of Norway which was particularly helpful in the cure of sleeping sickness. Downey, of Ker and Downey, famed white hunters and safari outfitters of Nairobi, had contracted the disease and had speeded his convalescence by going to Norway.

At Kasindi we crossed the border into the Belgian Congo. The customs official, an old friend of Cézaire's, talked to us awhile and asked about our plans. When I told him that one of my prime objectives was to see and possibly photograph gorillas, he told me about the new regulations concerning these much protected beasts. "No one entering any known gorilla country can carry a gun of any kind," he said.

In view of this news, I suggested to Cézaire that we might as well postpone the purchase of guns until after we had gone on our gorilla hunt. He agreed, but expressed the hope that meanwhile I would not get too close to any animals we might encounter. Temptation came our way, however, almost at once.

The customs official told us that a herd of buffalo and another of elephants had gone past the night before, heading for the nearby Semliki River. "I could hear them a mile away," he said. "If you want to follow them with your car, you might get some good pictures."

He sent a native boy in the car with us, and I got the cameras ready as we rode through the tall elephant grass toward the river. We stopped on a steep bank and looked down. There were a dozen or more hippopotami basking in the hot sun. I clambered down for a shot, but as I was scrambling up the embankment I heard Cézaire's shout from the car and saw a huge elephant lumbering toward us along the top of the ridge. He didn't see us or the car, apparently, for he shuffled along unconcernedly, his big ears pumping rhythmically to and fro. Still, he was less than two hundred yards away and could cover the

ground fast if he wanted to. We leapt into the car and Cézaire
started the motor. The tusker heard it, stopped short, then
veered off.

"See?" I said to Cézaire, "If we don't annoy them they go
away."

Cézaire didn't answer.

On the way back to Kasindi, circling around an acacia
thorn in the tall yellow grass, we spotted four elephants, their
backs just showing above the grass.

"Stop!" I said. "I want to get this picture."

"*Bwana*, be careful," the boy said. "You're in their wind."

"I don't think you ought to try it," Cézaire agreed.

But I wanted that picture. I didn't think the elephants
could see me in the tall grass and I planned to raise the camera
on its tripod to shoot them over the top of the grass. I moved
slowly to within a hundred fifty feet of the elephants and was
adjusting the camera when Cézaire shouted. One of the elephants was facing me, its trunk lifted, its great ears outstretched.
I didn't have to be an authority on elephant psychology to
understand that the elephant was seriously annoyed. I took to
my heels, and Cézaire speeded up the engine, let in the clutch,
as I reached the running board. When we were safely away,
Cézaire let out his breath, turned to me and said, "See?"

"One of them had young ones with her. I saw the backs of
the *totos* in the grass." This from the black boy.

"See?" I said to Cézaire. "She had young ones, otherwise——"

"But you didn't see them."

He could not dampen my own enthusiasm. Instead, I was exhilarated, feeling that I was meeting the primitive world I had
come to search for. This feeling was heightened, after we
dropped the boy at Kasindi and went on toward Beni, by the
sight of a beautiful waterbuck that dashed across the road in
front of the car, like chickens in America and—as I learned later
—like many other animals *and* tribesmen in Africa.

We had to cross the Semliki River on a pontoon ferry op-

erated by natives who hauled it over the water on a cable. While
they put their backs into it, they chanted in unison "Hi-ho, hi-
ho, hi-ho," in a mournful cadence, and then some of the crew
broke into a rhythmic recitative that Cézaire translated for me
on the spot.

"Our hearts will be broken to pieces,
  Our eyes will come out of our heads,
  If the white man does not give us the big tip he promised us.
  Don't be so lazy,
  The white man is in a hurry.
  Our stomachs are empty; they are flopping against our backs,
  We have not eaten for a long time.
  But the white man will give us money for food,
  The white man has a black heart and he will be kind to us.
  Put your testicles up!
  Pull hard!
  Our testicles will be broken because we are pulling so hard."

The others joined in with a "Hi-ho, hi-ho," as the ferry
reached the other shore. I'm afraid I actually overtipped the
crew, fearing to lose my black-hearted reputation for generosity
or to feel responsible for such irreparable damage to hard-
working men.

Despite the very modern hints about tips and the presence
of an old Chevrolet sedan, I felt happy. It took some people
weeks to get this far from civilization. Within a month my
search for the primitive was to be satisfying—and exciting—beyond my dreams. For I would stand face to face with a gorilla
weighing over four hundred pounds, with a camera in my hand,
a penknife in my pocket, and some distance behind me four
Pygmies with thin spears, three of whom ran away!

II

Gorilla!

THE natives call him Ngagi. The scientists have named him *gorilla gorilla beringei*. He is the smartest primate other than man, although his brain is half as large as yours or mine. His body, on the other hand, is twice as large—or larger —and ten times as strong. He has a reach of nine feet and can twist your head off as you would pick wings off a fly. He loves his wife and children and takes care of them as well as any human. He doesn't wittingly bother people who do not bother him. He may not be your ancestor, but his father was probably the brother of Adam's father. If you doubt it, look at his footprint. It shows a heel. Only yours and his, of all creatures, will reveal such a thing. He has a tremendous stomach—essential for a vegetarian of such size—but it's not much larger than that of many men I've seen. The biggest difference I noticed, in fact, is that he has hair everywhere *but* on his chest.

Until less than a century ago, he was a myth and a legend, like the Mountains of the Moon. And he turned out to be just as real as they. A few scientists began to take him seriously when they examined skins and skeletons sent from Africa by a sea captain. The world paid little attention, however, until Paul du Chaillu wrote his hair-raising tales of Africa, based on fact but sensationalized considerably by publishers' rewrite men. As more white men penetrated Africa, specimens were killed and examined. In time live young gorillas were captured for some of the world's great zoos, although most of these are of the smaller variety found in the forest plains of the French Cameroons. The giant mountain gorilla live only in the Eastern Congo. I was there, and I wanted as much as anything to see him in his forest home.

The odds were against me, I knew. Martin Johnson, Carl Akeley and others who knew the great ape best had taken at least two weeks of struggling through dense mountain forests before they caught a glimpse of one. Just a few years before, H. C. Raven, of the American Museum of Natural History, had spent a fortnight tracking with Pygmies on Mount Bugalamisa to see the gorilla. I could not devote that much time to this single project, but I headed optimistically for Bugalamisa, in the Tshibinda Forest a few miles southwest of Lake Kivu.

At the foot of the mountain we found the experimental cinchona plantation operated by the *Syndicat pour l'Etude de Quinine au Kivu*. The manager, Marcel Ernsterhoff, was a handsome young Luxemburger who lived there with his dog, Max, and a cat, supervising the hundred-odd native workmen. He greeted us with the enthusiasm of a lonely man who welcomes anyone coming fresh from the outside world, and offered his full cooperation. We could use the plantation as our base, and he would try to find Pygmies to lead us up the mountain to the heights of eight or nine thousand feet at which the gorillas usually lived.

But he warned me sharply and seriously about the new government regulation concerning firearms. Carl Akeley and other scientists had convinced the authorities some years before that the gorilla was in danger of extermination. Akeley had persuaded the Belgian king to set aside forever the huge tract of primitive land called the Albert National Park as a refuge for all animals, above all the gorilla. Despite this, gorillas still were shot. Hunters and scientists returned from expeditions into the gorilla mountains claiming that the huge beasts had charged them. They had to shoot in self-defense. Sometimes the statement was perfectly true, sometimes it was not.

There was only one sure way of making the world safe for the gorilla, as officials had determined to do—forbid all firearms.

If an explorer objected, saying it was dangerous to go near gorillas unarmed, the answer was, "Then don't go."

No one had gone, so far as I could learn, since the ban went
into effect a short time before my arrival in Africa. That's why
Ernsterhoff stressed that I would go up Mount Bugalamisa
strictly on my own responsibility. Even though I carried no firearms, I might get in trouble if the Pygmies with me killed a
gorilla with a spear despite a convincing plea of self-defense.
In the first place, Ernsterhoff said, it was almost inconceivable
that a group of Pygmies could withstand a gorilla charge without one or two of their group being killed before the ape was
put out of commission. Then I would be held responsible for
the death of the Pygmies as well as that of the gorilla; an embarrassing investigation would follow, and I would be subject
to a stiff fine and perhaps imprisonment.

Once Ernsterhoff was satisfied that I fully understood the
seriousness of the situation and the danger of going into gorilla
country unarmed, he was as helpful as he could possibly be.
He sent one of his boys into the forest to look for Kasciula, chief
of the Pygmies in that area, and some of his men. Kasciula was
already a familiar name to me, for he had guided Attilio Gatti
on his gorilla-hunting expedition, and had helped H. C. Raven
and W. K. Gregory, of the American Museum of Natural History, in their successful search for the big ape. Ernsterhoff assured me that I could not possibly find anyone more skilled as a
forest tracker, more courageous in the face of danger. And he
knew the ways of the gorilla better than anyone. He had lived
in the same forest with them for years, and claimed to know
some of the old man apes individually.

From the plantation clearing I looked up at the mountain
that towered above us, wearing a thick mantle of dark green
that hid from view elephants, gorilla, leopards and a score of
other animals. Yet it could not be so dreadfully dangerous, I
thought, if for centuries men had lived there, too, as the Pygmies had. The lower stretches of the mountain, leading to the
plantation, were covered with a wall of vines and underbrush so

dense that I did not see how it would be possible to penetrate it.

That evening the talk was of gorillas, of course. Ernsterhoff, as if tactfully giving me some good advice, pointed out that men still disagreed about the psychology and temperament of the great ape but that all were emphatic in saying the creature was as dangerous as any alive—certainly not to be approached without weapons. Carl Akeley who, more than anyone else, insisted on the essential gentleness and mild temper of the gorilla, nevertheless took every precaution when he was in gorilla country. He had said that anyone who allowed a gorilla to come within fifty feet of him was a damned fool. Although Akeley was convinced that often a gorilla charge was largely a bluff intended to frighten men or other animals away, no sensible person would wait to see whether or not the beast attacked. If it did, there could be only one result.

"Akeley always pointed out," I said, "that gorillas would keep out of a man's way if given a chance. He said that they would charge only if cornered or persistently followed, suddenly surprised while feeding or when protecting their young. I'm inclined to think that most animals are like that. That's why I feel reasonably safe without a weapon. I'm not going to irritate the gorillas on Mount Bugalamisa."

"You're going to be tracking them down," Ernsterhoff said, "even if you only want a look. They may not understand your motives."

I felt he was right and probably knew more about gorillas than many of the experts. But he did not say that they were vicious beasts, attacking and killing wantonly for the joy of it. He knew that Pygmies, going through the forest, made a wide detour if they heard gorillas ahead. At the same time, if gorillas heard Pygmies coming they moved some distance away, as if to avoid any encounter that might result in trouble. The forest on the mountain was the gorilla's domain, where he lived at peace with all other animals except the leopard.

Sometimes the gorillas came down the mountain and raided banana groves or vegetable gardens. But a gorilla would consider the bananas as being his as much as anyone else's. When such incidents occurred, the Africans attacked the marauder with sticks and loud shouts. Certainly this did not sound as if they thought the gorilla was overwhelmingly dangerous. Usually the assault was successful and the beast was driven back into the forest, but there were numerous cases on record of the killing or wounding of some natives in such brawls. Some Pygmies were also a bit leery of being the last man in a line walking along a trail in gorilla country. The great ape has a little trick of hiding beside a trail and taking a bite of the last man filing along. Some have been known to circle back onto the trail when being followed, so as to charge the intruder from the rear.

"The gorilla can charge with terrific speed," Ernsterhoff told me, "and that's surprising in such a bulky animal. And some people get so paralyzed with fright at the sight of a gorilla and the sounds he makes that they cannot move."

He told me the story of a professional hunter from Colorado who came to Tshibinda Forest to hunt gorilla some years before. He finally encountered a band of gorillas, without being able to see them in the moving foliage on either side of his path. Suddenly a big male emerged and screamed at him. The hunter, who had faced lions and elephants without a qualm, was so stricken with fear that he could not move. Fortunately, the gorilla ambled away, gathered up his family, and went on. The hunter, regaining his senses, quickly retreated down the mountain to the plantation, where a violent reaction set in. He vomited on the floor and was miserably sick all the following day.

Ernsterhoff also told me about his strawberry patch. He had started it on the edge of the clearing and watched the little berries grow in size and redden in the summer sun. Then one night, just before he planned to pick a nice batch, the gorillas appeared and ate every single one of the ripe red berries, after which they scurried up the mountain again.

"Actually, gorillas don't give us much trouble, however," Ernsterhoff said, "despite the fact that we are so close to them.

Leopards are a far greater problem. They often kill for the love of killing."

Several of his workers had been killed by leopards in the forests, when they lay down at night to sleep on their way to visit their native villages. Only a few days before we arrived, one of his men had been attacked in broad daylight by an unusually bold leopard which dragged the body into the nearby bush and ate, according to custom, first the genitals and then the intestines. The natives, knowing the animal would return for the rest of its meal, laid a trap for it, but the leopard was clever enough to avoid the trap and managed to finish off what remained of the body during the night.

While we were talking to Ernsterhoff the next morning, a native reported that a leopard had been sighted, perhaps the man-eater itself. Ernsterhoff went off with his gun immediately, a fiery light in his eye. His hatred of leopards seemed like a deep personal grudge, and he hunted them down as ruthlessly as they hunted down their prey. I would have liked to go with him, but I knew that I could see leopards elsewhere and this was my one big chance to see gorillas. I wanted to stay and wait for the Pygmies to arrive.

The next morning they were there—fourteen of them, some with thin ten-foot spears, others with small bows and arrows. They were not quite as small as I had expected, for these were not pure Pygmies. There had been some admixture of Bantu blood and, while some of them were under five feet in height, a few were a bit taller. These Pygmies were probably Batwa, whereas the pure-bred Pygmies of the Ituri Forest are called Bambuti.

The small forest men were led by Kasciula. He was no longer young, and a short greying beard fringed his chin. He stood, relaxed but alert, waiting for our palaver. There was a keen, darting look in his eyes, and an air of complete assurance about him, despite his shyness. By our standards, I suppose he was rather odd-looking, with his spindly legs, pot belly, gray kinky hair and small bulbous nose, but somehow he gave me great confidence. I felt sure I would be safe in his hands and that he could find a gorilla if anyone could.

This kind of situation arises time and again in any explorer's activities. You must have native help for many undertakings, and you must size up in a minute or two the quality and character of the human being into whose hands you are entrusting your life. With the barrier of language and a different framework in which one's thinking is done, different standards of behavior and values, this is not always easy. But Kasciula left no doubt in my mind. He was all right.

The chief spoke some Kingwana, enough for Cézaire to settle with him the terms of our agreement. If he and his men led me to the gorillas, they would receive three sacks of salt and two dozen tins of tobacco—both items highly prized. If they failed, I could then give them whatever I chose—an eminently fair arrangement.

He then made a suggestion that proved to be a blessing. Many gorillas were on the mountain, he said, but they were constantly changing their feeding grounds. He would send six men up to reconnoiter and report back when they had found a group. Then we could go directly to them. The six set off at once and the rest of us sat down to wait—for how long none of us knew.

That afternoon Ernsterhoff returned triumphant from the hunt, followed by two natives carrying a pole from which hung a hundred-fifty-pound leopard. The planter greeted the Pygmies who had remained behind, then called one over to me.

"If you have any doubts about what a gorilla can do, look at that arm," he said.

A nasty looking wound scarred most of the native's left forearm. He told us that he had been hunting with a band of other Batwa when a gorilla suddenly materialized from nowhere, seized him and bit him. Two of his companions had hurled their spears at the great ape, who let his victim go and ran off, screaming. He thought himself very lucky to have escaped, even though he would never again have full use of that arm.

The following afternoon the Pygmy scouts came down the mountain to report that they had found a band of gorillas near the summit. They would most likely be somewhere in that vicinity for a day or two. Kasciula announced that we would start early in the morning.

Cézaire and I had a hearty breakfast of eggs and several cups of delicious coffee with Ernsterhoff, and then set out with the fourteen Pygmies, Kasciula in the lead. The heavy mist was just lifting under the rays of the rising sun as we walked along an avenue of cinchona trees, crossed a swamp, and plunged into the tangled underbrush. I was keyed up, inwardly excited, and perhaps a little afraid of the adventure I was walking into. Within ten minutes, however, it didn't seem much like an adventure. Cézaire and I were crawling half the time instead of walking. All thoughts and feelings were driven away by the concentrated effort to fight through that jungle up a steep grade. The lianas, creepers, saplings, bushes, ferns, bamboo and branches of large trees were so intertwined and matted that they presented what was to me an almost impassable barrier. I watched in amazement as Kasciula seemed to pull back a slit in the barrier, slip through, and disappear. Behind him, I couldn't find the opening at all. The Pygmies got busy with their *mgoosu*—implements with long wooden handles, with an iron chopping blade on one side, a sort of scimitar-shaped sickle on the other. Deftly they cut a tunnel into the vegetation, and I followed. But a Pygmy-sized tunnel is considerably lower than I am. I found myself moving forward half-crouched, trying to ignore the long nettles and branches that snatched at my clothes. The Pygmies, of course, wore nothing but breech-clouts.

It was hot and semidark in the jungle. We didn't see the blue sky until we were near the summit. Once, when I was going on hands and knees beneath a fallen tree, I saw a chameleon on a vine beside me. His tongue darted out and bull's-eyed a passing insect, then he slithered away. The grade gradually became steeper, and I found myself panting, slipping back every few steps. When I slipped, Kasciula stopped and held his spear back to me so I could grab it and haul myself up again.

After two hours my heart was pounding hard against the walls of my chest, my head was throbbing, and I panted heavily. Looking back, I saw that Cézaire was having just as much trouble as I was. The Pygmies, on the other hand, moved effortlessly. It was obvious that they were moving at half their normal pace just to accommodate us. I had to signal for a brief rest. The Pygmies waited patiently but with an air of amiable condescension towards these two white men, supposedly so superior, who had so much trouble just climbing a mountain. As we rested, I looked about in the dark gloom of the forest and wondered why I had bothered to bring my camera along. Even with the best lens and fastest film, it was impossible to take a picture in such a dim light. If I ever saw a gorilla, I could not photograph him unless he walked into an open glade, of which there were a few here and there on the mountain. I understood why most of the pictures of gorillas in the books of hunters and explorers showed dead gorillas propped up against a tree or in the supporting arms of the hunters. They had to shoot the gorilla and get him out into the open for a camera shot. Carl Akeley had been the first to photograph gorillas in the forest with a movie camera, and he managed that only once in years of gorilla hunting.

Shortly after we started up again we came upon an elephant path and followed it for some distance, so the walking was easier despite the steep grade. Then it veered off to the side and we hacked our way through the wall of vegetation again. The altitude as well as the exertion was getting me, but I kept on, although calling for three-minute rests at more and more frequent intervals. Once we stopped a bit longer for a bite of lunch.

Near the summit of the mountain we ran into more elephant paths. We could see the tracks but they were not at all fresh. The ground finally leveled out and I knew we had reached the ridge along the top of the mountain. The walking was easier, the trails more frequent. The Pygmies moved more cautiously now and with absolute silence. I tried to walk the way they did, but twigs snapped under my feet, leaves rustled as I passed, and I felt that every wild creature within half a mile would know that a white man was coming.

Kasciula stopped and pointed to the ground. Elephant spoor, but not fresh. We went on, and again he stopped and pointed. But this time there was an air of expectation about him. I looked and saw the track of a gorilla. There was the print of the heel, and the marks made by the beasts' knuckles as he went along on all fours. A slight shiver went up the back of my neck as I realized that only a short time before a gorilla had walked down this trail.

A dozen yards farther along we saw dung, gorilla dung—and it was still steaming! Kasciula nodded his head and smiled. There was no doubt about it now—we were close to some gorillas. The path circled around an outcropping of rock, across a tiny glade not ten feet across, into which bright sunlight streamed. Beyond the glade Kasciula pointed again, and we saw gorilla beds, three of them rather close together. A gorilla makes its bed by sitting down in a thick clump of saplings and bushes, then pulling other saplings and branches down around him, tucking them in, tying them, and arranging them into what looks like a gigantic bird's nest. They looked quite comfortable. When there are leopards around, mother and babies go up into a tree and fill a comfortable fork with branches, leaves, and moss; papa sleeps at the base of the tree, his back against the trunk, head sunk on his chest. Nothing is likely to get past him.

Kasciula stepped forward on the trail again, after motioning for silence. It was comfortable now, walking along the ridge on more or less level ground, and we were accustomed to the altitude. But I could not walk silently, no matter how hard I tried. Even the two fourteen-year-old Pygmy boys who had been brought along to gain experience, were more adept than I was. The gorilla spoor was plain before us as we moved ahead, showing trampled grass, broken bamboo, and the stalks of green shoots from which they had stripped the most succulent parts.

I saw light ahead, and we came out of the forest onto a kind of rocky plateau with nothing but low scrub growth on it. The bright sun almost blinded me, but it made me feel a bit happier about my prospects for some pictures. If only we could spot a gorilla in an open area like this!

We walked to the other end of the open space, and for once I was almost as silent as the Pygmies. Stopping, we looked down and saw the thick forest growth that started a hundred feet or more below. Then Kasciula pointed. He had obviously spotted something, but I couldn't see a thing but vegetation. I kept staring where he pointed, and I saw some leaves move. There came a crackling of branches, the sound of something moving among the trees. Then there was a lashing and whipping of the branches in one place. I stared in eager expectation —and I still saw nothing but vegetation.

Kasciula grunted. From his expression, I knew he had seen something. It was a few seconds before I located it—an almost black head emerging cautiously from the green leaves. A long hairy arm reached out and pushed some branches aside, then the gorilla hunched himself on all fours into the open.

I was prepared for something big, of course, but the massive solidity of this great ape appalled me. I was filled with a mounting excitement and exhilaration. Jubilant over our good fortune in locating so quickly this most seclusive of beasts, I felt awe, fear, and admiration at the sight of his bulk, the epitome of brute strength. As he moved along the edge of the trees, his head wagging from side to side, there was something of grace in him despite the superficial awkwardness of movement. Even though his knuckles touched the ground at every step, he was startlingly human—not a burlesque of the human, such as you find in many monkeys and baboons. I felt like saying, "There, but for the grace of God——" and for a fleeting moment I felt myself back in the primeval days of my own ancestors, watching warily this offshoot of my own family that had grown so much stronger physically than I but whose intellect had been standing still for thousands of years.

He must have heard us, or caught our movement, for he stopped, turned in our direction, and looked. Curious, he stood up on his feet and peered more intently. He saw us, all right, but he did not seem perturbed. Still standing, his fist went to his chest, and I heard the sound for which gorillas are most famous. There was no cry, no roar, no scream—just a pounding tom-tom sound as from a muffled drum. And that's precisely what the beating of the chest was—the signal of a drum. There was nothing menacing in it, nor was there anything of anger in the sound and movement of the arm. He was just using that big barrel of a chest as a sounding board and opening his mouth so the sound would come out. It was a signal, plain and simple, indicating to others behind him that he had sighted something and wasn't sure what the devil it was.

Three other gorilla heads emerged from the green leaves, then disappeared again. We heard more chest-beating, and the same sound repeated farther away. The warning signal was relayed to all the gorillas in the neighborhood.

The first gorilla was apparently as interested in us as we were in him. He stopped beating his breast and grabbed an overhanging branch with his long arm. His legs were very short and seemed a bit unsteady. I saw the crest of furry, thickened skin on top of his head, the shiny black leather of his face and upper chest, his flat wide-flaring nose. Suddenly I remembered my camera and raised it. But at that moment my gorilla friend decided he had looked at us enough and dropped down, moving away slowly into the shadow. I snapped the shutter, but was certain that the beast had been lost in the darkness.

As he lumbered back among the trees, I felt a touch on my arm. A wizened old Pygmy, less than five feet tall, with brittle, spindly arms and a grey wool fuzz on head and chin, nodded his head toward the other side of the ridge. His expressive eyes told me that there was something interesting to see over there, so I followed the old veteran of many a gorilla hunt. Another Pygmy and the two boys on their first gorilla hunt followed, while Kasciula, Cézaire, and the others stayed at their post to see if our first gorilla friends would come close again.

Old greybeard led me to a ledge of rock that rose about three feet above a grassy glade sloping down toward the thick jungle growth. There on the edge of the grass, in the deep shade cast by the trees, stood four gorillas—apparently father, mother, and two youngsters. Mama and the little ones were busy eating, but the old man had heard us and looked up inquiringly. He dropped a succulent stalk on which he had been feeding and turned to his family. Although I heard no sound, he obviously communicated a mild warning to them, for they glanced up, without showing any fear, and retreated a few steps among the trees. When he saw that they were safe, he turned back toward us and stared.

I readied my Leica. Could I possibly take a picture of this gorilla? At that moment there was nothing I wanted more. The desire to record our meeting on film became so compelling that all other thoughts fled—even thoughts of my own safety. Quickly I calculated the strength of the light and its sloping angle toward the glade. But the gorilla was in deep shadow, where the film could catch him only as a dark mass against a larger dark mass.

Then he started to move forward, away from the trees and into the open stretch below us. He walked on all fours, deliberately and without menace, apparently motivated only by curiosity. If he kept going he would enter a bright patch of light where the sun's rays cut down across the tops of the trees.

I could not wait calmly as he shuffled slowly towards us. What if he should stop short of the lighted area, then retreat to the dark forest? I would lose this one great chance for a picture of a live gorilla in his own mountain home. This was unthinkable, of course. If I should leap down from the ledge and advance onto the sloping glade, I'd meet him halfway, as it were, and get close enough for a good picture if he stepped into the patch of light.

I was acting as soon as I thought. I clambered quickly down the rocky ledge and ran swiftly across a dozen yards of green grass—breaking the most elementary rule in dealing with all wild animals, which is *Never Run!* In this case I broke the rule in the worst possible way by running *toward* the gorilla's family. I later realized there was only one interpretation he could put on my actions—I was charging to attack his mate and his children. He reacted to that thought as quickly as I had reacted to mine about making certain of my picture.

But I was so engrossed with the camera that I did not see or sense the sudden change that had come over the lumbering brute. Curiosity was instantly converted to fury, the strongest imaginable fury which erupted like an explosion set off by the gorilla's deep protective instincts. Through my view-finder I saw him raise himself to his full height, turn his body toward me, and open his mouth for a cry of rage. As I pressed the shutter button his scream split the air. It was a blood-curdling shriek of such intense, blind, unadulterated fury that I was terrified. I had to get out of there in a hurry!

I turned to run back to the ledge and caught one glimpse of the maddened gorilla as he dropped on all fours and started for me. He obviously intended to seize me in his vise-like hands and literally tear me to pieces. Fear, excruciating and almost paralyzing fear, struck every part of me. I thought that my knees would buckle and that my heart would stop beating. I wouldn't have thought it possible for a human being to be so frightened and retain consciousness.

But somehow my legs moved, and I raced for the ledge with a speed greater than any I've ever attained before or since. I didn't dare turn my head to see how close the gorilla might be, and I expected at any moment to feel the overpowering clutch of long hairy arms. A gorilla possesses deceiving speed, and this one was in a hurry. But for one thing, he would surely have caught me before I could reach the ledge and clamber up—one accidental little quirk of the terrain. Between me and the gorilla, when I took his picture, there was a depression in the ground, a kind of shallow gulley with fairly steep sides. Coming directly for me, he had to run down into it and climb up the other side again. It was no serious hazard for a gorilla, but it slowed him up just the large enough part of a second to give me precious time.

Then something happened which almost cancelled out the advantage given me by the gulley. I had reached the ledge, dismayed to find only the old wizened Pygmy standing there. Where were the others? I wasn't too confident that a three-foot ledge and one thin Pygmy spear could stoop an angry gorilla, but at least it was the first step to safety. I grasped the edge and started to swing my right leg up when I felt my shoe slipping off.

It may sound foolish, I know, to save a shoe at the possible cost of your life, but my action was almost automatic. I knew I couldn't run without the shoe. Anyway, I reached down and shoved it back on my foot, losing precious time. The old Pygmy veteran not only stood his ground but reached down one bony arm toward me. I grasped it, and it was just the leverage I needed to vault up on the ledge. There, in the instant before I whirled round to face the gorilla, I saw that Kasciula and the others were racing across the ridge toward us, apparently summoned by a call from my old friend.

The gorilla was still coming, only about ten paces away from the bottom of the ledge where I had been a moment before. When the other Pygmies suddenly appeared he stopped, scowling, snarling, his eyes burning with fiery hatred. Several Pygmies lifted their spears high, ready to fling them when he came a bit closer. Others braced them against the ground, their sharp points forming a protective fence in front of me.

The gorilla stood and glared at us. Finally he turned and ambled slowly back toward his family, looking back occasionally to threaten us with furious snarls, warning us not to follow, not to approach his family again. When he was a few feet from the trees he turned once more and barked at us. Yes, it was a bark halfway between a hound's and a seal's, not too loud but penetrating, not menacing, like the scream, but not at all friendly, either.

His family in the forest took up the barking, and then I saw that his two youngsters had climbed into a tree to watch the shindig while mama stood at the bottom. They all barked at us, and then their friends and neighbors for miles around took up the cry, and the air was filled with a cacophony of shrill barks.

Kasciula and the Pygmies relaxed. Then the Pygmy who had disappeared from the ledge when the gorilla charged me, started bawling out the two boys who had also been there. They had been so terrified at the gorilla's scream that they had taken to their heels, with the adult after them to haul them back and teach them how to act in the face of a gorilla attack. They were supposed to train themselves for gorilla hunting, but they had broken the first rule and run away. The man read the riot act to them, and they hung their heads in shame.

Then Kasciula spoke to Cézaire and me gravely. "The gorillas may still attack if we stay here," he said. "But we will do whatever you want—stay and take the attack or go after them. What do you wish?"

He seemed almost eager, and so did some of the others. I knew that they loved gorilla meat and that their chief sport was hunting. But I was in no position to agree to an attack or even a bold stand, if that might result in the death of a gorilla or some of the Pygmies. I would be held responsible by the authorities. Anyway, I felt that I had enjoyed all the contact with the primitive that I cared for right then—especially the primitive in the form of gorillas. I ordered a retreat and a return to the plantation.

As we walked down from the summit into the forest, the barking of the gorillas subsided. In the thick growth we could soon hear nothing. When Kasciula signalled that he considered everything safe, we stopped for a brief rest and a smoke. I passed out cigarettes to the Pygmies, too, and they puffed away happily. I felt elated, once I caught my breath and my knees stopped trembling, and the Pygmies seemed just as happy as I. They were pleased to know that they had helped me accomplish what I so much wanted, that they had made it possible for me to go into gorilla country unarmed, face a charging gorilla, take a picture, and get away safely.

The descent of Mount Bugalamisa was much easier than the climb up. I steadied myself with one of the Pygmy spears, careful to heed the warnings of Kasciula not to impale myself or the men with me. Back at the plantation, Ernsterhoff was delighted at our success, of course, and relieved that everyone had come back safely. I paid off the wonderful Pygmies with an extra bonus, and said good-bye to them. My admiration for these little men was tremendous—for their tracking ability, their woodsmanship, their consideration, and their bravery in facing a gorilla, their willingness to attack it if I gave the word. They had given me a rare experience, and I knew that on my first trip to Africa in search of the primitive I had achieved my primary goal even if I saw little else.

III

Animal Kingdoms of Africa

AFTER my experience with the gorillas, I was inclined to disagree with those who insisted they were near extinction. Kasciula estimated that there were close to a hundred gorillas barking at us on Mount Bugalamisa, and probably more elsewhere on the mountain. And that is only one spot where the great apes are found. If I could encounter so many in just two days, the gorilla could scarcely be considered a rare creature.

Nevertheless, it is a sound idea to protect them. When you recall that the vast herds of American bison were completely wiped out in a short period, you know that the gorilla could disappear quickly if big-game hunters and natives went after him in full cry. Provision should be made for the preservation of all wild animals in their natural environment, perhaps gorillas first of all.

In the past three decades Africa has set apart many huge tracts in which wild game can live safely—at least so far as man is concerned. But how long will the animals there remain wild? Today the lions of Kruger National Park in South Africa are so accustomed to men and automobiles that they don't bother to move when civilization rolls close by. But other sanctuaries in Africa are different, and the men in charge are determined to keep them truly wild. Too many roads and tourists will convert the wild life into semidomestic animals, but on the other hand a reasonable number of visitors will drive away the poachers who might in time kill off the wild life. A delicate balance of opposing forces is involved and game officials mean to maintain it.

New sanctuaries are being created all the time, either as

definite parks where all game is protected, or as restricted and
controlled areas in which certain species may not be hunted. In
the period between my first and my most recent expedition in
Africa, for instance, half a dozen or more huge tracts have been
set aside to remain forever in their natural state. Shortly before
my 1954-55 trip, the Queen Elizabeth National Park had been
opened in Uganda, a wild and beautiful area of about seven
hundred square miles between Lakes George and Edward, ad-
joining in part the even larger Albert National Park in the Belgian Congo.

The Kazinga Channel between the two lakes is a favorite
haunt of hippos. The park's varied terrain, ranging from a group
of extinct volcanoes to endless grassy plains, is ideally suited to
the elephant, buffalo, Uganda kob and dozens of other species
living there. The Queen Elizabeth Park officials welcome tourists and provide rough but comfortable accommodations for a
limited number; a few roads and trails have been cut through
the great reserve—but not too many—so that the visitors may see
the animals in their natural surroundings. The wild creatures
near the roads will soon forget much of their fear of men and
automobiles, but there are still vast areas far from all roads in
which the animals have no contact with human beings.

The Congo contains four great parks, in two of which no
tourists are allowed up to this time, and scores of special reserves. The first and largest, Albert National Park, stretches for
186 miles along the Albertine Rift, enclosed on both sides by
tall escarpments and at the southern end by Lake Kivu. Most
of its animal inhabitants never leave its confines except for those
inveterate long-distance travelers, the elephants. Some areas are
prohibited to tourists and ordinary travelers, such as parts of
the Virunga volcano region where gorillas abound. Special per-
mits for scientists are granted occasionally, but not often enough
for the wild animals to become accustomed to man as
something as harmless as a tree.

When I first visited the Albert National Park in 1937, it had
been established only a little over ten years, and the tourist

traffic was almost nonexistent. A genuinely primitive area about two-thirds the size of Connecticut, it contained just about every kind of vegetation, terrain and environment any African animal might want—tropical rain forests, mountains, broad savannahs, upland jungles, glaciers, rivers, swamps and half of fish-rich Lake Edward. Already its animal population was increasing, not just because hunting had been forbidden, but because beasts from surrounding territories were migrating to it. The jungle grapevine had carried the word of this fertile and now relatively safe area.

Safe from attacks by man, that is. The lion and leopard and wild dog still kill the many species of antelope, while the hyena and the vulture take care of the remains. The park authorities thus allow nature to "balance" itself. But, you may ask, isn't man part of nature, too? Modern man with a gun, with bulldozers and road-scrapers and dynamite and structural steel—that man is *not* a part of nature as naturalists use the term. Man as a primitive hunter may belong, and that's why the Pygmies remain in the region while many other native settlers have been evacuated to other locations.

The Albert National Park was the dream of an American, Carl Akeley, who saw the animal life of Africa diminishing and retreating during the two decades he traveled there in the interests of science, people and wild life. He wanted to make sure that a sizable chunk of the primitive was left intact, and he found a sympathetic listener in King Albert of the Belgians, who was an ardent outdoors man. The King had been deeply impressed by Yellowstone National Park on a visit to the United States in 1919, so Akeley's proposals were welcomed. The Park was established by decree in 1925, and has been added to since that time. Fittingly, Akeley lies buried within its boundaries on the slopes of gorilla-infested Mount Mikeno.

Our own encounter with gorillas had occurred some miles to the south, on Mount Bugalamisa, but Cézaire and I headed for the Albert National Park after this adventure. Since guns were not allowed within the animal haven, we decided to post-

pone again our purchase of weapons. Then it occurred to me
that we really didn't need guns at all, so I discussed the matter
with Cézaire.

"If we lived through the gorilla hunt without a gun," I
said, "we can get along without them entirely. I don't anticipate
being in half as much danger from any other animal ever
again, so why should we carry weapons of any kind? We're going to see more wild animals in the Albert National Park, without guns. I think it would be a good idea to make the whole
trip unarmed."

Cézaire had never heard of such a thing, but he could not
deny that we had managed to do rather well without weapons so
far. At the time I did not realize just how unusual my proposal
was, but later, when many people commented on my making
an expedition through primitive Africa without a gun, I titled
the lecture which I gave throughout the United States,
"Through Africa Unarmed."

I never had reason to regret my decision. I was not interested in killing animals, but in seeing and photographing them. I
wanted to avoid situations in which it would be necessary to
shoot. Although I took many chances during my three trips, I
can't think of a single one where my possession of a gun would
have altered the odds for or against me. So I never carried a
weapon in the course of my three African trips—except on my
1954-55 journey, when officials required me to wear a revolver
as protection against—not wild animals, but men—the Mau Mau
terrorists of Kenya. In certain circumstances, notably when
photographing lions close up, I was covered by professional
hunters with guns, but not one of them ever had to shoot to
save my life.

One of the first spots we visited in the Albert National
Park was the Rutshuru River, famous as the home of hippos.
There I obtained one of the most unusual film shots ever taken
—unfortunately one that cannot be shown to the general public.

We drove over flat savannahs toward the river—grasslands
with swampy patches and a few trees. Here and there we saw

mudholes and from each hole a set of parallel tracks, quite deep, as if a small cart with wide wheels, heavily laden, had retraced the route many times. They were hippopotamus tracks leading to the river from favored feeding places. Since an adult hippo may weigh as much as four tons, it was not unreasonable to find deep tracks.

A hippo isn't afraid of anything, not even another hippo. He can break a lion's or a crocodile's back with one crunching bite of his gigantic jaws. He'll try his best to do the same to another hippo if he thinks his mate or his favorite sunning place on the bank of the river are being appropriated. And the Rutshuru River in some places is so crowded that the better locations on bank and sand bar are taken.

Cézaire stopped the car on a high bank above the river, and I gasped at the sight below me. There were literally hundreds of hippos in the river, along the muddy banks, on little islands and sandbars. The water seemed to be full of them, too, diving, squirming, snorting and cavorting. One would sink below the surface with contented gurgles, emitting huge bubbles, only to burst to the surface a few yards away puffing and blowing. Another would dive and be gone, apparently forever. A hippo can remain submerged perhaps ten minutes—some authorities say much longer—can swim underwater with grace and agility, or walk along the bottom.

I found a spot where the reeds and bushes along the shore grew thick and high, so that I could get near the hippos without being seen. Not far away a tremendous bull hippo slept with his head resting on another's back. A huge scar, looking red and fresh, ran down his side, the memento of a recent battle. My camera was going, and I suddenly saw in my view-finder something riding on top of the water. I let the camera run for a bit, to make sure of getting this shot even though I didn't know what it was. Then I took the camera from my eye and looked. It was a hippo baby, small and almost pink, riding on the back of his mother, who was sedately swimming downstream with only her snout showing. No crocodile was going to get *her* baby.

She deposited the young one on a sand bar and nudged away a few friends to make room for him. Then she lay down herself and almost squashed her baby to death. The baby squealed, the hippos nearby shifted slightly, reluctantly, and the baby went to sleep.

I turned to my left, where I heard some thrashing in the water. There I saw a pair of hippos not more than fifty feet away. Only the back and ears of the female showed above the water, and the male was in an undignified but for him quite natural position. Turning the camera on its tripod, I caught them with the telephoto lens *in flagrante delicto*. The amorous gentleman must have heard me, for he suddenly stopped his thrashing, turned his head in my direction, and hurled toward me a look so nasty that I felt I should apologize for having intruded. Taking his not-too-subtle hint, I clambered up the bank and into the car. We departed, and they continued their love-making undisturbed. I had a rare motion picture shot.

On later expeditions, my hippo encounters were less intimate but more exciting. One of the most unusual came about through my work with the fabulous Commandant Ernest Hubert, director of the Albert National Park in the Congo. Stories about this man's amazing dealings with wild animals had been circulating for some time. Negley Farson, author of two excellent books on Africa, had not quite believed them but finally saw with his own eyes that Hubert turned away menacing creatures by throwing chunks of mud at them. Since I always sought out those rare individuals who have an uncanny, almost instinctive understanding of wild animals, I was eager to meet and work with Hubert.

On my 1946 trip, he welcomed me to the Park with great warmth and charm, heightened, I think, because mine was the first expedition since the beginning of World War II and he was a bit lonely. Slight, compact, energetic, witty, and absolutely fearless, he offered to help me in every possible way and set out immediately to find herds of buffalo, hippos, and elephants for me to film. Our first jaunt was down to the Rutshuru River to see hippos. We went in my truck, with one of his native boys walking ahead. The truck proceeded slowly because of rocks and anthills hidden in the tall grass, so the boy was a couple of hundred feet ahead. Not far from the river, a big bull hippo materialized from a mudhole, looking like a gigantic self-propelled piece of the wet earth he had been lying in.

The hippo was to the left of the truck and some distance ahead of us. The boy was directly between the hippo and the river, and the hippo didn't like the idea at all. He headed for the boy on the run. Although his gait was awkward and lumbering, the beast covered the ground at a remarkable speed. The boy started running back toward the truck, but it looked to me as if the hippo might cut him off before he reached us. Hubert apparently thought so, too, for he leapt from the truck and ran toward the hippo. He had no gun or weapon of any kind, of course, but still he ran toward the four-ton monster as if he intended to put it across his knee and spank it.

When he was about seventy-five feet from the hippo, Hubert stopped, waved his arms wildly, and shouted at the top of his lungs, "Hey! Hey! Hey!" The big brute slowed down, came to a stop, looked at Hubert and then at the boy, who had just about made the truck, and turned off to one side in a huff. It was difficult to credit my eyes, but I could believe, now, the story about the angry lion that charged Hubert. The gentleman just held up his hand imperiously and shouted, "Stop!" The lion stopped.

Hubert came back to the car without a word, acting as if he had done nothing unusual. And I guess he hadn't, by his standards. When we reached the river I saw even more hippos than on my first trip and, under Hubert's guidance, got quite close to some of them. They were all rather busy, swimming and diving just for the fun of it, and they looked not at all like the unmoving lumps of flesh in most of our zoos. Hippos don't find food in the water they spend so much time in. The river is just a daytime rest-home for them, where they can swim and doze and fight. They are nocturnal creatures, really, climbing up the river banks at night and wandering for miles if necessary in search of sweet grasses and plants.

As I looked, some of the swimmers came ashore for a nap. Two big bulls began disputing a sunny spot on the sandbar a little way out, and neither one would back down. Soon they were having a battle royal, each one opening his scoopshovel of a mouth wide, showing vast pink interiors and wicked looking teeth. The one animal a hippo has the most trouble biting, however, is another hippo. Although these two bulls thrashed the water and tore up the sand, they did little damage to each other that I could see. Other hippos reluctantly moved out of the way, but the scores of pelicans walking up and down the sand bars paid no attention.

After lunch that same day, we went out in the truck again, and as we crossed the plains I saw innumerable waterbucks, cobs, topis, reedbucks, and other kinds of antelope. With these delicate morsels in such profusion, I knew there must be lion about, but on my first trip I had been unable to catch sight of a single one in Belgian Congo. East Africa had made up for the lack, of course. I asked Hubert about lions.

"Yes, we have plenty of lions," he said, "but you'd rarely see them out at this time of day. Just before and after dusk is the best time."

I tried every evening I was there, but still saw no lions in the Congo. I heard them in the middle of the night, in the midst of all the other night noises the primitive world offers. The hyena's is one of the most chilling, but the most baffling is the noise made by a hippopotamus scratching itself against a tree close to your *rondavel*, or visitor's cabin, in the Park.

On our second day in the Park, while we were scouting around the Ruindi plains with Hubert, we spotted a large herd of elephants. Approaching them on the lee side, we came fairly close in the truck, then stopped and began to walk. This was against the rules of the park, dismounting from a car anywhere, but as the guest of Hubert I could do anything he did. He was as eager as I was, it seemed, for me to get dramatic movie shots. I told my cameraman to lag behind us somewhat, in an effort to get some shots with his six-inch lens showing me taking pictures of the elephants. I was producing for Hollywood this time, and just plain elephants are not really enough. You have to show man in relation to elephant, especially a man being somewhat foolish and getting too close.

Because of the demands of a feature film, I took far more chances on my second trip than on my first, but when I was with Hubert I never really felt that I was risking my life. I had such confidence in his judgment and in his knowledge of animals that I never hesitated to do whatever he suggested.

As we walked closer to the elephant herd, I saw that there were big ones and little ones both. I looked questioningly at Hubert, and he nodded casually, indicating that he thought it perfectly all right to proceed. I got closer to elephants than I had ever been in the wilds, taking many feet of color film as they grazed, flopped their ears, and shifted position slightly. Behind me, the cameraman was photographing the scene too, of course. That sequence came out quite well and in "Savage Splendor" you can see Hubert and me uncomfortably close to the herd. But I don't think they ever found out we were there.

When we were back in the truck, I asked Hubert how he kept elephants from charging. I didn't think shouting "Hey!" or throwing chunks of mud would suffice. He agreed, and said that a racing automobile engine was the best thing to divert them when they were angry. The horn seemed to have little effect, but a roaring motor really baffled them.

"If I didn't know better, I might think this herd looked like a bunch of circus elephants," I said, "as tame as you could want them."

"That's why the elephant can be the most dangerous animal here," Hubert said. "He looks so peaceful and well-behaved that your caution is apt to be lulled. Then you run into one with a grudge against men. Elephants travel long distances, you know. The other animals may stay within the confines of the Park—it's so big—but elephants regularly take little jaunts of a hundred or hundred and fifty miles. One of them may get wounded and walk around with a bullet in him or suffer from tusk-ache. This makes him short-tempered and he will charge without question when he gets the smell of man again. You never know when one of those bad-tempered boys will be in a herd."

I was happy that Hubert had brought up this subject after, not before, I had filmed the herd so close.

Hubert drove me about twenty miles to a big hyena hideout, which looked like a huge pyramid of dried underbrush. We got out of the truck and Hubert picked up a big stick to beat against the mound. Shouting and pounding away for only a few moments he roused everything within a mile's distance. Suddenly a dozen or more hyenas darted out of the mound, streaking by us with very unpleasant snarls and disappearing in the tall grass. They were so fast that I couldn't get a picture of them, but not too fast for me to smell them. They have the odor of rottenness about them, perhaps from the fact that they eat carrion, like vultures. They are scavengers, and some native tribes still put out their dead for them to dispose of. The hyena follows the lion to take what the king of beasts may leave. He follows wounded animals, waiting patiently for them to die. He will pursue for hours or even days a female antelope about to give birth to young. He wants to be on hand when the calf is born so he can devour it. The hyena is a coward and he has been known to bite sleeping natives in the face.

When he doesn't have a hideout of brush, he goes underground for the daylight hours. He doesn't trouble to dig a hole for himself, however. He waits until a wart hog has left its hole to go about its morning business, then backs into the hole hindend first. This may account for the fact that his shaggy coat always looks as if it needed a good brushing. When the wart hog comes home in the evening, the hyena snarls and bristles, so the poor wart hog has to rush off and dig another hole in a hurry before sunset brings out the lions and their keen appetite for wart hogs. Many natives believe that the hyena is a hermaph-

rodite and that the male suckles the young. Actually, the confusion is due to the resemblance between the male and female
genitals.

From a distance the wild dog looks something like a hyena,
but the character is quite different. The wild dog is a killer, not
a scavenger. He is brave, willing to tackle something three times
as big as he is, even when alone. Usually of course, the dogs
travel in packs of five to twenty, although some hunters have reported close to a hundred in a single pack. Short-haired, big-eared
and spotted irregularly with black, white, and tan, the wild dog,
or lycaon, is not a handsome animal. But he is built for speed
and endurance and can outrun almost any wild animal on the
plains. And he is a killer, implacable, vicious and filled with a
lust for the slaughter in addition to a voracious appetite.

When they are chasing a fast antelope, baying like real
hunting hounds, they adopt a technique of community effort
that no single animal can beat. One leader sets a very stiff pace,
right behind the fleeing prey, while the others of the pack lag
behind a bit. When the leader tires he drops back and another
takes over. When the antelope begins to falter, all the dogs
come alongside and slash with their teeth at the flanks of the
doomed animal, ripping the skin until the intestines come out.
I've never heard of wild dogs attacking a human being, but I
always noticed that the natives gave them a wide berth.

The most dangerous animal in all of Africa, in my opinion,
is the buffalo, and he is Number One or Two on every hunter's
list. The gorilla will usually keep out of your way, and anyway
you have to go looking for him on the mountains. The lion? No,
he attacks and eats only when he is hungry and doesn't always
pursue the battle once he has knocked his enemy down. The
elephant can be deadly in a charge, but he is more apt to move
off a little rather than pick a fight. The leopard may come close
to the buffalo as a dangerous creature, but he is largely nocturnal
and most sensible people do not wander around in the open at
night where leopards are known to live.

You'll find buffalo almost everywhere in Central Africa, although the herds are not nearly as big as they were in the old days. One buffalo alone, however, can take care of you neatly and thoroughly. He is close to a ton of hard muscle, with sharp horns whose roots meet in the middle over his forehead to form a protective armor plate in this most vulnerable spot. On top of all this, he is smart, fast and often bad-tempered. His sight, hearing and smell are all excellent and his truculence seems to increase mightily when man is brought into his ken through one of those sharp senses.

Hunters with the best high-powered guns have great respect for the African buffalo. In the first place, when he charges, he is never diverted by a noise or a shot that hits him—unless it kills him, too. And when he charges, he presents a mighty small area of vulnerability. Hunters have pumped four or five bullets into a buffalo and had him keep coming at full speed. And even when wounded, he is smart enough to backtrack and sneak up behind the hunter to catch him unawares. There is a long list of white hunters who have been killed by buffaloes.

And I was asking Hubert to lead me to a herd of buffalo so I could take pictures of them—without any weapon, without any hunter behind me to cover me with a gun! We were in the sanctuary and no guns were allowed. That was one factor in my favor, of course. Very likely the buffalo in the park had experienced no hunters for many years, unless they were migrants who had come to this animal haven for safety and because they hated hunters so much.

Hubert was reassuring, however. He did not minimize the pugnacity of the buffalo, but felt that those in the Park would be less likely than others to charge readily. Then he found a herd for me, and we went together to film them.

The buffalo were grazing in the grass, which did not obscure our view of them. We saw them as black dots from where we parked our truck and started walking toward them downwind. I followed Hubert's instructions carefully, walking at first just a

few paces ahead of him. My cameraman stayed a hundred feet
behind us to get pictures of us and the buffalo together.

"To the left a little," Hubert whispered. I veered slightly to
the left.

"Stop," he cautioned, and I stopped. One of the buffalo had
looked up. When he saw nothing move he went back to his
munching again.

"Now forward carefully," Hubert indicated and I stepped
slowly toward the buffalo. I suddenly thought of something and
looked around. There wasn't a tree in sight. Glancing back to
see if my cameraman was in position, I noticed that the truck
was now about half a mile away. If the buffalo charged, we had
no chance whatsoever.

"Stop," Hubert signaled, for I was too far ahead of him
now for him to speak without disturbing the grazing herd.

Two buffalo looked up and saw us. They were only about
a hundred feet away from us and I could tell that even Hubert
had no thought of going any closer. I don't think you ever go
any closer without asking for trouble.

One of the leaders turned toward the rest of the herd, and
the other turned toward us. He stretched out his neck, as if
sniffing. I had my camera ready and started the film running
through. The sound of it must have reached the buffalo, for he
lifted his head a little and stared more intently, more ominously.
He was obviously not pleased.

He waited, as if to see whether we would come any closer.
Suddenly I felt as if I could put myself inside that animal's
mind and feelings. I knew what he was thinking. We didn't belong there, and he didn't like us. We had disturbed his feeding.
If we went away, all right. But if not, he'd give the signal and
take care of us. But he couldn't quite make up his mind what
he should do.

Hubert and I did not move. If we had started back, the
movement might have been the trigger of decision for that
buffalo. The best procedure was just to stand there and hope he

would be convinced that we meant no harm. Maybe he would figure that they should move on to another fresh patch of grass, anyway.

That is exactly what he decided. At a signal which I could not see or hear, the twenty-five or twenty-six big black buffalo turned slowly and wandered off into the grass. We stood still until they were out of sight, and then I felt as if I hadn't breathed for a long time. I relaxed, and turned to smile at Hubert. He appeared to be calm and pleased that I had obtained the pictures I wanted. Actually I was more interested in the pictures my cameraman got of the whole scene.

They did turn out well, all right. In the film you can see me and the buffalo in the same scene, even in the same frame. You can see the lead buffalo staring at me, his head covering almost the entire screen as he debates what action he should take. I see those thoughts in him every time I look at the film, and other people have told me they have seen them too.

Only two years later, Tom Marvel, in his book *The New Congo*, told how Hubert took him to see a herd of buffalo. Hubert told him that the park buffalo did not charge any more, except on very serious provocation, and nobody ever gave them that in that sacrosanct domain. This means that the buffalo are getting used to men. More and more people have been visiting the Park since my trip after the end of World War II. Before too long, the buffalo there will be like the bears in Yellowstone, a little unpredictable but really not dangerous. But I can't believe that they will ever stop tourists' cars and beg for sweets. Africa may be getting civilized in a hurry, but it can't go that far.

IV

Visits to the
Stone-Age Pygmies

A T first glance, Pygmies are caricatures of human beings, miniature imitations fashioned by a clumsy hand. I caught myself looking at them as I might at circus freaks or zoo animals, until checked by the thought, "How do I look to them?"

If a Pygmy looks like a wizened ten-year-old in my eyes, he must see me as an awkward giant. My figure must seem unalluringly straight and flat, lacking the many curves that appeal to a Pygmy—balloon-like belly, sway back, and outsize, impudent buttocks. His golden-brown skin no doubt seems just right to him, a proper compromise between the brown-black of his Bantu neighbors on the edge of the forest and the pasty pallor of the occasional white visitor. He may suspect that I'm not that color all over, but how can he tell when, instead of wearing a sensible liana G-string with barkcloth apron, I cover all but hands and face with layers of cloth and encase my feet in heavy leather boots?

On several occasions I lived in the Great Ituri Forest with Pygmies who had rarely seen white men—some of them never had. Once one grew so bold as to rub an exploratory finger over the back of my hand, to see if the white came off, like the paint he and other natives sometimes smear on faces and bodies. Pygmies show more curiosity about white men than most primitive tribes I've encountered. They felt my clothes, examined my tent and stared at my cameras. When I prepared food I had brought along, they surrounded me in a respectful and silent circle to watch me eat, glancing occasionally at one another and grinning. Once I opened a can of bacon and fried some, its aroma filling the little forest clearing. The crowd was larger that day, and those in the front row even drooled openly. They never asked for anything and there were too many present for me to distribute my small allotment.

Despite his curiosity, no Pygmy feels that he understands a white man—those incredible creatures who would rather take pictures of animals than kill and eat them. He is acutely perceptive of the white visitor's *feelings*, however, sensing anger, impatience or happiness almost as soon as the emotion is felt. And he is respectful and cooperative, for white men invariably bring gifts—above all precious salt. Hold out a handful of sugar and a handful of salt to a Pygmy and he will snatch the salt, cramming it into his mouth as if it were candy. It is the one serious nutritive lack in his lush forest.

When you first meet a Pygmy, you cannot help staring at him with a kind of disbelief. The true Pygmy, the Bambuti of the Ituri Forest, averages four feet in height, and for most of us the only humans that size are children. Pygmies, however, are obviously *not* children, in spite of a certain childlike quality, a naive directness about them. Some have grey kinky hair and chin whiskers, and faces wrinkled like a butternut. There are three-foot-nine-inch matrons with babies on their hips, suspended in a kind of sling from the shoulder, and the shortness of the mothers is accentuated because Pygmy babies are normal size, as large as ours at the same age. Pygmy children just stop growing when they are about ten years old.

It is confusing to look at a female the size of your niece in the fourth grade and note that she is a toothless old hag with breasts like long empty leather pouches. Or to see a young fellow apparently too young for his first communion and realize that he may have slain fifty elephants by hamstringing their hind legs. Your preconceived notions about values and relationships collapse—which is one good reason for exploring.

If you live and work with Pygmies long enough, in their own forest, this first startling impact of their juvenile size diminishes and even disappears. They are so perfectly adapted to their environment, to their work and play and houses and weapons, that they strike you as just about right. If you think of size any more, you think of your own awkward bulk, entirely too cumbersome for skillful forest tracking. When that time comes, you can finally begin to see the Pygmies with a true unjaundiced eye, as human beings with a different heritage, background and set of merits and faults.

But can any white man get to *know* them? I think so, though it is customary for travelers and explorers to deny it. Even some who have lived among Pygmies longer than I did say that we cannot possibly bridge the evolutionary gap of several thousand years separating us from these living "fossils" of the Paleolithic Age. I suspect that this is a fine piece of rationalization, however, to explain away failure. Certainly Dr. Paul Schebesta, the great anthropologist who lived with Pygmies for long periods, came to know them very well. Perhaps I'm fooling myself, but I know some Bambuti Pygmies in the Ituri Forest better than I know some New Yorkers with whom I associate fairly regularly. The Pygmy never hides his true self behind a wall of pretense or inhibitions.

You cannot know much about Pygmies if you merely stop along the road from Irumu to Mambasa and have your picture taken with what are now called "Cook's Pygmies" because they have become a standard tourist attraction. In the thirties, when I first visited Africa, the road was relatively new and few tourists traveled that way. For one thing, there was only one garage on a stretch of about six hundred miles cut through the primitive tropical jungle, a strip so thin that the forest could have reclaimed it without a trace in a few months. As you sped along it, you might *know* that Pygmies, okapi, elephants, leopards, aardvarks, monkeys, parrots, chimpanzees and pythons lived behind the green wall on either side—but only by hearsay. You'd probably never see them. A movement, a flutter of leaves, would tell you that something had been there a moment before you looked, but what?

Sometimes, if you traveled at night, you might find your way blocked by several elephants, and you'd hope they would just go on across the road and act as if you were not there. At other times, especially at dawn or dusk, you might see a mother baboon scampering out of the way with her youngsters, one clinging to her back. And if you traveled the road often enough, you might eventually come upon a group of Pygmies, who would flee behind the green wall at your approach. If you had with you a guide who spoke Kingwana, the Ituri brand of Swahili that Pygmies are likely to understand, and if one Pygmy was braver than the rest or happened to know your guide, perhaps he would venture within twenty paces of you, looking as frightened as a wild animal, hungry for the food you might give him but fearful that you mean to capture or kill him. Reassuring gifts of salt could bring him closer and even entice from the forest some of his companions. At best, however, the interview would have been brief and no more rewarding in human understanding than a ten-minute visit of a Martian to Earth.

Now, of course, changes have been made. After the road came clearings made by the Bantus, little villages where they grow plantains and beans and rice. Since some Pygmies occasionally visit those villages, a few have become more familiar with the road and the incredible men and machines that travel on it. They may pose for pictures or even stage a lackluster dance.

All this is really not as bad as it sounds. One narrow road cutting through a few thousand square miles of primitive forest does not bring civilization. If one of the Bantus of a roadside village should venture a mile from his home without a Pygmy guide, he would never return. Not long ago, a Bantu woman was lost for two days in the forest, wandering frantically in circles. The first miracle was that she still lived at the end of two days; the second that a Pygmy who knew her chanced upon her.

He led her to her village, which was only a few hundred yards away all the time.

The Bantus of the villages and the Pygmies have developed a strange interdependency. Only through the Bantu villagers can one make contact with the Bambuti Pygmies of the Ituri. For a half century every explorer, every government official, has found it necessary to use the village Bantu to reach the Pygmies. Even missionaries such as my friends Bill Deans and William Spees and the lone white settler in the Ituri, the late Pat Putnam, came to know the Pygmies first through the good offices of nearby Bantus. Long after they had become firmly established as friends of the Bambuti, they had to conduct all important affairs through the proper Bantu overlords.

If you want to buy a Pygmy bow and arrow, a spear or a headdress for a souvenir, you cannot buy it from the Pygmy who seems to own these things—no matter how much you offer. You must purchase it from the Bantu who "owns" the Pygmy. If you need Pygmy guides or hunters, you negotiate with the Bantu "masters."

None of these terms is quite correct, nor do they give the right impression of the relationship of Bantu and Pygmy. The little Bambuti are not slaves, by any means—they are, on the contrary, fiercely independent and jealous of their rights and prerogatives. A Bantu may say that he "owns" a certain number of Pygmies, and he always refers to them as "my Pygmies," but he does not own them in the sense that *ante-bellum* Southerners owned slaves. He could not, for instance, remove the Pygmy from his section of the forest if he tried—and he would never dream of trying.

The Bantu is contemptuous of the Pygmy and at the same time afraid of him. He considers himself as far above the forest dwellers as most Americans consider themselves above the village Bantu. He laughs at the Pygmies, and explains to the white man that they are not really human beings; they are animals, perhaps a cut above the chimpanzee, but still animals because they live in the forest like animals.

Bantu villagers have partially domesticated these wild creatures for the usual purpose—to obtain useful goods and labor.
From the Pygmy hunters, the villagers obtain meat to eat and
ivory to sell, plus some manual labor in the gardens during the
dry season. In return, they have used the good American advertising technique of creating a demand and then satisfying it.
For centuries the Pygmies lived completely self-sufficient lives
in the forest; then the villagers introduced them to bananas and
manioc and sugar cane, to iron for arrow and spear heads, to
tobacco and hemp for smoking, and to more salt. The Pygmies
succumbed to these luxuries, although they seem to have rejected all others such as the paying of taxes, clothing and, in
the main, religion.

The Pygmies have mortgaged themselves for the sake of
their new appetites. If Bambuti society had been more advanced, both Pygmy and Bantu might have developed their relationship through commercial channels alone, through straight
barter and trade. The forest hunters could have brought their
meat and ivory to the market and sold to the highest bidder.
But the Pygmy had no concept of commerce and could think
only in terms of individual relationships. If he gave meat to a
village Bantu, that man gave him bananas and arrow heads
made of iron. So he dealt with that Bantu alone, and perhaps
persuaded his brother and his cousins to do the same. In time,
no Pygmy could get along without a close tie-up with a villager, and some villagers found themselves "owning" from three
to twenty or more Pygmies.

It was a good arrangement for the villagers, who proceeded
to rob the poor Pygmies blind. A hunter might bring in ivory
tusks which the villager could sell to the licensed ivory dealer
for two hundred dollars; the man who risked his life to kill the
elephant might receive the equivalent of ten dollars, while the
middleman villager kept the balance. In a week's time, of course,
neither Pygmy nor villager had anything to show, since both are
spendthrifts. Tomorrow? They don't think about that.

The Pygmy knows, most of the time, that he is getting a

raw deal. He complains, verbally abuses his Bantu overlord, and tries to haggle over the price of the next thing he brings in. But he never contemplates staying away from the village entirely. He could disappear into the forest and no Bantu could go after him and find him. But if he fails to bring in his supposed quota of meat or acts recalcitrant in any way, the Bantu master withdraws his marijuana or beer and that makes the Pygmy knuckle under quickly. He may retaliate by sneaking down to the village in a heavy rain, when all villagers are in their huts, and stealing fruits or vegetables from a garden—usually the garden of another Bantu, not his master. If he is caught, his master must pay for what he stole.

Even though the village Bantus look on Pygmies as animals, they will take Pygmy women as wives readily enough, especially if their Bantu wives are sterile—an increasingly common condition resulting from that early fruit of civilization, venereal disease. Intermarriage works only one way, however, for no Bantu woman ever marries a Pygmy. She could not possibly stand the nomad hunter's life in the forest, and no Pygmy male would abandon his natural home for life in the village.

Many Pygmy women who have married Bantus find, in time, that they must return to the forest. They run away from the villages and go back to their families in the Ituri. Once, when I was staying with the Pygmies in the forest, two young men from the village came to visit their Pygmy mother who had run away from her Bantu husband. There was a noisy and joyous reunion, then the sons returned to the village. They were thoroughgoing villagers just as their mother was, despite a few years' exile, a forest Pygmy. The husband did not really mind; he had his sons, which was the chief object of taking the Pygmy as wife. She was never as good a housekeeper as his Bantu wife, anyway.

The unusual symbiosis of Bantu and Pygmy is a fortunate thing for the traveler who wants to meet Pygmies, who trust only those strangers introduced under the auspices of their Bantu masters. At the approach of anyone else, the Pygmies simply disappear into a few thousand square miles of forest—a place that even the Arab slave traders of the last century dared not penetrate. A Pygmy can still be a deadly opponent to anyone poaching on his territory without permission. Stanley found the Pygmies as "vicious" as any native enemies he encountered in Africa, and even today their Bantu masters maintain a healthy respect for Pygmy bows and arrows. They look like toys, but the twenty-inch bows are accurate in Bambuti hands and the arrows are dipped in poison. Which poison depends upon which book about Pygmies you read; some say it comes from strychnos and euphorbia trees, others from dried snake venom, still others from the roots of swamp orchids or the decayed bodies of insects. The chances are that Pygmies use all of these and perhaps others, depending upon what is available in their part of the forest at the time. In any event, the poison is effective, as are many of the thousand other herbs and plants used as medicines and charms.

I met my first Pygmies in 1937 with the help of Kalumé, chief of a Bantu village on the eastern edge of the Ituri Forest, between Beni and Irumu. The Bantus are made up of scores of different tribes, of course. Those in this region were the Bandande, among whom Kalumé was an important leader, a genuine Sultani with numerous *capitas*, or subchiefs, beneath him.

Kalumé greeted me with friendliness and courtesy, a tall and well-muscled man in a long cloth toga. He smiled broadly as I made my speech, which had been written out for me in phonetic Kingwana by Commander Attilio Gatti, who had known Kalumé some years before. The sounds I uttered haltingly meant nothing to me, but much to my surprise they seemed intelligible to Kalumé. I was prepared to fall back on the interpretive resources of Cézaire, but it tickled my vanity to have conversed at least once in Kingwana on my first trip to Africa.

Business with Kalumé was easily conducted; a little something for him and his *capitas*, salt, palm oil and other gifts for the Bambuti Pygmies—that was all. Would we prefer to visit with the Pygmies here in the village or go to them in the forest? There was a Pygmy clearing not too far away, and the path leading to it was well worn for an Ituri forest path.

I much preferred Pygmies in their own homes, in their natural surroundings. A Pygmy standing self-consciously on display in a Bantu village would be too much like a lion in a zoo or an elephant in a circus. He would blink in the unaccustomed light of the bright sun and probably get a headache, since the Bambuti complain that they dislike leaving the forest because the sun hurts their heads. I'd give him salt; he'd stuff it in his mouth and grin; there would be an exchange of fatuous questions and answers through an interpreter—and that would be that.

So we walked a few miles through the Ituri Forest, after Kalumé had sent a messenger in advance to let the Pygmies know that white men were coming with gifts. I had hoped that the Bandande chief would summon some of his Pygmies by drum, as I knew they did in many places. But in this area, the Pygmy clearing was near the village—only a few miles away— and the path was sufficiently plain for a villager to follow. Later I was to hear plenty of drums—drums deep in the forest that summoned more than five hundred of the Bambuti. They never failed to send a little shiver down my back and transport me a few centuries backward in time. Everyone must carry somewhere in his genes a memory of the primitive life from which he was sprung, and drums seem to awaken some of those long dormant memories. It is not a thought or picture that returns at such moments, but rather a feeling, a feeling foreign to everything else in his life, but somehow vaguely and disturbingly familiar.

A walk of three or four miles doesn't sound like much of a chore, unless you are speaking of the Ituri Forest. There the jungle seems to resent your intrusion and make every effort to push you back, trip you up, and hold onto you to prevent further progress. Later, when I followed the Bambuti deep in the forest, I knew that this first path had been an easy one. But at the time it seemed impassable in spots and difficult going all the way. True, our Bantu guides slipped along fairly deftly, and they were far from expert woodsmen, but they made my efforts look laborious and clumsy.

This was one of the first excursions I made into tropical jungles, so I shall never forget it. Thorns reached out and snagged my clothes, holding fast until the tough cloth tore, nettles stung my face and hands, giant ferns slapped my face wetly, looping lianas wound themselves around my body like the tentacles of an octopus. This sort of thing was particularly bad during a detour of only a few hundred yards around a giant mahogany tree that had toppled across the path when lightning struck it.

The crashing of the huge tree—a good eight or nine feet in diameter—at least enabled us to see a patch of sky for a few minutes and to take a few pictures. Everywhere else there was a thick green roof overhead which reduced the bright sunlight to a greenish twilight haze. I knew that within a few years that brilliant, dazzling patch of sun and sky would be obliterated by one of the many trees struggling upward to take the fallen monarch's place. But other patches would be opened up as other trees, some growing as high as two hundred feet, were destroyed by termites or were simply overcome by the weight of many years.

We saw one huge nest of termites that might do the job. It stood over ten feet high and must have contained billions of the tiny creatures. The sickly white insects live inside, guarding their queen, an immense bloated egg machine, many times larger than her royal guards. The workers, unable to endure the light, never emerge, but toil ceaselessly to cultivate the fungus on which they all feed. When I tapped the mound with a long pole, however, an army of soldiers poured out, searching frantically and pugnaciously for the enemy and squirting streams of viscous liquid from their head-syringes to entangle and trap any insect invader.

Back on the so-called path I was amazed to strike a stretch

relatively free of undergrowth, but in its place was swampy, gooey mud clinging with the tenacity of glue. Here I would have welcomed some sturdy lianas by which I might pull myself along, but the only thing to grab was air. This, of course, was so heavily laden with moisture that it seemed to have substance.

Once past the swamp the ground seemed to rise somewhat. In the forest it is not easy to distinguish hills because you cannot get enough perspective to see a hill; the enveloping foliage is too close. You feel yourself bending forward slightly as you walk and realize that you are doing this because you are ascending an incline. In ten minutes, by the same sort of feeling, I knew that I was going down the hill. Aviators talk of flying "by the seat of your pants." I was handling my body by the feel on the soles of my feet.

As we went deeper into the forest, we began to see a little of its wild life. Splashing across a narrow, crystal-clear stream, I saw a long snake slither into the underbrush, but my glance was too brief to tell me for certain what kind it was. When I described it later as being very thin—only about the size of my thumb—but incredibly long, perhaps eight or nine feet, I learned that it was probably a black mamba, considered one of the deadliest of all African snakes.

I slipped and fell on a rotting log that lay lengthwise in the path, and a parrot screeched above my head, as if making fun of my awkwardness. The cry was taken up by other parrots some distance away, and I heard above me the whirring of wings and the rustling of leaves. But I could see nothing. Then we came to a space clear of undergrowth and I made an excuse to stop and catch my breath. Some pink and white orchids suddenly fascinated me and I examined them most carefully until my heart stopped pounding. As we started on again, a cloud of huge butterflies rose up and circled hysterically toward the high branches. A familiar sound came to me, and I stopped again. It seemed as if I were in the bird house at the zoo in Central Park, except that I smelled flowers and rotting vegetation instead of

that obnoxious odor which exists in all zoos. Weaver birds
wheezed, parrots squawked, and the tiny sunbirds tittered their
high, wiry tones.

Sometimes you can walk through the forest for an hour
without hearing a sound except the racket you are making as
you break branches beneath your feet and stumble over hidden
roots. You stop and hear only the strange emptiness which is
absence of sound, like that on the other end of a dead telephone
connection. At such times, not even the air moves to stir one
leaf so that it rubs against another. So far as you can tell, the
forest is uninhabited by living things. Then at other times there
will come a bedlam of sound, a turmoil of movement. Birds
screech, sing and cheep while fluttering from branch to branch.
Black and white colobus monkeys argue and scold as they swing
in panic far above your head. A covey of guinea fowl takes off
like a squadron of bombers. A sudden crash of branches and
tossing of leaves make you realize that some big creature not
ten feet to the right has bolted in terror, and you wonder—leopard, elephant, okapi, wart hog? This brings mixed feelings, for
you would like to see the rare okapi, dread an angry elephant.
Never mind, you do not know what it was and never will know.
It was not a Pygmy, you may be sure; he would not have made
so much noise.

I finally got my second wind and at the same time seemed
to acquire a certain amount of agility and grace in walking
through the forest. Perhaps the Ituri gave up its attempts to
keep me out, since I'd come so far, but at any rate I stopped
stumbling and managed to evade clutching thorns and embrac-
ing lianas more frequently. But by this time the mosquitoes
and other insects were almost unendurable. They had been with
us right along, but we kept accumulating more as we progressed.
Perhaps the insects have a forest telegraph like the Pygmies'
drums and sent word of our arrival ahead. They stung, bit, and
buzzed about our heads in clouds that moved with us. When I
complained loudly, Cézaire remarked that we were fortunate not

to have encountered any safari ants. The Ituri was saving them for later.

Despite the hardships of our little hike, I was excited. I had wanted to find the primitive—and here I was. The walk was only three or four miles, but it took me back—how many thousands of years?

Well, I am not a paleontologist or anthropologist, but my dictionary and encyclopedia give clear, concise definitions of the various ages of Man. In the Paleolithic Period, man had achieved a rudimentary speech and social organization, but had no settled homes, engaged in no agricultural pursuits. The following Period, the Neolithic, saw the development of agriculture, the domestication of animals, usually settled homes, and the use of metal. To my mind, this placed the Bambuti Pygmies squarely in the Paleolithic Period, for they live by hunting alone, cultivate no crops, have no domesticated animals except their small hunting dogs. They have used iron for only a few decades and obtain that from their Neolithic neighbors, the Bantus, who also make earthen jars for the forest nomads. On my 1937 trip, I saw only a very few such jars in Pygmy camps nearest the villages, none at all in more remote areas, where meat was hung over the fire and green bananas roasted in the coals. On subsequent trips, I found more and more jars being used by the forest people.

As for speech, Pygmies usually talk the language of their Bantu masters. A basic rudimentary language called Kilesi, or sometimes Kimbuti, probably derived from the original Pygmy tongue about which nothing is known, is spoken by all Pygmy tribes in their relations with each other. Their form of Kingwana, the *lingua franca* of Central Africa, is so simple as to be a kind of Pidgin Kingwana, which sounds remarkably like noises that animals make.

Social organization? The family, somewhat extended, is their organization—no more.

Aside from a few recent borrowings from the Bantus then,

the Bambuti Pygmies obviously live today as in the Paleolithic Period. My authorities say that this is the earliest period of man on earth, extending from the beginning up to about twenty thousand years ago.

Yes, three or four miles took me back twenty thousand years!

I was mulling over this awe-inspiring thought when a light almost blinded me. We stepped from the half light of the forest into a clearing, where shafts of the sun's rays cut the gloom like a shining sword. I stopped, blinked, and looked at a dozen leafy beehives about four feet high and six feet in diameter—Pygmy homes.

I stood beside Kalumé, his two *capitas*, and Cézaire, waiting for the Pygmies to appear. But not a creature stirred. We could hear nothing but our own breathing.

My eye caught a movement of a leaf on the other side of the clearing, a glimpse of a coppery face, then nothing but leaves. I realized that dozens of eyes were staring at us, and it gave me an uncanny feeling. If we were enemies and the Pygmies had not wanted us around, what a perfect target we would have made! We might have had a dozen arrows in us without once seeing an assailant.

But Pygmies under the benign influences of approaching civilization don't kill people any more—except occasionally each other. On the other hand, civilization may find that its influence boomerangs. Not long ago two Pygmies were seen selling fresh meat near Mambasa. This was strange, since all Pygmies sell goods only through their Bantu masters. And then a purchaser of one piece of meat thought that it had a familiar shape, remarkably like his own thigh. The authorities came and arrested the two Pygmies. Yes, they had killed a man—a Bantu of another village—and had cut him up to sell the meat. Why? They needed money, money with which to buy metal. One of the Pygmies wanted to get married, and the father of the girl was demanding metal goods in payment. When civilization introduces new wants, it can expect strong reactions. When I first saw the Pygmies in 1937, they knew nothing of money, and the only metal they desired was iron from which to make tips for spears.

But even if you know that Pygmies rarely kill people any more, it is a strange sensation to know that you are being watched by so many persons you cannot see, whom you will never see unless they choose to reveal themselves to you. Some white men have traveled several days in the Ituri, with Pygmy guides, knowing that other Pygmies were walking parallel with them, keeping them under surveillance at all times. When they backtracked they saw tiny footprints, fresh and new, but never the little men who made the prints.

Finally Kalumé called out, "Aputo! Manzaele! Nzala!" and cried to the unseen Pygmies that the *bwana* had brought salt and was a friend. In a moment the leaves parted at several points as three small figures appeared, hesitant, watchful, dignified but shy. They stopped fifteen feet in front of us and stared.

"Itiri!" said Kalumé, saying hello in their own Kilesi tongue.

"Itiri bonocha," replied one of the little men, to let Kalumé know that the Pygmies were glad to see him.

At this exchange, other figures emerged slowly from the forests, until a group of about thirty Pygmies, men, women, and children, stood in the clearing.

I was looking at Adam's cousin, at a remnant of "dawn man." Just as glaciers have preserved intact examples of mammoths long extinct, so the impenetrable forest had preserved, alive, these fossils from an ancient time. Civilizations had risen and fallen in many quarters of the globe without leaving a mark on these people. Perhaps evolution, too, had passed them by. At any rate, I stood face to face with the primitive, just as I had wanted, and it stared at me wonderingly, then smiled. I smiled back, and twenty thousand years began to fade away. If two human beings can smile at each other, they have much in common. I knew that these Pygmies and I were more alike than different.

V

Quiet Day in the Pygmies' Ituri Forest

EACH time I returned to Africa I visited the Bambuti Pygmies of the Ituri Forest. Only one other tribe lured me back that often—the Masai of East Africa—and I spent far less time with them than with the Pygmies, who are so thoroughly primitive that even three long visits failed to satisfy my curiosity about them.

No one from the outside is capable of entering the depths of the Ituri to live as the Pygmies live—hunting elephants with twenty-inch bows and slim spears, finding their way unerringly and in a straight line from one point in the hostile, cluttered jungle to another many miles away. They eat roots which our stomachs cannot digest, drink water which, without boiling, would make us deathly sick, and devour with gusto anything from caterpillar and ant grubs to bats, snakes and, on occasion, snacks of humans. Who else can scoop handfuls of honey from a bees' nest without getting stung by the clouds of angry bees? Or swallow handfuls of sand when hunger's pangs are severe and no food is at hand? Who else dines upon and makes belts from the okapi, so rare a beast that until about fifty years ago it was considered a legend, a tall tale of superstitious natives?

If you have a rugged constitution and an iron stomach, and bring in some of your own supplies, you can live for a time *with* the Pygmies and under their protection, but you cannot live *like* a Pygmy. Getting to know them sometimes seems like trying to understand a creature of a different species, with the unique

72

advantage that this creature can speak. But speech is a mixed
blessing, for Pygmies, like many primitives, tend to answer questions not with facts but with statements not really intended to
deceive but designed to make the questioner happy. Naturalists
looking hopefully for unusual animals have been promised fan-
tastic creatures by the amiable Pygmies. No wonder they
thought that the okapi, described as a cross between a giraffe
and a zebra, represented just another Pygmy story designed to
warm the heart of white visitors! Then the okapi turned out to be
real, and the Pygmy description of it remarkably accurate. Obviously, some Pygmy talk is fanciful, some true. The difficulty lies
in deciding which is which. Anyway, it is safer to judge Pygmies,
as well as other people, by their actions rather than their talk.

This takes a little time, however. Pygmies reveal little of
their natures while standing for inspection, even after gifts of
salt and palm oil. You would not act very natural under the
penetrating gaze of a Martian, either, though he might have
passed out ten-dollar bills. But if he stayed around long enough,
you would return to your normal life. You'd become accustomed
to this more or less permanent fixture observing you and, if he
were at all acute, he would begin to see what made you tick—at
least enough to go back home to Mars and write a book about
you.

I could learn a good deal more about the Pygmies, after
living with them for some time, than the Martian could learn
about me. After all, we *are* of the same species. We spring from
the same stock. A Pygmy could give me a blood transfusion,
and I'd get along fine. After a time, the startling differences
between us, which at first made him seem so remote, dwindled
in importance. They were only patterns of behavior dictated
largely by his environment. His inner drives were essentially the
same as mine. He was stirred by the same emotions that stirred
me, even though the stimuli were sometimes different. He was
afraid of lightning and the hoot of an owl, which didn't bother
me. I was afraid of elephants and getting lost in the forest,
which didn't bother him. But we both felt fear. We both hoped

for good hunting, although we hunted different things. He seethed with anger when someone stole a forest antelope from his trap, just as I would boil if someone took a good piece of insurance buiness from me by unfair tactics. We both wanted to avoid death, which he ascribed generally to something unseen, such as an evil hex, while I ascribed it generally to something unseen, such as a virus or germ. We both loved, bragged about and became annoyed with our women, using only slightly different ways of expressing those feelings. The Pygmy generally was a monogamist but had played around considerably before marriage—and that sounded familiar. We both loved music and dancing, but he managed to find much more time for these pleasures than I did.

You might say that you could *never* understand someone who voluntarily smears himself with elephant dung. The Pygmy does this to confuse the keen smell of the elephant, which he hunts for food and ivory. "Civilized" people sometimes also go to almost any length to earn a living.

Maybe I can't see things through a Pygmy's eyes, as when he looks at a bat and sees food. Certainly I can't smell things through his nose, as when he sniffs a putrifying elephant dead four days in tropic heat and gleefully hurries to the feast. "I eat the meat, not the smell, *bwana*," he explains. But even if I cannot put myself in his place, I can feel hunger, which lies behind his actions and mine.

Feelings—they are the heart of both of us, the bridge of understanding, the common language. Customs are just the costumes with which emotions clothe themselves to fit environment and heritage. The Pygmy's customs are as well adapted to his world as his dress—and when I realized this, when I recognized the feelings beneath them, I was at home in the Ituri, visiting friends who put on an amazing show for me just by being themselves. I witnessed a reasonable facsimile of the lives led by the ancient ancestors of all of us, with but minor changes in height, color, weapons and species of beasts hunted and roots eaten.

On my second and third trips, I had to do more than try to understand the Pygmies. I had to capture some of that understanding on film, feature-length films in color to be shown throughout the civilized world. When you make a travel picture, you try to accomplish two things—hold an audience's attention and interest with the picturesque, the colorful, the unique and the dangerous aspects of your journey, and at the same time invest all this with the warmth and humanity which will bring it home emotionally. Sometimes that is easy. A charging rhinoceros or lion, obviously heading directly for the cameraman and hence for the audience, is colorful and dangerous; the vicarious fear, which the audience feels if the picture is a good one, is thoroughly human.

With the Pygmies, there was plenty of unique and picturesque material, of course, but most of it was so very different that adding the human touch for an American or European audience proved difficult. It would be easy to treat the Pygmies condescendingly as half animals, or poke fun at them as freaks, but neither treatment would be honest or informative. Just as my own travels were motivated by more than sightseeing and thrill-seeking, so I wanted my moving pictures to give viewers at least some deepening and broadening of their understanding of human beings and even animals. For Hollywood I had to pack in thrills, danger, action, drama. For myself I had to add something of what I searched for—better understanding of the seemingly different.

One day, during my second trip, I got a wonderful shot of an old Pygmy, grey-haired and wrinkle-faced, talking. That's all he was doing, just standing there talking to a group of other Pygmies and to us, including an interpreter who managed to give me a brief running translation of the old gentleman's comments. But I scarcely needed the words, for the man's grimaces and gestures told me plainly that he was being highly critical of something or somebody. He was fed up to the ears, he was disgusted, he could hardly believe anything could be so bad. Indeed, it was so bad that it was almost funny—and he laughed. He mut-

tered the Pygmy equivalent of "Phooey!" and gave an Ituri Bronx
cheer. For almost five minutes he went on, oblivious of the
grinding camera, expressing emotions that could be understood
anywhere in the world. No one could look at pictures of the old
man without knowing his feelings, and that was precisely what
I wanted.

Actually, the old man was talking about his wife. She
nagged him, she didn't work hard enough, her cooking was no
good, and she didn't know the first thing about bringing up
children. Women? Phooey! In spite of his voluble talk, he kept
a watchful eye out to make sure his wife was not within
earshot, stopping occasionally to look around, then going on
with his tirade when he saw he was safe.

When it came time to cut and edit the footage for our
picture, we could not figure out, at first, how to work in this
marvelously human sequence. There was no place that could
lead, naturally and understandably, to a man's talking about
his wife. Then we realized that, from his expressions and gestures, he was just being highly critical. We switched the object
of his criticism from his wife to a dance being put on by the
younger men of his group. We showed part of the dance, then
cut to the old man and his disparaging grimaces, cut back to
the dance again. When the old man was really looking to see if
his wife were listening, we had him turn to look at the dance,
then turn back to the camera for further belittling comments.
They think they know how to dance? Phooey!

I doubt that anyone who saw "Savage Splendor," will ever
forget the old dance critic. Even though the film relocated
him, I never felt that we were playing tricks on the audience.
What we wanted to show was a Pygmy expressing feelings instantly recognizable by human beings everywhere. The scene
made Pygmies come alive as people, which was well worth the
small bit of literary license we took to fit it in as part of a longer
continuity.

That particular dance was the highlight of the scores of
dances I saw Pygmies perform, for it was the elephant dance.

The day before, a group of hunters had killed an elephant, about which I'll tell more later. They had brought home to the village many big chunks of meat, which the women had cooked with roots and herbs of various kinds, while the men and children stood around uttering anticipatory shouts of pleasure, jabbering delightedly, twittering like birds, squawking like parrots, chattering like squirrels in a mounting bedlam that suddenly ended with the serving of the food on big green phrynium leaves.

I stared aghast at the quantities of meat that disappeared into Pygmy stomachs. I have shopped and cooked and camped enough to judge the weight of meat fairly accurately, and I know that seven or eight pounds of elephant meat went down the throats of most of the men there—and not a great deal less into those of the women and children. The skin over their bellies was stretched tight until it seemed it should hurt, and I knew why that portion of their anatomy was always distended. When Pygmies have a lot of food, they eat all they can possibly hold, as if they might have to go three days without food—which sometimes happens. They have neither the facilities nor inclination to keep anything for the next day—except inside themselves.

As they finished eating they appeared to be drugged, supremely happy but anesthetized. They sank back where they sat and fell asleep, one by one. There was no dancing that night. There were not even many loud quarrels the next morning. And no one went hunting the next day. They loafed and slept and talked about the good meal of the night before.

By noon however, they had regained strength that matched their high spirits, so they danced. Obviously, the dance had to re-create the elephant hunt, with the actual hunters as dancers. Luck was with me, for the sun was bright and the time was noon. In the depths of the forest itself I could not shoot pictures at all because of the continual dusk; in the small clearing of a Bambuti encampment I could take pictures for two or three hours around noon, if and when the sun were shining down through the small hole in the vegetable roof. It was like taking pictures in the bottom of a well, so I viewed every chance to film as a special dispensation arranged through the joint efforts of Fate and the weatherman. Often, of course, nothing photogenic occurred during these rare periods. For the elephant dance, however, everything came together like the pieces of a jigsaw puzzle, and I got one of the best sequences I ever filmed.

We had plenty of time for our preparations, for the Pygmies had to build their elephant first. It was significant to see how, in the reconstruction, they cut him down to size. Their model of the huge beast was no taller than the Pygmies themselves. Two upright sticks driven into the ground were the legs, a larger log between them the body. For the tail, the dancers used the actual tail of the elephant they had killed the day before—a little out of proportion but realistic. The tail holds a special significance for the Pygmies. The chief hunter of the group always cuts off the tail of a slain elephant first, before anyone else touches the animal. He throws it into the forest, which I took to be an offering to the spirits, since they always throw part of each piece of game to the jungle spirits. But I learned that the tail was thrown away because, if a Pygmy woman saw it, she would become sterile. In spite of this, here was the tail attached to the wooden model. Only the tail of a freshly killed elephant, I found, carried its dread power over fertility.

Huge phrynium leaves at the front end of the log made realistic elephant ears, but the best touch was the curved banana stalk which served as a trunk. This admirable figure stood in the center of the clearing, and the hunters retired to the edge of the forest. They were armed with their frail spears, thin shafts of straight-grained hardwood with iron tips that glistened from the careful sharpening their owners had given them against smooth stones. I noticed that the hunters had either stuck bright parrot feathers in their short hair with a kind of gummy resin or donned small head-dresses of feathers and flowers.

The drummers began a low, slow beat—so slow, in fact, that I did not realize at first that there was a definite rhythm. I heard

one muffled thump and then, several seconds later, another muffled thump. When the five hunters led by their leader, Edodo,
appeared at the edge of the clearing, I realized what perfect
stalking music it was.

The hunters appeared as Pygmies always do when they
move through the forest, silently and suddenly. One moment you
see nothing but leaves, lianas, and tree-trunks forming a wall.
The next moment you see a Pygmy standing on this side of that
wall, without apparently having disturbed a leaf. They were all
wary, cautious and eager as they searched for the elephant, looking first this way, then that, as they spread out slowly, seeming
to cover much greater distances in their movements than they
actually did. With a flick of the hand, one hunter signaled another to follow him. Two notes of a bird's song came from
Edodo, and the rest turned in his direction. They were following
elephant spoor through the jungle, and had momentarily lost the
trail, had spread out to seek it again, signaling to each other all
the time. Edodo found the trail again and gestured to the others,
who fell in behind him.

The acting of these Pygmies was as expressive as any I had
ever seen. They not only told their story convincingly but projected to the audience the emotions they felt in the hunt. Every
muscle of their bodies was tense. Their eyes seemed to bore
holes in the air and give the ground a microscopic search. Their
faces showed excitement, eagerness and extreme caution at the
same time. A suppressed joy brought quick smiles as they found
the trail again, and they moved forward together. At this point,
the drums increased their tempo, indicating plainly that the hunters were on the march once more, not casting about for the trail.

Bodies bent over, spears ready, the hunters moved toward
the center of the clearing in tiny steps, turning in a half circle to
the left, then curving back toward the right, indicating that they
traveled many miles through the forest after their prey. As they
tracked down the big beast, the drums went imperceptibly faster,
and I found my breath following suit.

Suddenly came a moment so electric in its impact that I

jumped and almost stopped turning the camera. The drums gave one louder boom and Edodo jerked erect, threw his arms back, and stared with both fear and elation at the dummy elephant, which somehow became, in our eyes, a true mammoth quietly eating grass and ferns in the jungle, his back toward his small attackers. A long moment of silence followed, as the other hunters stared over Edodo's shoulders at the beast. Then came a flurry of movement, jittery and nervous, as the hunters retired seven or eight paces to consult on strategy. The drums took up a very soft but rapid beat.

The hunters put their heads together, talked, gestured, looked up at the elephant, talked again, then separated to form a kind of half circle closing in on the animal from the rear. Edodo was the leader, the hunter chosen to cast the first spear, as he had on the real hunt the day before. There are several methods used by Pygmies to kill elephants; these had obviously used spears into the stomach rather than the hamstringing technique. The first hunter creeps up on the big beast from the rear, and downwind. In addition he is smeared with elephant dung to cover his own scent. Finally, he dashes in close, plunges his spear into the elephant's soft belly, pulls it out, and runs away. The elephant bellows and whirls on him, but at that moment another hunter from the opposite side dashes up and drives his spear into the beast, which turns to counterattack on that side. A third hunter snatches this moment to dart in, and so on until the elephant's stomach has been cut in four or five places. The animal decides to get away from his tormentors, and plunges into the woods. But after a short distance, his viscera begin to drop from his sliced underbelly; he tramples upon them until he disembowels himself and falls to the ground. The Pygmies, who have been following him, finish him off with their spears.

This was the dramatic scene the dancers were about to reenact. Edodo crept up close behind the dummy elephant, hesitated, looked suddenly terror-stricken as if the elephant might have started to turn, darted back to the edge of the forest in a rapid shuffling step. Then again he cautiously, dancingly, moved toward the make-believe beast, every feature of his face and every muscle of his body displaying the excitement of the chase, the danger of his position. And the drums kept pace with his movements, mounting in tempo as he came closer, dwindling away as he retreated. Three times Edodo approached, three times ran back, then on the fourth sally carried through the first attack. With a whoop he plunged his spear with both hands forcefully under the body of the dummy elephant. Wrenching it free, he raced for the woods, as a second hunter approached from the right to follow suit. One after another the hunters speared the motionless dummy, until it almost seemed that it twisted and turned. The drums beat loudly and rapidly now, and I thought they had reached their peak. The other Pygmies were beginning to shout, to cheer and to laugh.

The hunters pantomimed the brief tracking of the wounded elephant, then fell upon him all together, plunging their spears at the dummy ferociously until they knocked it over. The drums boomed and the whole village cheered, chattered, laughed. With abandoned frenzy the hunters danced around the fallen mock elephant, and several little boys dashed from the crowd to join them. The entire village took up the dance, jumping and cavorting around the clearing in perfect time to the drumbeats but in no kind of pattern that might be called an organized dance. It was not particularly beautiful, but the joy of the dancers made it a delight to watch.

I had stopped the cameras by this time. I had the elephant dance itself on two cameras, and the light had been fine. When it appeared in "Savage Splendor," it was considerably cut, but it was still one of the memorable sequences of that film. Seeing the whole dance was an experience I'll never forget. It carried more meaning, more significant dramatic impact, than any dance I have seen in all my travels in Africa. I know that if I could have brought those hunters and their drummers to the United States and put them on tour they would have been a sensation. They had unknowingly staged a ballet of universal appeal, a dance that could be understood and appreciated by people all over the world.

The day of the elephant dance was marked with red, and there were not many like that. For every lucky day when all the essential factors for interesting picture-taking jibed there were weeks of waiting, walking, talking and learning. Many of these days were interesting to me, even if they were not productive from the point of view of Hollywood. I lived with the Pygmies in their village, stayed long enough for them to get used to me, then watched and listened and learned that important first step in picture-making—deciding what scenes to photograph.

In 1946, I had plenty of variety and all the stars and extras I could hope for. Perhaps the largest gathering of Ituri Forest Pygmies in one spot took place, largely through the help of Bill Deans, the American missionary who for more than twenty years has given help, friendship, and encouragement to every outsider who came near the Ituri with serious purpose. I had met him in Stanleyville, where I was waiting for the balance of my equipment for trips to photograph the Wagenia, Mangbetu, Watussi, Pygmies and other native tribes in and around the Belgian Congo. These trips were to be followed by jaunts into Uganda, Kenya and Tanganyika for pictures of more and different natives and as many animals as I could get near. Meanwhile, Armand Denis was busy in other sections of Africa with his own crew. Between the two of us we covered a good deal of territory, and shot more than enough footage to make "Savage Splendor," which we co-produced for RKO.

Bill Deans was so devoted to the Pygmies that he was particularly energetic in helping anyone who wanted to picture them honestly and sympathetically, and he knew them so well that he could make many valuable suggestions as to scenes I might shoot. On top of that, he made arrangements in advance with the proper Bantu chiefs and *capitas* to call their Pygmies together—"I'll have at least a hundred for you," he said—and assembled the necessary palm oil, salt, dried fish, and so on for gifts. By the time I arrived at his headquarters in Bunia, Bill had gone on to Irumu, but my supplies were already loaded into his one-ton truck. We followed him in the truck, crossed the Ituri River on a pontoon bridge, then drove on about ten kilometers along a narowing road into the forest until we came to Bill's original mission, now supervised by Mr. and Mrs. Searles and their son Tom.

These missionaries always amaze me, above all those working with the Pygmies, who seem to be as highly resistant to civilization's religion as to civilization itself. I don't see how men can continue year after year in this difficult and sometimes dangerous work, with such meagre results in the way of conversion —or conversion that really sticks. The nomadic life of the Pygmies makes regular missionary work on a particular group almost impossible. And even when converted, a Pygmy rarely gives up his old way of life. But in spite of discouraging results for formal religion, the missionaries achieve great things for humanity, for understanding and warmth between different peoples. The medical missionaries, especially, are saving lives and reducing serious sickness, in spite of the fact that most Pygmies still prefer their own medicine men, amulets and herbs. Missionaries must have limitless patience.

I was certainly grateful to the missionaries who persisted, for their presence and their knowledge made things easier for me many times. In this case, the groundwork was laid, but I still had the big job of living with the Pygmies and filming their activities. From Bill Deans' mission there lay miles to be covered on foot, through that thickest of all jungles, although I noted that as we penetrated further there were occasional patches in which the undergrowth seemed to have been completely choked out and all one could see were the lofty branches of trees up to two hundred feet tall. The going was slow, however, because we had with us about thirty Pygmies and their wives to guide us and carry in our supplies and gifts. It was incredible to see what big loads those tiny women could haul, bundles supported by lianas across their foreheads in the tump-line style of our Indians and other primitive people all over the globe. And most of the wives carried a baby on one hip, babies who jogged along placidly, staring with wide eyes at the passing scenery or falling asleep.

After about an hour we came to one small Pygmy clearing, with ten or eleven beehive huts in it. I saw no resident Pygmies, and the ashes looked quite dead. It must have been an abandoned camp—the general messiness and smells indicated that, aside from the absence of humans. Pygmies aren't very clean and care little for good housekeeping or civic pride. When a camp becomes too dirty, or when the game in the region is thoroughly hunted out, Pygmies just move on to another location. They have so few personal or household goods that moving is no great chore, and housebuilding takes only an hour or so.

Villages are not the correct term for these settlements in the forest, because they are so temporary and also because they do not contain a heterogeneous group of men and women. In any one settlement, all the residents are members of the same family; cousins, brothers-in-law, uncles and aunts are included, but there is always some close relationship. Such small groups have no need of governments, so there is no real chief or headman. There often is a hunter who is looked up to more than anyone else; his opinion carries great weight, but he is not a chief in the usual sense.

In another encampment a few miles away, you will find another family group. Group A may also have some blood ties to Group B, but they live and hunt separately and generally keep out of each other's way. While there is no actual association of family groups into what might correctly be termed a clan, a working arrangement exists between them—daughters of one group marry sons in another; they may "belong" to Bantus of the same village; they do not—now—engage in serious quarrels over hunting territories.

Each pseudo-clan, however, has a very definite territory in which it hunts, roams and lives. Fifty miles farther into the jungle there may be another grouping of families in different encampments. Wars between the so-called clans formerly were quite frequent, and there are still clashes when anyone trespasses. Individual fights and minor feuds break out even in families, but intertribal war has diminished because the "clans" are more inclined in recent years to stay within their own territories. All Pygmies know just where these boundaries are, although there is no marker of any kind. Moreover you cannot persuade or bribe your Pygmies to guide you across that boundary. They talk not only about the enemy, but about evil spirits, strange and fearsome beasts that throng the forest which is unfamiliar to them.

This situation has prevented any white man from exploring the whole Ituri Forest. He cannot arrange to have himself passed on from one tribe to another, as many early explorers on this continent did with the Indians. If you start out from one side of the Ituri, determined to cross it, your Pygmies will accompany you only so far and no farther. There you are in the middle of the jungle, with little men who refuse to go another step, and no other little men on the other side to guide you on another leg of your journey. You are limited to the territory of your original Pygmies, but that may be a thousand square miles of land—enough to tell you all you want to know about Pygmy life and environment. And there is no significant difference between the tribes. On my three trips I went to three different locations, worked with three different groups, and never could have told one tribe from another.

On the long walk to our movie "location" we passed two more abandoned settlements. I believe the last one was occupied at the time, but not by anyone I could see. I saw some pottery jars near fires that looked as if they had been burning recently. I asked if this camp belonged to our guides. They said no, and volunteered no further information. The inhabitants may well have been looking at us as we passed through and returned to their homes as soon as we disappeared.

In the afternoon I saw some light through the trees ahead, a startling sight after hours in the forest. Even the settlements were not large enough to let in more than a thin shaft of light.

But here was something more, I could tell, and as we emerged from the trees, blinking and squinting, I saw a clearing such as I had never expected to find in the Ituri. It was fully two hundred feet across, with only a few tall trees standing inside it. I grinned happily and looked sympathetically at my camera. Now perhaps it would have a chance to show what it could do, with a little good light!

I settled down for a long stay with the Pygmies, except for one short trip outside for supplies and a little respite from the claustrophobic effect of the deep forest. I pitched my tent at one side of the clearing. There were already about twenty Pygmy huts on the other side and my Pygmy guides and their families started at once to build their own houses near these.

The women did most of the work, but some of the men helped while others bossed their wives. From the nearby woods they brought supple saplings about eight feet long, while the man of the family drew a circle on the ground to mark the dimensions of the house. The thick ends of the saplings were driven securely into the ground along this line, about a foot apart, except for a small opening that would later serve as the door. The women then bent the saplings over toward each other, interlacing them and tying them together in a rounded arch. With all this bracing of one sapling against the other, the framework was quite sturdy.

It was too late in the day to take any pictures of this activity but I wandered about the clearing, looking around for activities that could be filmed when the opportunity arose. I stopped at one house under construction to watch a Pygmy hunter who obviously fancied himself as a first-class architect. He limited his help to suggestions, advice and orders to his wife, but there were plenty of those. As I watched, I was struck once again with the fact that language is often no barrier whatsoever, especially when one is dealing with such expressive people as Pygmies. I did not need to understand a word in this case to know exactly what was going on.

No, that sapling should bend over that way, the imperious gentleman gestured, and his wife did what he said.

No, no, these are too close together. She made them farther apart.

That is not tied tightly. It will come loose in the middle of the night and then a leopard might come in. She tied the vine tighter.

The next step in construction was fitting phrynium leaves into the latticework of the saplings, starting at the bottom and overlapping them as she progressed upward, much as we place shingles. In this process, the man found her work abominable. She left openings, didn't overlap properly, and generally did a sloppy job. To his specific corrections of his wife's work he added a few general denunciations of her as a wife, mother and workhorse. Through all this she just kept working steadily, and I thought she was doing a remarkably fast and efficient job. But, of course, I was not going to have to sleep in the hut, and he was.

Suddenly he leaned forward and snatched away a big leaf she had just fixed in place. With that, she had enough. She turned on him—all three foot six inches of her—and glared. From her lips there burst a volcano of sound, shrill, rapidfire and filled with venom. Again, I needed no words to understand. She was telling him off as beautifully as ever that the job was done, telling him that he was a lazy good-for-nothing, that she did all the work and did it well, that all he did was get in the way and act like a big shot—and he wasn't even a very good hunter! I could even tell when that last shot hit him, for he recoiled as if struck in a vital spot. Anger blazed in his eyes and he started to talk back, but she picked up a good-sized stick and waved it at his face. He stepped back, a little bewildered, glanced at me and looked ashamed, then walked away, muttering. The woman proceeded to finish the house in short order, tucking in leaves until the whole thing looked good and waterproof to me. The little door was so low that I don't know if I could have gone into it even on hands and knees, as the Pygmies did. I learned later that one reason for the small door was to make it difficult for evil spirits to enter.

A couple of smooth logs to sleep on, the family jars or pots, the man's weapons—bow and arrow, spear, and perhaps a knife— were the total furnishings of the Pygmy home. At night the occupants usually started a fire inside to drive away the chill dampness of the ground, and to keep away insects and leopards. Insects were a perpetual menace, but leopards were relatively rare. I heard several times, nevertheless, of leopards breaking into Pygmy huts and making off with a child, although I never obtained firsthand information of such a tragedy. There is no reason to doubt the truth of the stories, however. The leopard is clever, more silent and cunning than a Pygmy, and desperate when hungry or cornered.

The next morning, I found about seventy-five Pygmies in and around the clearing. During the evening of our arrival I had heard the drums, and knew that the message was going out that the *bwana bukuba* had arrived, the white man bearing many gifts. The newcomers would have filled up the clearing with their huts, but I needed plenty of clear space for pictures, so persuaded them to retire to other clearings near by or make new ones. They didn't quite understand, but they were happy to oblige. The third day more Pygmies arrived, and the day after that still more. By the fifth day at least five hundred Pygmies had established themselves in and near the big clearing —far more than I could possibly use for pictures, so many that they got in each other's way. Bill Deans, who had hoped to get a hundred together for me, was astonished at the number and made a conservative if unofficial census.

Bill was delighted, for he had never obtained the ears of so many Pygmies at one time. He held meetings and preached the gospel to them, and most of the Pygmies listened attentively, for Bill spoke in their language. But in my opinion most of the good missionary's ideas floated right over the curly heads to be lost in the tall trees. The concept of a single all-powerful, ever-present, and merciful God was one their minds could not grasp. In whatever religion they had, the Pygmies were not very concerned about the Creator and the good God; I'm not sure that they envisaged such a Being, but if they did their idea was extremely hazy. In any event, they felt they did not need to worry about a *good* God, but only about the bad spirits, of which they knew plenty.

Even though I now had more Pygmies than I could possibly use, I could not disappoint them in their expectation of delicacies. Some had traveled scores of miles through the forest to reach my clearing, obtain the gifts, and help in any way they could. Each day I handed out presents to the new arrivals, which gave me some good pictures but also necessitated a trip out of the forest for more supplies.

When the Pygmies lined up for distribution of presents, there was never any pushing, arguing or shoving. They were all quiet and orderly, but smiling broadly, talking to each other in low voices, rolling their always startled eyes, smacking their lips. For the moving pictures, I poured out a big sack of salt on leaves, then gave each person in line a handful as he stepped forward. Each Pygmy shoved the salt in his mouth greedily. Although I tried to make every handful just about the same, once in a while there was a noticeably small batch. Never did the Pygmy getting it object, but I received a searching look several times. The palm oil came in big five-gallon tins, and to receive this the Pygmies all obtained big shiny phrynium leaves which they held cupped in their hands while I poured in the oil. Most of them ate this at once, too, licking the leaves hungrily to get every drop. Some of the women saved theirs and took it to their earthenware pots. They like to cook herbs and greens in the oil and it is one of the Pygmies' favorite dishes. Obviously, these forest dwellers have retained the faculty possessed by many animals and originally by man of knowing instinctively what their bodies need for good nutrition. Palm oil is one of the richest sources of Vitamin A in the world, for instance, and salt is a necessity. They don't know, in their minds, that they need these things, but their appetites are true reflections of their needs, not just of their desires.

The dignity and consideration of the Pygmies in the food distribution was so striking that it brought back to my mind an incident from my first visit with them. Then I had salt and oil, but only a few cigarettes. When I learned that they liked to smoke, I passed out what cigarettes I had, about three-quarters of a package, and though there were few Pygmies present then, I had not nearly enough to go around. Each Pygmy who received a cigarette broke his in two, to share it with someone who had missed out. The act was a simple, uncalculated one, based upon an elementary fact of life for the Pygmy—what one member of the family group had he shared with others.

In addition to the first gifts for the five hundred Pygmies, I had to give them their *posho* while they were in attendance—or rather, a small part of a *posho*, a word which stands for rations for one week given to bearers, guides and other full-time workers. I handed out salt and bananas regularly, but that is all. Since the Pygmies were living in their forest, they continued to hunt for game, and the women gathered berries, roots and green leaves resembling spinach, which all Pygmies enjoy. The *matabishi*, or pay, came at the end of my stay in the forest. I didn't really feel called upon to pay all five hundred, but handed out dried fish, nuts, and more salt to each family. To those performing dances and other special acts for my camera, I gave larger amounts.

It rained a great deal during my stay in the Ituri, but fortunately the downpours came chiefly at night. Many a day I just sat, or paced back and forth, however, praying for the small patch of grey sky overhead to turn blue, for the murky light to grow clear and bright. Even when there was no rain, the forest dripped almost continually as the moisture of the heavy air condensed on leaves and branches. And when the sun finally did appear, the forest floor exhaled misty clouds that hung in the clearing, coated camera lenses, and penetrated clothes, bedding, shoes and soul. Half of the time I was wetter than the Pygmies without clothing, and when I climbed into my saturated pajamas at night I almost envied the Pygmy who lay down as he was on a couple of smooth logs. The fire he burned in his hut all night filled the place with smoke that would have suffocated me, but it dried the air a little and drove out all but small attack forces of the man-eating insects.

In spite of these photographic and personal difficulties we managed to take pictures of many scenes of daily Pygmy life and a few more exciting events especially staged. We filmed the making of huts; women going off into the forest for firewood, greens, and herbs, each with a baby rocking on one hip. A mother never puts her baby down on the ground, even for a moment—there are too many animals at hand ready to snatch such a succulent morsel. This explains, of course, why Pygmy women always kill one of twin babies the moment it is born. They just cannot handle two babies at a time. With one baby on hip, the women can perform any task—house construction, cooking, gathering food, working in the garden of their Bantu "owner" in the village. With a baby on each hip, they could do little. In some districts of the Ituri, the dead baby is buried under the floor of the hut it was born in; in others it is put in a jar and left out in the woods, where a variety of creatures will soon dispose of it. Pygmy women never eat the tiny double bananas about the size of one's finger because they think it will cause them to have twins—and the only thing worse than this is sterility.

I filmed the making of bark cloth, a task in which the men often join the women. Pygmies use the bark from six different trees and nine different vines for this purpose—the one selected depending upon what is at hand and in good condition. The bark is stripped off in long pieces, soaked in water, then pounded with a small stone against a larger flat stone. Alternate soaking and pounding produces a broad, soft, and fairly tough cloth rather like felt. But the pounding must be done with care, to avoid poking a hole in the material, to make the web of interlacing fibres of about the same thickness. The final cloth is a dark brown, but many Pygmies like to dye it by boiling it with berries and roots that turn it a dull purple.

Men wear the bark cloth like a rather full diaper, fastened to a liana G-string in front, passed between the legs, and fastened again in back. When the cloth is large, the effect is almost that of old-fashioned bloomers. The women's dress is much briefer, and often consists of big leaves rather than bark cloth, tucked under G-strings front and back. I once followed some women into the forest when they were looking for food and saw several of them shop for new costumes while there. Coming upon some particularly large and glistening green leaves, one woman plucked them, removed the old leaves, and fitted the new ones in place. Several others followed suit, and some tucked small red flowers in the waistbands, too.

One of the vines used for bark cloth is called, in English, the trellis-work fig tree, a powerful parasite. One of these vines will start growing up the trunk of a huge ironwood tree which is just about the hardest wood known. The vine circles and climbs and clambers, growing thicker and thicker as the years go by, branching out along the lofty branches of the tree. Soon the trunk of the vine is as large as that of the tree, and in time the tree is choked completely. In its place stands a huge trellis-work fig tree, strong and proud as if it had done the job of growing all by itself.

Later I saw some Pygmy children playing a game which they call by the name of the vine. One child, who is "it," stands in a circle of other children. The encircling children dance around the one in the center, chanting a kind of song and gradually closing in. The "it" child answers with its own chant and tries to break out of the circle. "It" is the ironwood tree, and the others are the trellis-work fig tree that will not let it loose. I never could figure out how the game ended or who won. I have an idea that there was no such thing as winning a game among the Pygmies, for there is no competitive spirit within the family group.

During the course of filming routine events I learned what superb actors most Pygmies are. They are real hams who enjoy nothing quite so much as acting out a part. They do not, like some amateurs, try to steal the show or upstage each other, nor do they posture before the camera with self-conscious grins. They really *act*. At first, I thought it might be impossible for them to understand what I wanted, since the very concept of enacting a role might be completely foreign to them. They did not, I am sure, comprehend the purpose of cameras or the nature of picture taking. Pictures themselves are meaningless to most Pygmies. You can show a good photograph of himself to a Pygmy and he will recognize nothing; he may even hold it upside down. I thought that this might result from the fact that a Pygmy, lacking mirrors, never sees himself. But he does not recognize his wife or even his own hut in a picture.

Although they may not have understood my purpose or the whirring boxes my cameramen and I held, they caught on immediately to the suggestion of acting out certain scenes. The most difficult, perhaps, was the reenactment of my arrival in the Pygmy country. For this I selected about fifteen hunters with spears and with bows and arrows, and we all traveled some distance through the forest to the Ituri River, where it was broad enough to let in a fair amount of sunlight. At this point we had arranged to have two dugout canoes, for our arrival.

I was in the lead canoe, paddled by several Bantus, while my cameraman rode in a following craft, filming my approach to shore. Faces peered through the thick foliage of the edge of the stream, disappeared, showed themselves once more. We obtained shots of the Pygmies from a camera set up on land about twenty feet from shore; this caught some of them trotting toward the river as if eager to look at the stranger reportedly arriving by dugout. One of the Pygmies turned, right in front of the grinding camera, as if to motion to someone behind him to hurry along. He did not once look at the camera or the cameraman which would have spoiled the illusion.

Between shots from one dugout and others from on shore,

we reenacted the entire scene, even to having one of the Pygmies extend a welcoming hand to help me on firm ground from the canoe. It was a good scene, showing a bit of the thick Ituri, of the river and close shots of the Pygmies as they moved among the trees. But it could have been awkward and phony without the excellent acting of the Pygmies.

One day, after some reminiscent talk by a few oldsters about fights between tribes in the old days, which was translated well enough by Bill Deans for me to get most of the story, I asked if the Pygmies thought they could put on a battle for me, acting as if two groups had come upon each other in the forest, two enemy groups that started fighting until one group was routed. They seized on the plan eagerly and talked among themselves about how to stage the war. The job had to be done on the edge of the clearing, rather than in thick woods, so I would have enough light; between us we settled on the membership of the two groups. One old boy, who must have been over seventy and was crippled with rheumatism, insisted on being part of the play because he had fought in many wars in his youth. So vivid was the acting the next day that old age and rheumatism seemed to be thrown from him in that glorious moment of the charge against an enemy. He was just as spry as the rest of them.

The realistic acting of the Pygmies frightened me for a while in shooting this sequence. If you had seen the looks on their faces when the two groups met each other, you would have thought they were in deadly earnest, that nothing would have pleased them so much as to kill their supposed opponents. The happy, carefree, smiling little folk of the forest suddenly became vicious and savage warriors, bent on spilling the blood of the enemy. I understood why Stanley had thought them as bitter enemies as any natives he encountered, why the Arab slave-traders kept a respectful distance, and why the Bantu "owners" felt as much fear as contempt for the Pygmies.

With shrieks and whoops that would unhinge the spine,

they tore at each other, shooting their arrows with what looked like fair accuracy. But not an arrow hit a man; all sailed cleanly over everyone's head—although a couple came rather near me.

No matter what I asked the Pygmies to do for the camera, they performed brilliantly, so long as it was some act that was natural to them. They would have been dismal failures if they had tried to enact some unfamiliar routine, so I could not have faked anything if I had wanted to. I don't consider as fake the reenactment of something that does in truth take place—a procedure that must be followed often in the forest for reasons of lighting if for no other. An act that normally occurs in deep, dark woods must be moved to the clearing for picture-taking.

On several occasions at the outset of my second trip, I had to delay the start of filming because of one huge tree which held back the light about half an hour. After consulting Bill Deans, I decided to have it cut down. The Pygmies turned out to be poorer lumberjacks than actors, even with axes we supplied, but they finally chopped most of the way through the big trunk. I set myself to get a picture of the toppling of the big giant, calculating the direction of its fall as well as I could, and placing myself in what appeared to be a safe but advantageous spot. The Pygmies had tied a very long liana halfway up the tree, extending to the ground at an angle, where a dozen of the little fellows were going to pull, then hop out of the way as the trunk began to fall of its own weight. I was about twenty feet to one side of the line of fall, hoping to catch the tree falling *almost* directly toward the camera.

A final few hacking strokes with the axes, a mighty tug by the men on the ground, and the tree tipped toward me. I had the camera at my eye and started it, watching through the viewer as the tree majestically—as if in slow motion—keeled over. Suddenly I realized that I was getting *too* good a picture. The tree was falling *directly* toward me, not almost toward me. I pulled the camera away from my eye and stared up. Someone was yelling to the Pygmies on the ground to pull hard toward them, which would have made the tree veer away from me. But they could have exerted little influence on it at that point, so great was its weight, as it gathered momentum.

It was too late for me to run anywhere, either. I just ducked and thought fleetingly that this was a hell of a way to die. A small branch whipped across my bent back—and that was all. Amid a roaring and snapping of branches, a trembling of the earth, I felt one small branch across my back. I looked up and breathed again. Another smaller tree, a dozen paces to my left, had caught the full impact of the big giant and had deflected its final fall away from me. Luck is one commodity an explorer cannot have too much of.

Out of the many days I have spent in the Ituri Forest, a kind of composite day emerges from my memories. I keep aside as special days those on which the elephant dance took place, the days of bridge-building (which I'll come to shortly), and the occasions on which I went hunting through the forest. I think of a normal, quiet day in the Ituri, when I stayed at the clearing, watching and listening, taking such pictures as presented themselves when the light was right. There were many days like this.

In the morning I awaken to the sound of the loud voice of the chief hunter, or headman *pro tem*, calling out the day's plans to the whole encampment—which groups will hunt on which trails and with which weapons, what special chores the women may have, and so on. Other voices come to me as the Pygmies emerge from their houses, and in a few minutes one or two voices are raised in anger. Soon some of the men are quarreling violently. Curses and imprecations fly back and forth. I pull on some soggy clothes and step from my tent to feel the splash of a huge drop of water that has fallen from a branch above. The smell of the Pygmies assails me at once. During the day my nose will become numbed so that it no longer perceives this odor, but on first awakening, with my senses keenly perceptive, the smell is strong. What is it like? It is hard to define, but seems combined of sweat, dirt, dung both human and animal, half-spoiled meat, joined by the forest smells of damp rotting wood, stagnant swampy ground and thousands of flowers.

Soon another smell covers this pervasive odor—the more pleasant fragrance of woodsmoke and cooking food, which makes me look at my own fire cold and dead. Everything is so damp that getting a fire going is quite a task, but we manage it and prepare breakfast. Meanwhile, I listen to the mounting sounds of quarreling, for now a few of the women have joined in and their voices are shrill, piercing, strident.

The morning is dark and gray, with no blue showing in the open space above. This accounts for the excessive disputes. Pygmies are as easily depressed as elated. A rainy or dull day puts them in bad humor as they awaken, and the entire village seems to get up on the wrong side of its logs. Since no Pygmy can conceive of repressing even the smallest and most insignificant emotion, he snaps at the first chance when he feels snappish. The one snapped at snaps right back, and that starts it off. By the time the snaps have grown to loud curses, a friend of Pygmy A joins in to say something nasty to Pygmy B, whereupon Pygmy B curses him and Pygmy A tells him to mind his own business, he can handle his own battles.

The wife of the interrupter thereupon feels called upon to add her bit, although she is supposed to be busy getting breakfast. Husband tells wife to shut up, so wife yells at husband, calling him mean to the children, a lousy hunter with poor aim, and a philanderer. Thus we have a second battle going, which overlaps onto the first on occasion.

What started the first quarrel? No one knows by this time. At first I made inquiries through interpreters, trying to learn what kind of thing brought on such battles. Once or twice I learned, but could not quite believe that such trivial matters would erupt into such loud fights. Usually, the chief combatants did not know the origin of the snapping three minutes after it began.

Rarely did the quarrels mount above the verbal into the

physical. Once or twice I saw one man hit another, and just once I saw a hunter grab up his bow and arrow and shoot at the fleeing figure of his opponent.

This clamorous quarreling makes the Pygmies sound rather unpleasant, I suppose. And while it is going on I feel very annoyed with them. Bill Deans and other missionaries have told me that when they live in the forest with the Pygmies, they pitch their tents some distance away from the huts because they cannot stand the noise of the quarreling. When I feel like spanking the Pygmies for being so childish, I remind myself that they have no ulcers, no neuroses and apparently no high blood pressure or coronary thrombosis. Our society has imposed upon us the necessity of restraining most of the unpleasant emotions that we feel over trivial things; we have gained and lost something by this. Pygmy society imposes no such restraints, possibly because they live in relatively small family groups, all of whose members are really closely bound together in deep affection.

As I eat my breakfast and listen to the bedlam, I also tell myself to wait five or ten minutes. By that time the Pygmy breakfasts will be served and the air will clear. Breakfast takes some time to prepare because it is a big meal, often as big as dinner the night before. It must be large enough to sustain them through the day, for they take no other food.

I can tell when breakfast is ready at hut after hut without looking, for the noise diminishes somewhat and alters its tone completely. There is talk and chatter all over the clearing, but it is happy, anticipatory. I look and see two men who have just quarreled violently sitting side by side on the ground, dipping boiled bananas into a common pot of palm oil sauce, looking at each other with wide smiles, chewing rapidly and happily.

This quick change of mood, this lightning switch from anger to affection, from bad spirits to happiness, makes the Pygmy sound childlike—and that is what almost every visitor says. Childlike, happy, and carefree are the common terms used about Pygmies and, to a certain extent they are true. They give only a superficial picture, however. How can one call an elephant hunter childlike? How can I follow hunters for two days when game is scarce, watch them track as no other humans do, and say they are carefree? The looks of terror on Pygmy faces when an owl hoots at dusk are not the looks of happy people. It is better, I think, to say that they are temperamental, that their emotions are readily and easily expressed. Being completely expressed, they are out of the system, so anger can quickly be replaced by affection. Annoyance flew from the Pygmy's breast upon the stream of curses he hurled, and none was left to rankle. Pygmies are childlike, happy, carefree, gay—and also courageous, persistent, terror-stricken, devoted. They possess most human qualities and display all of them as the occasion warrants.

As breakfast ends there are loud sighs of contentment, cheerful talk of plans for the day, jokes. Three or four young men take up their bows and arrows and start a kind of target practice, shooting at a broad leaf on the other side of the clearing. It is too early for me to get pictures of this but I persuade them to have another practice later in the day. At this time, I recall something I read in Schebesta's great books on Pygmies and ask them to shoot at bananas thrown into the air. They are delighted and show remarkable accuracy, one banana being pierced with three arrows almost simultaneously.

The work of the day begins. There is no big hunt today, so I decide to stay in the clearing and get what pictures I can. Two or three groups of hunters go off into the forest, and the women of the village leave to gather food, followed by some of the older children. I wander about from hut to hut, walk to some of the nearby clearings to see how some of the recently arrived Pygmies are getting along. There I am delighted to find a group forging iron spearheads. Few Pygmies know this art but prefer to buy their ironware already fashioned by the Negro villagers on the edge of the forest. These Pygmies have obtained their iron from the village, since they cannot smelt their own ore. One significant evidence of change in this field, however, is indicated by the fact that even most of the villagers have forgotten how to smelt iron. They now use the leaves of broken automobile springs. I would not have found a piece of spring in the middle of the Ituri Forest in 1937, when I first went there. By 1955 that was the standard raw material.

The Pygmies who are forging their iron have made a bellows from the skin of an animal, which is pressed open and shut to bring the flame to white heat. The iron is heated, then pounded with a stone hammer into shape. The work is neat and attractive. Later, the hunters sharpen the point on another stone, then affix it to the thin hardwood shaft.

In another clearing I see men compounding the poison for the arrows. I cannot recognize the root they pound into a pulp, but I note the care with which they handle it. Looking closely at some of the arrows, I see that they are notched about an inch behind the point—just like the darts of the head-hunting Jivaros in South America. The purpose is the same, too—to prevent a monkey's pulling out the arrow as soon as it is struck. When it pulls, the arrow breaks at the notch, and the poisoned point stays in the flesh long enough to kill the animal.

Back in the main clearing I come upon two boys, who must be eight or nine years old, wrestling in front of a sizable audience. There are cheers and shouts of encouragement for both battlers, who are sweating and enjoying themselves immensely. When the match is over, several boys decide to go hunting. They go into their huts for bows and arrows, disappear into the jungle talking excitedly. Occasionally, they actually return with some small game, although frogs and caterpillars are more frequently their prizes.

Behind one hut I see a boy and a girl talking. They act startled when they see me, but I pretend not to be looking at them. They are about eleven or twelve years old, although this is an age that is difficult for an outsider to determine. Pygmies are usually fully grown at that age, so one must guess the age by a juvenile look. The girl's breasts are quite small, have obviously just begun to develop. Breasts are the standard Pygmy clue to a woman's age, but by the time a girl is twenty they are likely to sag considerably for she may have had four or five children by that time.

The boy and girl, after a furtive look or two around, walk toward the woods together. Sexual relations between youngsters is promiscuous but not flaunted. I have heard that some mothers try to keep a watchful eye on their daughters, primarily because the birth of children before marriage can cause difficulties. But generally the fact of free sexual relations among boys and girls is accepted without much thought or concern. All this changes drastically at marriage, however, for fidelity stands high in the Pygmy moral code. Husbands and wives guard each other jealously and the only crime worse than adultery is stealing game from another man's trap. Only these two violations of the code may lead one Pygmy to kill another in these relatively peaceful days. The more common procedure, in the case of adultery, is a thoroughgoing beating administered by husband to the wife, and perhaps to the offending male although the latter may make amends by paying over a certain number of arrows or a spear.

There is one fear husbands no longer feel about their wives —cannibalism. William Spees told me about one very old Pygmy who said, "When I was young, you had to keep your wife right beside you all the time, or someone would grab her, kill her and eat her." Because of this old custom, he had enjoyed many wives —and so, apparently, had his enemies, although in a different manner.

Just why cannibalism has died down, if not out, is not entirely clear. I believe that the existence of a strong government in the Congo has exerted considerable influence, even though the Pygmies seem beyond its reach. The government cannot take a census or collect taxes; it must carry on what contact it has with Pygmies through their Negro overlords. But somehow the word has filtered through that there *is* a strong government of the white men out there, and one of the things they disapprove of most is cannibalism. On the other hand, this same government's

disapproval of hemp-smoking has had little effect, probably because the Negroes surreptitiously continue to supply the
Pygmies as a means of control over them.

To get back to my quiet day in the forest, I watch the boy
and girl disappear into the jungle on their own errand, then
turn toward another cluster of Pygmy huts, just in time to see a
boy of about six overturn a jar of water while trying to roll a
hoop made from a liana. His mother, who is busy pounding bark
cloth, jumps up in a sudden red rage, grabs a piece of firewood
and brandishes it as if she would bash in her son's head. But he
is too quick for her and runs howling at the top of his lungs toward the forest. She races fifteen or twenty steps after him,
then gives up and flings the wood at him, missing badly. She
returns to her work on the bark cloth as if nothing had happened, although she can hear the hyena-like howls of her offspring in the woods. They continue until I think of trying to
find the boy and calm him down, but some other women go into
the forest after him. I hear the yells turn to sobs, then silence. In
a few minutes the boy returns with the other women, showing a
few startlingly clean areas of face where tears have washed dirt
away. He glances cautiously at his mother as he approaches his
hut, but she pays no attention, so he takes up the hoop again and
continues to play.

In spite of this scene, I will state flatly that Pygmy mothers
and fathers are as devoted to their children as parents anywhere.
For every act of anger against a child I have witnessed a dozen
scenes of great love, which is all the more striking when one
realizes that men and women never display any signs of affection
for one another in public. I can only conclude that kissing,
fondling, hugging and such acts are refinements of civilization,
conjured up as substitutes for the sex act. If a Pygmy feels love,
he knows just one way to express it in action, retires to some
privacy and does so. Minor expressions of that emotion have not
entered into his sphere of emotional concepts.

There is a good deal of affection between parents and children, however, probably developing from the almost constant

physical contact between mother and child during infancy. There comes a point at which the child is definitely finished with such things, and the mother knows it. His love is directed elsewhere and she pays little attention. For one thing, she probably has had several other children since the wandering twelve-year-old was astride her hip, half of whom have died. Infant mortality is high among the Pygmies, although missionaries and government authorities believe the Pygmy population is increasing.

Speaking of affection felt by parents for children, I witnessed one scene which seemed to present evidence against it. A child three or four years old did something the mother did not like. She gave him a smack. Father objected, and picked up the wailing child. Mother resented father's objections and tried to snatch the child back again. There ensured a tug of war between parents, the child being the tugged object. I really thought they would pull him asunder and couldn't help running up to interfere. Both parents were so startled that they dropped the child, who picked himself up and scampered off a little way until he knew that everything was safe again.

Yet I still insist that Pygmies love their children devotedly. But there is a difference which I had to learn between their ideas and ours. We want to train our children, plan for their futures, make certain that they will become successful members of their communities. Such an idea could not occur to a Pygmy. Pygmies cannot plan for the future beyond the next day's hunt, and there is no need for them to think about the future of their children. The lives of their children will be like their own lives, just as all Pygmy lives have been approximately the same for centuries. The child's security is no worry, for it is a member of a family-group which operates on a communal, collectivist principle, in which every member shares what everyone else has—so far as the essentials of life are concerned.

Since there is little conscious training of children, there is no real discipline. Boys play with small bows and arrows and spears, and thus learn to track and hunt. Girls learn to gather vegetables and cook, to make bark cloth and houses along with their mothers. There is no conscious teaching of these arts. Children just absorb them. Beyond that, what need a Pygmy child learn? Only to run faster than mother or father when parents are really angry.

By noon on my quiet day, I see that the sun is shining brightly and I must not lose the opportunity to take pictures. I have heard that the Pygmies enjoy a game of tug-of-war and decide to film it, if I can persuade them to participate. This is never a difficult task when it comes to games of any kind, but when I start to select about twenty-five men and twenty-five women—this is to be a battle of the sexes—there is a sudden shyness over the big crowd in the clearing. As soon as the game begins, however, all those not selected act rather neglected, as if they had been punished for something they did not understand. When I decide that some of the shots would be better if taken from an elevation, I have a dozen eager volunteers to help me make a platform about ten feet high. It is a little shaky, but firm enough once my cameraman gets set. I handle a camera on the ground and direct my actors, who try to pull their opponents across a little stream that wanders through one side of the clearing. At first they tug hard and earnestly, but then their gaiety gets the best of them. Some fall down and knock others over, laughing and shouting. Eventually the men pull the women through the stream and everyone cheers. I thank the players and pass out an extra *matabishi* of salt.

One reason for the tug-of-war being between the sexes is that men and women almost never touch each other in public, not even in their dances. Since each person on a team grabs the one in front of him around the waist to form a tugging chain of humans, teams are not mixed. I do not know the reason for this very definite lack of physical contact because there is no false modesty nor prudery among the Pygmies. The only thought that seems reasonable to me is that physical contact between man and woman suggests only one thing to Pygmies, and they reserve that for the privacy of the hut.

The marriage relationship among Pygmies is complicated

by many factors and fraught with numerous difficulties—surprising in a primitive society. In many groups the task of locating a potential wife is a serious problem for young men, because of the economic value of women. Women may be valued for individual qualities, but as a whole they are looked upon as essential workers and as the producers of more Pygmies. A family group, as tenacious of its collective life as the individual of his own life, will not let a girl go without acquiring another in return. Thus there has arisen the "head for head" system, called in Kingwana *kichwa-kichwa*. A young man of sixteen or seventeen may find in a neighboring group a girl of thirteen or fourteen he would like to marry. The basis for his choice may depend in part on her beauty and figure, but her aptitude for hard work carries more weight. The young man must not only win the consent of the girl's father and pay over to him a purchase price, but he must also become match-maker and persuade a girl in his own family group to marry a young man in the same neighboring group. In this way, neither group will lose strength.

This is not always as easy as one might think, since some groups are quite small and there are not always available girls near the marrying age. One group may produce primarily boys over a period of a few years, and these fellows are going to have a really rough time finding wives. Among Pygmy groups living near the villages, Bantus select some of the Pygmy girls as their own wives, which further depletes the supply of girls without giving any in return.

Let's assume a young man has overcome these preliminary difficulties, arranged a match to meet the requirements of *kichwa-kichwa*, and gained the consent of the girl's father. They settle on a price for her, which might be six arrows and a spear, or eight arrows and so much bark cloth, or four arrows and a good piece of iron. The deal is made, and the girl goes home with her husband, without any ceremony of any kind. But this is far from the end.

Whenever the wife bears a child, the husband makes an additional payment to her father. Even if she has no child, he makes a further payment at the end of six months or a year, when both parties to the marriage decide that it will probably work out all right. If the girl should prove sterile, or if the young couple should decide the marriage is no good, the man can return the girl to her father and get his payment back. This return is complicated, however, by the other couple in this exchange, who may want their marriage to continue. Although Pygmy marriage might be called trial marriage, very strong factors are brought to bear to make marriages stick. Only complete sterility is deemed complete justification for return of a wife, or the taking of another wife.

This all sounds businesslike, cut and dried. But there is love among the Pygmies. Many marriages are based on affection as much as on economics. And sometimes a love affair will develop that goes against economics and *kichwa-kichwa*. If a young man and girl love each other but cannot arrange a balancing head-for-head match, or if the young man has nothing with which to pay the father, they may elope. The girl's father will track them down and bring the girl home, but the man may persist and abduct her again. About the third or fourth time, parents of both boy and girl begin to realize that there is something big to cope with, and they may come to terms, foregoing the head-for-head arrangement. If the boy has nothing to pay the girl's father he may live in the girl's village and work and hunt for her family until he has discharged his obligation. It is rare, however, for love to overcome convention among the Pygmies.

Even after many years of happy, successful marriage, a girl's strongest ties remain with her original family group and never with her husband. She knows that her family will welcome her back happily at any time—and the husband knows it too, which puts some brake upon his dictatorial powers over her. A wife is looked upon as property; she is there to work and everyone knows it. It is perfectly all right for her husband to beat her once in a while, if only to remind her who is boss. But there are limits beyond which he cannot go. If he beats his wife too hard or too often, if he philanders regularly, if he fails to provide moderately well, if he is constantly mean to the children—then the wife will just walk back home to her family. The family will welcome her and protect her, unless she is just being too sensitive about an occasional smack on the head, in which case her family tells her to go on back to her husband. Usually, however, a wife leaves her husband only for good cause.

The abandoned husband finds himself in a difficult situation. He is suddenly without the chief workhorse—the person who made his house, gathered his firewood, brought his water, searched for his vegetables, cooked his meals, took care of his children, helped him hunt with nets. In short order he realizes that a wife is an absolute necessity, so he goes to win her back. He can succeed by making a further payment to her family and promising to avoid the acts which drove her away in the first place.

I have heard of some unscrupulous families that milked a man dry by having the wife run away with fair regularity. In the main, however, the practice is not abused and serves only as a mild check on a husband's complete dominance over his wife.

The sun has dipped below the treetops on the western side of the clearing, and in about an hour the hunters come home—one with a monkey, another with a snake, and a group of three with a young antelope. There is laughter through the clearing, and I know that the same scene is being enacted in all the clearings near by where my five hundred Pygmies are established. With that number, however, this section of the forest will be cleaned out of game in a very few days.

The game is divided according to standard regulations that have apparently existed for centuries. The first and prize portions go to the hunter who actually struck the fatal blow. A piece is tossed into the woods for the spirits. If the hunter used another's bow, the owner of the bow gets a prize piece. The owner of the hunting dog, if there was one, gets a special piece. Other members of the hunting party come next, and then all others in the family group of the village.

Fires flicker in front of the beehive huts as the women and girls prepare the evening meal, the men watching and talking to each other with animation. Some hungry children are crying for their food, but the older ones stand near the fires, looking, sniffing and waiting impatiently.

Dinner is served on leaves on the ground, as always, and the Pygmies eat as long as there is anything in the pot. The women clean up as the men lie back and stretch. Some get up and walk about the clearing, others come to watch me eat my dinner. A group comes in from a neighboring clearing for a chat. This is the happy time of day. No bickering, no screaming now. The only sounds are sounds of happiness and contentment.

The dusk deepens and someone begins to tap out a rhythm on the drums, while a reedlike flute or whistle makes unmelodious melody. I see some young men tapping their feet, waving their hands with the rhythm of the drums, but no one rushes out to dance. I sit and wait, knowing what will happen. One of the men who taps his foot steps away from the tree where he has been leaning, and does a little jig, claps his hands, laughs. The fellow next to him does the same, and the desire to dance spreads around the clearing like an engulfing wave. Soon there are fifteen men and women following one another around in a circle, waving arms, singing, laughing, stamping their feet. The drums are inspired by the dancers and the pounding rhythm pulses through the forest. Children join the dancers, and finally some of the oldsters.

Pygmies can go on dancing for four or five hours when they are enjoying themselves and have good drummers. They can dance all night long when the moon is full and no outsiders are there to watch. For the Pygmies have two kinds of dances, one like those I have watched, another obscene dance in which the rule against physical contact between men and women is broken and broken resoundingly. How do we know? Some of the few Pygmies who have been converted to Christianity have told the missionaries, substantiating the rumors that everyone had heard. When I have seen the frenzy and complete abandon of their respectable dances, it is not difficult for me to imagine their being carried away one step further on the drumbeats of strong emotions.

On my quiet day in the forest, however, the dance ends after about two hours. It is completely dark now. Some of the fires are taken inside the Pygmy huts to drive out insects and keep away marauding beasts. One by one the families disappear through the tiny doors. I sit for a while, staring at the tiny spots of red that glow here and there, listening to the sounds of the jungle. There are not many at night, for the birds and monkeys and parrots are still. Occasionally a leopard screams, a hyena emits its weird and unpleasant laugh, an owl hoots, and peepers try to imitate birds. On one occasion, a lemur kept me awake most of the night with its eerie, human cry.

Finally I, too, turn in and fall asleep before I know it. Some time later something awakens me. My eyes are wide open and I listen intently, wondering what sound caused me to wake out of such a deep sleep. I hear nothing. The silence is as vast and broad as the sea. A mixed feeling of awe and pleasure comes over me as I realize that I am in the heart of the Ituri Forest, living among the remnants of prehistoric man.

Then I hear something like a huge sigh far away. This is a familiar sound to me now, after a week or two in the forest. A storm is coming. The first signal is a sudden high wind in the treetops, and that is the sigh I hear from miles away. I hurry out of my tent to see if my stakes and ropes are strong and secure. I tighten them, test as best I can, for once in the middle of the night my tent had collapsed and I found myself in the deluge.

Back in the tent again I listen to the sigh which has now grown to a roar. The branches overhead begin to stir uneasily, whispering to each other that the big, big wind is coming. They toss and twist and turn—then suddenly the big wind arrives, like a huge wall of irresistible energy. Branches groan, snap, and crash to the ground. My tent tugs at its ropes, trying to take wing and fly across the continent. Not far away, a giant tree, writhing under the lashes of the wind, topples over, and the ground shakes beneath me as in an earthquake.

One minute behind the strong wind, the driving rain arrives. It pelts against my tent like pebbles hurled by a blast of dynamite. Inside, I feel the fine spray on my skin as the drops are vaporized and filter in. It sounds like Victoria Falls outside, as water pours from the leaves, falls into the clearing in sheets.

Far away the deep bass boom of thunder begins, rolling across the universe slowly and majestically. Every half minute I hear it, but there is nothing menacing about it. Then I see the flashes of lightning that cause the thunder, and by the time between them I know it is still some distance away. I become fascinated counting the seconds between the flash and the rumble as the storm comes closer and closer, until the lightning is a devastating blast of power and the thunder a menacing roar that threatens to split the earth open. I peer out through the tent flap and see a lake where the clearing was. As I look, the black sky is torn apart by a jagged bolt of lightning that reaches down to the top of a tall tree. I actually see it touch the tree, which towers above the others, before the brilliance temporarily blinds me.

I hear the mighty tree crash, taking a dozen others with it in its fall, and I feel safer, for the tallest trees act like lightning rods, drawing the full force of the electric shock from the skies.

Lightning and thunder, wind and rain, all combine at once to concentrate their forces on our clearing, pounding my tent and the Pygmy huts like fragile things on an anvil. But for all the high voltage striking around us, the noise of atomic blasts, the violent wind and lashing rain—for all of that all we get is wet. And we are used to that.

Now I begin to count the seconds as lightning and thunder are separated in time once more, the storm passing beyond us. One second, two seconds, three seconds. It seems as if the wind is dying slightly, although the rain pours steadily. Bright flash, four seconds, crash-boom-rumble. Five seconds. I never get beyond seven seconds, for I am asleep.

VI

Bambuti Hunters and Builders

I HURRIED along an almost imperceptible forest path trying to keep up with three Pygmy hunters. The little man in the lead held up his right hand, and the others stopped. One, who was in the process of taking a step, actually kept one leg in the air until the leader signalled again. Perhaps the sound of some animal had been heard, in which case it was essential to make no noise—even that of placing one bare foot on the soggy leaves covering the forest floor.

But there was no animal. The leader had merely lost the trail of the wild pig they were following. Immediately the three hunters set about the task of locating it again—and quickly. They were serious, alert, their eyes darting now to the ground, now ahead, now at their fellow hunters.

The first man dropped to the ground, moved a few leaves, felt the earth with the palm of his hand. The second stepped to the left, the third to the right—both disappearing behind the foliage. I stood still, feeling useless and on the verge of being lost, as I realized that if the leader took four or five steps and vanished, I would be alone in the jungle without even a glimpse of the sun to guide me. The lack of light also prevented my taking pictures of this fascinating example of tracking.

I heard a soft, low whistle to my left. The leader turned, beckoned to me to follow, and in a moment we were proceeding as before, three hunters and panting explorer, on the path of the wild pig which hunter Number Two had found. Within an hour

111

they had their wild pig, dispatched with spears as it charged. I was as pleased as they were, because I had not slowed them down or made so much noise as to spoil their hunt.

When an outsider goes hunting with Pygmies, they *must* slow down for him. Nobody else can move through the forest that fast. When the Bambuti take an outsider along, whether sightseer like me or big-game hunter, they adjust themselves to a slower pace. At first my restricted experience with a Pygmy hunt made me think they had a sixth sense for such work, but then I realized that such talents or instincts must once have existed in all human beings. Civilization has dulled them or caused them to atrophy completely in most of us.

I did not go with Pygmies on many hunts. For one thing, I'm not a big-game hunter myself; I had neither desire nor weapons for killing any animals. I just wanted to watch the Pygmies at work, which I did in the course of two or three hunts for okapi, which we never got, two elephant hunts, and the one for the wild pig. I saw them track, stalk, and kill half a dozen different creatures. I heard them use their wooden whistles to attract the game—whistles in three sizes hanging from their necks. And I saw the work of their wonderful if unattractive dogs.

The dogs are mongrels that look as if a bit of hyena and fox has been grafted onto the family tree, with permanently built-in moths to make their short coats splotchy and full of badly darned holes. But no canines can beat them at their jobs and I doubt that many can match their courage. When they accompany their masters on the hunt, they can follow the spoor even more surely and swiftly than the Pygmies, unless the prey crosses a good-sized stream, and even then they may pick it up on the other side. They never get too far ahead of the hunters but that the men can hear the clop-clop of the little wooden bells tied around each dog's neck. Since the Pygmy dog has no bark, the bell is essential.

No "man's best friend" relationship exists between master and dog, so far as I could see. Never did I witness a pat or other sign of affection. But no Pygmy would underestimate the value of his dog, and a dog would give his life for his master, as shown by one experience I heard about but in which, I am happy to say, I was not a participant.

Three Pygmy hunters were moving swiftly through the forest on the trail of some animal, and their dog was just a few feet from the first hunter. Suddenly a leopard sprang from a low branch upon the first Pygmy, who was quick enough to dart beyond the reach of a man-killing first blow but not quick enough to avoid a slashing of his right shoulder and arm. He flung his spear at the leopard, but his bleeding arm could not guide it right. The spear missed its mark, and the Pygmy managed to clamber up a small tree. The leopard might have gone right after him, but its attention was diverted by the charge of the second hunter. The leopard swerved toward him just as he aimed his spear, so that it too missed, and broke against a rock.

Luckily for the second hunter, the leopard saw Number Three and went for him, enabling the second to climb to temporary safety. The third hunter kept hold of his spear and tried to plunge it into the leopard as it sprang. The spear merely sliced the leopard's leg a bit, serving only to make him angrier than before. Then the leopard and hunter Number Three battled it out, the hunter struggling to keep the leopard's claws from his throat and at the same time maneuvering to get in another thrust with his spear.

He would have been slashed to ribbons if it had not been for the dog. The mongrel rushed at the leopard from the side and from the rear, snapping at the big cat's legs and flank, then racing away as the leopard turned away from the hunter momentarily to get rid of the pesky dog. The two hunters in the trees could do nothing to help; they had no weapons and one was badly wounded and bleeding profusely. All they could do was watch man and leopard struggle, with the dog snarling, rushing in and out. Once he sank his fangs into the leopard's tail and tugged. The leopard whirled, howled, and obviously decided to kill the pest once and for all. That gave the third hunter just

the chance he needed. He lunged with his spear, which pierced
the leopard's side, cut into its heart, and dropped it. By this time
the hunter was so badly wounded that he could hardly stand,
but all three men managed to get back home. As their wounds
were cleaned and dressed, they all sang the praises of the dog,
giving him full credit for saving their lives. But they did not
once pat him or show him any affection.

The dogs are helpful, too, when the hunters go out with nets
—and so are the women and children. This method of hunting
involves the entire village—the hunters themselves for fixing
the nets; the dogs, women, and children to act as beaters, driving the game into the netted area. The nets themselves are fine
examples of workmanship; made of thin lianas, they are woven
into lengths of twenty to thirty yards, tough, strong, durable.
With five or six nets hooked together, a big semi-circle can be
made among the trees, an enclosure almost invisible. The hunters
station themselves along the outside of the net, in hiding, while
the noise-makers have formed a semicircle a few miles away—
an arc that slowly closes in toward the net. Small forest antelope
are the most likely catch for the nets, although occasionally
there is a small buffalo, a wild pig or an armadillo.

Pygmies also dig pits and camouflage them with saplings
and brush—usually along well-established animal trails, which
one can see here and there crisscrossing the forest. Poisoned
stakes are fitted into the bottom of the pit, if they want their
prey killed. Elephants, okapi and the lovely Bongo antelope are
caught in pits. Smaller beasts are often taken in noose traps
made of long, thin lianas. Then there are spear traps, with a
pointed and poisoned log suspended over an animal path to a
natural salt lick or watering place. A thin vine across the trail
releases the spear when it is touched, so that it plunges into the
beast below. Elephants and buffalo are the chief victims of this
technique.

One of the most depressing experiences I went through was
an unsuccessful hunt. Just as the Pygmies are hilariously gay
and happy over good things, so they are cast down and dejected

beyond belief by disappointment. On the way back to the clearing, my hunters even muffled the wooden bell on the dog. When
he raced ahead into the clearing there would be no sound to pro-
claim the return of the hunters. And they themselves trooped in
silently, with heads cast down. The faces of the women fell, but
they said no word about the hunt.

After a good hunt, feelings are high, of course. Despite the
great weight of the wild pig, which the hunters had to carry
several miles back to the village, they laughed and chatted all
the way. One snatched at a flower and tucked it in his waist,
and they all beamed with pride and anticipatory hunger as they
marched into the clearing. Women and children ran up, exclaim-
ing with pleasure, and no one could wait quietly until the
butchering and division of the meat occurred.

One thing will divert Pygmies from their hunting—the finding of a bees' nest with honey. Once I watched them scramble
up a tall tree, where there was a hive hidden in a big hole. They
used a heavy liana looped around the trunk to help them in their
ascent, much as a telephone linesman uses a wide strap. Once up
even with the hive, the first hunter enlarged the hole with his
spear, as hundreds of bees swarmed about him. Then he plunged
in his hand, brought it out full of honeycomb dripping with
honey, and crammed the whole mess into his mouth. One after
another, each hunter climbed the tree and ate his fill of honey,
and not once did a bee sting a man. I questioned several people
about this seeming immunity to bees, but could never learn the
reason for it. I was told that in some places, Pygmies smear their
skins with honey first, and the angry bees will not sting through
it.

The Pygmies' tree-climbing agility enables them to rob
parrots' nests of eggs and, principally, of baby parrots, which
they sell as pets to the Bantu villagers. Pygmy marksmanship
with the tiny bows and arrows is often amazing. Bill Deans
told me about a Pygmy who was set to guard a banana grove by
his Bantu "master," who wanted to end the raids of monkeys
and baboons. Suddenly a full-grown elephant lumbered from the

forest into the grove, confronting the lone Pygmy armed only with his twenty-inch bow and a few arrows. The little hunter knew that there was only one chance of killing the huge animal with his feeble weapon—a clean shot through the eye into the brain. And he would not have a second chance, for the elephant would be on him. He aimed the slender arrow and shot at the right eye—a tiny target in the massive head. It struck its mark, and the elephant dropped in his tracks.

Sometimes Pygmies shoot monkeys high in the trees, and the little creatures are caught in a lower branch as they fall. A Pygmy will scoot up the tree like a squirrel and bring it down. One day while I was there, some hunters caught a live monkey, bound its hands and feet, and brought it back to the camp with the idea of making a pet of it. But this monkey was determined never to be domesticated. It struggled continually with its bonds, thrashing about, rolling over, biting at its own arms and legs. After about three days it escaped, and I was glad.

The forest is full of hazards, and the biggest beasts are not the most dangerous. I was reminded of this fact recently by Bill Deans, who visited with me in New York where he had come for medical treatment of a disease he had caught in the Ituri.

"I remember sitting at your camp table in the heart of the forest," he said, "having supper. We looked around at the towering trees and thought how beautiful it was. And you might have thought at such a moment that, even though this was the jungle, it was really not so terrible.

"But in the Ituri Forest there are many dangers, seen and unseen. I'm thinking of *bilharzia*, for instance, which I've contracted and which I'm having such a hard time getting rid of. It is a pernicious disease, in which a microfilaria is introduced into the bloodstream and eventually the entire intestinal tract is seriously affected. You can get it just by standing in water or washing—water that the Pygmies drink.

"There's the tsetse fly carrying sleeping sickness, the

anopheles with malaria and blackwater fever, and the fly bearing *filaria bancrofti* which, introduced into my brother's body, caused his death in the Ituri. We do not see these dangers as we look at the forest nor the graves of many missionaries buried there.

"There are numerous deadly snakes—pythons fifteen to twenty feet long, and the poisonous viper that almost got me recently. I was sitting in front of my tent and a Pygmy suddenly darted up and crashed his spear down right at my feet. I was startled, and couldn't believe that he meant to attack me. Then he pointed to the viper whose fangs were only inches from my leg, now dead from the quick thrust of his spear. Yes, it is beautiful, but the Ituri Forest is a dangerous place."

Pygmies hate all snakes. Some tribes believe in reincarnation and think that the souls of departed Pygmies live in snakes —because they see snakes come out of the ground in which they have buried their dead. But even these Pygmies will eat snakes they have killed. Each tribe has one animal that is taboo, however, and is never eaten.

One of the worst snakes is the spitting cobra, which can shoot its venom five or six feet with deadly accuracy, aiming for the eyes. H. A. Hunter tells of a trip in the Ituri during which a spitting viper actually shot its venom into the eyes of the leading Pygmy, who fell to the ground writhing in pain. Immediate treatment was given by the stricken one's companions, who urinated directly into their friend's eyes. This seemed to give some relief, and further treatment of the same kind effected a complete cure. Pygmies ordinarily suck snake bites immediately, and they also possess several herbs which are obviously good antidotes.

William Spees told me of one exception to the general dislike of snakes among Pygmies. He knew one Pygmy who carried a live viper around in his loin cloth as a pet. Later he added a cobra to his collection, and kept both snakes in his house. He claimed that he owned a special medicine which rendered the snakes' venom ineffective. Spees could not really believe this, but he could learn of no other explanation of the man's immunity.

Another menace is the ant. Safari ants travel in solid columns a few inches across—a more dangerous enemy than many wild beasts of the forest and much more difficult to dispose of. Their bite is like the prick of a red-hot needle, which burns for hours afterwards. And no matter how many ants you kill, there are ten times as many ready to take their place.

Dr. Schebesta tells of an experience with ants and a monkey. One of his associates caught a colobus monkey and wanted to make a pet of it. The monkey was apparently not too averse to captivity, for the man fed it well and did not bind its arms or legs. One leg clamp and a long chain kept it close to a stump on which it slept.

One night Dr. Schebesta and the monkey's owner heard piercing shrieks from the pet, roused themselves and rushed to see what was wrong. The monkey was struggling to pull away from the stump, but it could scarcely be recognized as a monkey. It was a writhing mass of ants. The chain was a thick rope of ants, and the stump was alive with them. The monkey's owner put the little creature beyond torture with one merciful shot. By that time there was not much flesh left on the monkey.

The men wasted no time in trying to repel the ant invasion, for within a few hours the horde would have attacked everyone and everything in the camp.

Another explorer was awakened in the middle of the night by a persistent clicking sound. Reaching his hand out under the netting to find his flashlight, he felt his forearm burned as with red-hot pincers within a few seconds. Ants had invaded his tent, and the clicking sound was the noise of a million ant mandibles attacking food, shoes, and the net itself.

I have encountered ant armies on the march in the forest many times. When I did not see them in time to step over the long column, a hundred ants were swarming up my clothing in a flash. Only once was our clearing invaded, and then the

Pygmies saw the army just after it had emerged from the forest. Everyone snatched up a burning brand of wood from the fires and ran to the defense. Boiling water is a good weapon, even though temporary, but there is not enough of it in a Pygmy clearing to do much good. A line of fire across the path of the ants is best, although it must continually be extended as the ants try to outflank the fire. Four or five Pygmies stayed awake all night to keep the fires burning, and the next day was devoted to the extermination of the invaders.

Another Pygmy method of fighting ants was to break up the long column into smaller groups by starting fires at different spots along the line of march. But this was not enough. The surviving ants would have regrouped, found each other, and gone on their way with only a slight delay and a detour. It was necessary to track the line back to the ants' nest and destroy it with fire. When they finally found the big mound, with rivers of ants pouring down its sides, the Pygmies gathered dry leaves, twigs, and branches, and made a bonfire on top of the nest. Then they had to run to escape the avenging hordes that streamed from the mound.

The high point in Pygmy life is the elephant hunt. Not every male Pygmy is an elephant hunter; this most dangerous chore is reserved for the most alert, courageous and cool-headed. When an elephant hunter's reflexes slow down, he reluctantly gives up the chase for the mammoth and confines his activities to antelope, pig and okapi, like a baseball player who is dropped from the major leagues and goes to the minors or takes up coaching.

Every village, nevertheless, has a full quota of elephant hunters, and there is hardly a Pygmy family but has lost one of its members, at least, to the biggest forest animal. I tried to learn how many elephants an experienced hunter might have killed in his career, but it was difficult to arrive at any clear answer because Pygmies apparently have no numbers beyond ten. Several times, in answer to my question, "How many?" I

received the reply, "Without number." This might mean, to a
Pygmy, twelve or ninety or somewhere in between. From Bantu
villagers and missionaries, I gathered that many hunters kill fifty
to sixty elephants during their lives.

No Pygmy goes on an elephant hunt casually, as he might
for any other beast. The elephant demands preparation, the ap-
peasement of evil spirits, moral support from the entire village,
and a little something to bolster courage at the last minute.
Some Pygmies consult a medicine man the day before a projected hunt to learn if the signs are propitious. Actually, the
medicine man is not as influential a person among Pygmies as
among most primitive tribes. The idea seems to be borrowed
from the village Bantu, as few Pygmies themselves act the role
of medicine man. I did not encounter a single one. The Pygmy
groups most closely tied to their Bantu owners, which means
those who live on the edges of the forest rather than in its
depths, are most likely to come under the witch doctor's influence and consult him in case of illness, sterility, a need of good
fortune. None of my Pygmies, on my second trip, bothered to
consult a witch doctor before going out to hunt elephants.

They made other preparations, however. The day before
the hunt they went into the forest in search of kola nuts, large
and pink, which their women boiled, pounded and boiled some
more. This is the nut from which is extracted the flavoring for
all cola drinks, so Pygmies have enjoyed their "pause that re-
freshes" for centuries. Pygmy men also chew the kola nut for
greater virility, then spit the fibres on their arms to advertise the
fact to the girls.

The hunter drinks a potion of kola water when he awakens
on the day of the hunt. In his mind is the memory of the dance
put on by the women of the village the evening before, a dance
to inspire him to great deeds. A quick breakfast, and he is off
with his companions, who may number from three to five.

First, of course, they must find their elephants. But since
the forest is well populated by the big creatures, Pygmy trackers
rarely have much difficulty. By noon they may have located a

small herd. The hunt would be much less dangerous if they could find a solitary elephant, of course, but elephants travel in groups most of the time, numbering from four or five up. The Pygmies must worry not only about the beast they plan to slaughter, but all the others. Elephants often show remarkable intelligence and concern for their fellows. I've seen, for example, two elephants support a wounded brother on either side, leading him to safety as two soldiers might carry a wounded comrade from the battlefield.

When the Pygmy hunters locate their elephants, they study the terrain carefully, compare the elephants and select the one they will kill—usually the one with the largest tusks, for his ivory will bring the greatest rewards. The elephants are unaware of the Pygmies at this stage, for the hunters not only keep out of the wind but also smear themselves with elephant dung—of which they have found plenty along the trail.

When the hunters have studied the lay of the land sufficiently, they retire about a hundred yards, build a small fire, and smoke hemp, or marijuana, to take away their fear. Then they are ready. With the best hunter in the lead, they return to the herd of elephants, who may be asleep in the noonday heat or quietly munching grass. The hunters cautiously approach the elephant they have chosen, making certain to keep the wind just right, and circling if necessary to remain out of the vision of other elephants in the group.

At this point, the task looks almost ridiculous. A Pygmy is small by any standards, but alongside a huge elephant he looks so tiny, so weak, so ineffectual, that one feels like urging them to call the whole thing off before they make fools of themselves and meet sudden death. A mouse might just as reasonably try to slaughter a lion, or a squirrel kill a wolf. But Pygmy spears are razor sharp and Pygmy strength is greater than you might believe. Their biggest asset and most potent weapon, however, is courage, of which they have plenty even without the aid of marijuana.

If the elephant lifts its trunk and turns its head as if it

heard or smelled something, the approaching Pygmies freeze into immobility. The elephant sniffs only what smells like another elephant, lowers its head, and goes on eating. Then the Pygmies close in until two of them stand beside the hind legs of the elephant. The others place themselves to rout the other elephants and take up immediate pursuit of the selected animal.

At a silent signal the two leading Pygmies reach out with their sharp spears so the blades are just behind the elephant's knee joints. A sudden sharp slash and the tendon is severed in each hind leg. The two Pygmies dart away, the wounded elephant whirls to grab them with its trunk, the other Pygmies shout and jump and bellow to frighten the other elephants into a stampede. They rush away, and the wounded animal tries to follow. But it can barely drag itself along, since its hind legs are useless.

The beast bellows angrily, tugs itself painfully along the ground, its hind legs dragging. It reaches out and grabs a tree with its trunk to pull itself along, and rips up the tree by its roots. With the other elephants out of the way, the Pygmy hunters dart in as close as possible, trying to thrust their spears into the elephant. But the animal lashes out at them with its trunk, makes them keep their distance as it tries vainly to escape. Sometimes the elephant manages to go some distance, with the Pygmies following, waiting for their chance to kill it. But kill it they finally do, without fail.

Sometimes, of course, the plan goes wrong. Perhaps the tendons are not completely severed, and the elephant manages to snatch up one of the hunters and trample or gore him to death. Perhaps one of the other elephants refuses to panic and run, attacking the hunters instead. William Spees tells the story of one Pygmy hunter who was separated from his friends while trailing an elephant which had been wounded but not incapacitated. The elephant circled around to fool its pursuer and attacked the hunter from the rear, goring him in the side. The Pygmy dropped to the ground and, although bleeding badly, retained consciousness and his quick wit. He lay absolutely motionless, as if dead. The elephant approached, reached out with its trunk and poked the hunter, who remained limp and lifeless. Finally, after a good deal of investigating, the elephant decided the hunter was dead. Like all good elephants, it then had to bury its victim. The elephant dug a hole in the earth with its tusks, pushed the Pygmy into it with its trunk, then began to cover the hunter over with dirt, brush, and leaves. The Pygmy said later that this was his most difficult time—trying to keep his nose free to breathe without moving and showing the elephant that he was still alive.

But he succeeded, although he felt as if he would suffocate any minute. The elephant did not make things any easier for the hunter by going away when burial was completed. The beast must have been suspicious for it stood near by and watched the grave for a few minutes to make sure there was no movement. (Buffalo do the same thing after they have killed a man.) At long last, the elephant moved away and the wounded hunter pushed himself up into the air. Within a few minutes, the other Pygmy hunters came and found him. Fortunately, they carried him to the mission rather than to the Bantu witch doctor. Penicillin, cleanliness and rest healed the Pygmy's wounds and during the time he spent at the mission he became converted to Christianity. Spees thought that in view of this momentous change in his outlook on things, the Pygmy might give up elephant hunting. But the young man just shook his head. "No," he said, "once an elephant hunter always an elephant hunter."

When Pygmy hunters kill an elephant, the animal is usually many miles from the nearest Bantu village. But the hunters cannot touch the animal until the "owner" of the chief Pygmy hunter arrives to oversee the butchering and distribution. So one of the Pygmies races to the Bantu village to announce the news, another returns to the Pygmy village. Within a day, a huge crowd has gathered to watch and participate in the division of spoils. With the heat of the jungle, *spoils* is a term that can be

used in more than one sense. The elephant's big belly begins
to puff out like a balloon, bloated with the gases of decomposi-
tion.

During my second trip, I was most eager to get motion pictures of an elephant hunt. I soon learned, however, that the
hunt was almost impossible to film, as there was never enough
light in the forest to take pictures. I was beginning to despair
of success in this project, as the end of my visit approached.
But then luck, which has always seemed to balance things out
for me, came to the rescue. One group of Pygmy hunters killed
an elephant in a clearing close to the edge of the forest, near
the village of a Bantu chief named Pawanzas, of the Walese
tribe. They sent a runner to bring me the news and guide me
back to the clearing. Never did I travel through the forest so
quickly, for this was an opportunity that would never come
twice. According to my guide, the hunters had tracked the elephant for miles after wounding him, and had finally dispatched
him in a good-sized clearing where sunlight abounded. The only
growth was tall elephant grass, which would soon be trampled
down by the crowds.

As we hurried through the forest to the clearing, I hoped
that the Pygmy was not just saying things he knew I would like
to hear and when we came to the clearing I saw that he was
right. Plenty of sunlight, a little late in the day but good enough.
The only factor that dismayed me was the big crowd that had
gathered—between three and four hundred men and women,
about equally divided between Bantu villagers and Pygmies.
They were all relatives—some rather distant, I gathered—of the
Pygmy hunters or the Bantu overlord of the chief hunter. Luckily, the butchering had not yet started, as everything had to wait
for the arrival of the Walese chief of that area and the headman
of the village in which the Bantu "owner" lived.

While waiting for them I was able to clear a little space
for good camera shots. When the important personages arrived,
everyone turned to the Bantu in charge. He glanced around to
see that everyone who might claim a share of the elephant was

present, then lifted his hand in signal to the four Pygmies who had made the kill. They scrambled up on top of the big beast and stood on the bloated belly. At a second signal, the chief hunter plunged his spear into the elephant's side. A geyser of gas and stomach juices spurted into the air seven or eight feet, spreading an odor that made my senses reel. But the Pygmy hunters shouted and pushed their faces into the liquid, gulping it, bathing in it. This act was supposed to give the Pygmies some of the elephant's strength to aid them in their next kill.

In some instances, the first act of the hunters, upon making the kill, is to cut a hole in the abdomen, walk inside, and cut off small portions of the entrails. They emerge with these pieces, two or three inches long, in their teeth, and offer bites to the remaining hunters—teeth to teeth—as a token of victory in the hunt.

When the gassy geyser subsided, the hunters returned to the ground. Pygmies and villagers then lined up, each with a sharp knife. Behind each man stood his wife, ready and waiting with a big basket. At another signal, the Pygmies and villagers raced for the elephant, clambering up its sides, slipping, clutching for a firm hold—each one trying to reach the backbone first. The men yelled, the women shouted encouragingly, and the whole scene looked like a small riot. But there was organization and plan behind the bedlam, though I could not see it at first. When a man reached the backbone, he gained the right to cut a strip of meat down the side from that point. As I learned later, he did not necessarily get to keep all the meat he cut, but each man no doubt figured that the more he had the more he was likely to wind up with.

Shoulder to shoulder, Pygmies and villagers lined up along the crest of the fallen elephant and started hacking away at the meat. As one man cut a big chunk of flesh away he merely flung it back over his shoulder. He knew that his wife had her eyes fixed on him and was waiting to snatch whatever he threw, to deposit in her basket. Soon big chunks of elephant meat were flying through the air, women were rushing forward to grab the pieces, sometimes catching them even before they struck the ground. There was remarkably little bickering for such a confused scene. I suppose it was confusing only to me, and not to the Pygmies and villagers. But they *did* get in my way repeatedly so I could not get clear shots of the butchering.

Finally the meat was cut away from the exposed side and there was a lull in the proceedings while two Pygmies took an axe and chopped a hole through the elephant's ribs into the chest cavity. They then proceeded to take up their sharp spears and hop inside the beast. In a moment I saw two spear points sawing their way along the ribs, as the men worked from the inside out, cutting away more meat and flinging it out through the hole, along with heart, liver, and all other entrails—prized parts of the beast.

I could not quite believe that an equitable distribution of meat could be made among so many demanding men and women, but by the end of the afternoon the job was done and no one seemed angry. In fact, there was much hilarity among the entire group. The Bantu chief of the area received one huge leg as his share. The headman of the village was given a select piece. The "owner" of the chief Pygmy hunter kept some entrail delicacies for himself, as well as some solid meat and—perhaps most important to him—the ivory tusks. And he decided just how much meat should go to all the assembled villagers and Pygmies. No one, apparently, had the right to question his decision, so long as the chief and headman received their shares. The Pygmy hunters received most generous portions for their families, of course, and other relatives from their settlement came in for shares. Not a thing was wasted. At the end, even the tough skin was cut up so some of the Pygmy women could make soup from it.

Thus my second visit to the Ituri ended with a good deal of satisfaction on my part and, I believe, almost as much on the part of the Pygmies. An unexpected worry, however, came up at the last moment. A Pygmy messenger brought news that a large group of Pygmies from deep in the forest—*suba ndula*—had gathered a few miles away. Word had spread beyond the unseen boundaries of my Pygmies' forest that a white man with many gifts welcomed Pygmies. There were more than five hundred in the second group, making more than a thousand Pygmies gathered in that small area. But we were somewhat worried because the newcomers were enemies of my Pygmies and, although there had been no intertribal battles for some time, the enemy had actually invaded my Pygmies' section of the forest. I wanted to avoid all chances of bloodshed, so consulted with a few of the Pygmy leaders and their overlords in the village. As a result, my Pygmies agreed to strike camp at once and return to their homes by a circuitous route that would avoid the newcomers. And a messenger sought out the invaders to tell them that the white man had departed, had no more gifts, and urged them to return to their homes. He would come to visit them and bring more gifts when he returned to the Ituri another year.

I learned later that the two antagonistic groups had managed to avoid contact, so no blood was shed. At the time I sent the message, I had no intention of returning to Africa or the Ituri Forest. Near the end of such a trip, one always wonders why he got into such a hazardous and tormenting business as living with primitive people and trying to take moving pictures of them which would be acceptable to Hollywood. Within a year, of course, one forgets the ants, chiggers, mosquitoes, bad smells, doubtful food and worse water, the fatigue, the eternal dampness. What comes to mind are the sounds of the forest in the middle of the night, the sight of Pygmies dancing around a fire to the infectious beat of drums, of eighteen giraffes careening like rocking boats with tall masts along the plains, of pink flamingoes rising from a blue lake in mass flight, of a lioness playing with her cubs.

When I went to Africa in 1954-55 to make "Zanzabuku" for Republic Pictures, I had a proper expedition, with an assistant and four other cameramen, with a Dodge Power Wagon

and truck, kindly supplied by the Chrysler Corporation, and
with more time than I had ever taken before. I wanted to visit
the Pygmies again, not just for my own satisfaction, but to take
pictures of one thrilling achievement of these little people which
I had never been able to get. This was the building of a liana
bridge across a wide river.

It would not be an easy task, I knew. I had to find the right
spot on the right river, assemble a group of Pygmies and persuade them to tackle the really difficult job of building a bridge
for which they might not see any necessity, and finally arrange
to have all this take place where there was sufficient light and
proper positions for my cameras.

Lady Luck outdid herself on this occasion. During the better part of a year in Africa, on my third journey, I frequently
felt that she had abandoned me altogether, migrated to another
continent, crossed me off her list once and forever. There were
days, weeks of delay, frustration, rain, accidents and interrup-
tions. But when I returned to the Ituri, luck flew back and settled
down on my right shoulder.

The first spot selected was not right, for the river was narrow and the building of a bridge would not have looked at all
spectacular. Hollywood *had* to have the spectacular, so we
searched further, until we found the ideal stretch of the Ituri
River. At this point it was about ninety feet wide, and throwing
a liana bridge across that distance would make a spectacle indeed. For a quarter of a mile the river flowed in a straight
course instead of twisting and winding. Very tall trees lined
each bank—a necessity for the Pygmy method of bridge-building. But the undergrowth was rather sparse, leaving clear spaces
from which my cameras could obtain good shots up and down
the river.

Most important of all, however, was that right here the
Ituri River flowed from west to east. When the sun rose in the
morning, its light would not be cut off by two-hundred-foot trees
until almost noon. No, it would cast its beautiful rays right
down that straight mile stretch of river. And in the afternoon,

the sun would set at the western end of the stretch, giving me light until four o'clock at least. Each day would bring about three or four hours more of filming time than I had ever enjoyed in the forest. It was almost too good to be true.

Pygmies were assembled, given gifts and briefed on the project. They seemed agreeable, but I heard a few of them muttering *"Bumbafu! Bumbafu!"* and shaking their heads. When I asked the interpreter what this meant, he seemed a little embarrassed.

"Well, when someone tries to do something very difficult and daring," he said, "even though it may not seem very sensible, he is *bumbafu*. These Pygmies don't need a bridge here, because their camp and the village of their Bantu masters and their hunting grounds are all on this side of the river. But you want a bridge, even though it's dangerous and difficult to build one. So you are *bumbafu*."

"How would you translate it in a word or a phrase?" I asked.

"Crazy white man!" he said.

From the Pygmy point of view, I suppose they were right. Anyway, they were willing and eager so long as I gave them food and gifts. We set them to work at once clearing out some smaller trees that might get in the way of the cameras. Others went in search of long and strong lianas, and still others made a few platforms on which cameras could be mounted for shots from different angles.

We were never certain, of course, that the project could succeed. The Ituri at this point was quite wide, as wide as any river the Pygmies had ever spanned. I wanted the task to be difficult because that would probably make it more dramatic, but I hoped it would not be *too* difficult.

The crux of the problem in bridge building is the first long liana that must somehow be stretched across the river. After that the work is precarious but relatively simple. We selected a tree, tall and straight at the water's edge, from which the first attempt would be launched. Free of low branches, it looked like

a double-length telephone pole with another tree on top. Opposite this tree, on the other bank of the river, stood several trees
of comparable height with wide-spreading branches.

Looping stout lianas around the trunk of the first tree, one
of the more agile Pygmies worked his way up to the first big
branch, taking one end of a hawser-like vine with him. He
climbed out on the branch and tied the long liana securely to it,
using smaller vines as tough as wire to reinforce it. A second long
liana was attached about two feet away, so that two long and
supple wooden ropes fell to the ground. These were simply the
ropes for a giant swing, to which a small seat was attached. The
idea was to place a strong young Pygmy in the seat, set him
swinging, and hope that he could swing out far enough to reach
a branch of one of the trees on the opposite bank.

The swing did not look quite long enough to me, but I
deferred to the judgment of the Pygmies. I was no engineer, but
I could see that to reach across ninety feet of river, the swing
had to be at least ninety feet long. Allowing for slack and a few
extra feet on each side, a hundred and ten feet would be closer
to the required length.

None of the Pygmies seemed to be particularly eager to act
as the swinger. As the time approached for the first launching, I
think they looked at the river's width, at the great height of the
swing, and found themselves assailed by doubts. But they were
very vocal in their insistence that the job could be done, and
equally vocal in their modesty. Each one disclaimed any special
ability as swinger or bridge builder, and many pointed to other
men as experts in the field. We finally settled on a young fellow
of about twenty, named Meru, who seemed both proud to have
been chosen and afraid to get in the swing. But he looked like a
brave man, and I was told that he was one of the best elephant
hunters of the tribe. When I enumerated the special gifts of
dried fish, nuts and palm oil, plus several arrows, that would go
to the man who carried the first liana across the river, Meru
appeared more eager for the task.

The Pygmies had cut a clear path through the forest leading straight back from the tall tree, a kind of narrow alley in which the swing could be pulled back to launch Meru on his flying mission over the water. A long liana, tied to the seat of the swing, was led back through this path and passed up to two or three Pygmies perched high in the branches of a tree. The idea was for them to pull Meru back and up as far as possible, then suddenly let him go. He was equipped with a sharply curved piece of hardwood that looked something like a longshoreman's bulky hook. As he swung up close to the branch on the other side of the river, he was supposed to latch his hook over the branch and hold on for dear life. I was afraid that this movement would jerk him right out of the swing seat, but the Pygmies assured me that he would be fastened to it securely and would manage to scramble up on the branch once he caught hold of it.

Looking quite serious, the young man settled himself in the swing, hooked his arms around the supporting lianas, grasped his wooden hook, and watched carefully while others strapped him to the seat with small tough vines. Then the Pygmies in the tree back at the end of the cleared path began hauling on the long liana, pulling Meru back and up higher and higher. I had one camera on a platform filming this action and another on the river bank to shoot the flight of the swing across the river and—I hoped—Meru's grasping of the branch on the other side. I stationed myself near the base of the tree with the swing, where I could see in both directions and give the necessary signals.

Slowly and laboriously the Pygmies in the tree hauled Meru up on the back half of the swing's arc, until he was suspended, almost face down, near the far end of the narrow alleyway. Then I gave the signal, "Cut!" and one of the Pygmies in the tree cut the hauling liana. Meru's tiny body hurtled down and out at increasing speed, barely missing the trees beside the cleared area. In a fraction of a second he reached the bottom of the arc at the foot of the tree and sped out over the water and up toward his goal. But something was wrong! He didn't zoom upwards as he should. I heard the groan of a bending branch and looked up to

see the branch to which the lianas had been attached bending
from the force of the pull that had been exerted on it. Meru's
foot touched the top of the water, cut down his speed and prevented him from coming anywhere near the tree on the opposite
bank.

The swing arched back toward us, and the Pygmies grabbed
it, bringing Meru to a stop. The young fellow was obviously
deeply frightened, and I did not blame him. If the branch had
broken, he would have been a goner. Even if it had bent a little
more so that his body struck the water, he would have been
killed by the force of the impact.

He stepped from the swing rather shakily, and I put my
arm around his shoulder in an effort to calm and reassure him.
He kept shaking his head and muttering to himself something
that sounded to me like *"Zanzabuku! Zanzabuku!"* I had no
idea what it meant at first, and neither did anyone else, for it
was apparently a word or phrase in the original Pygmy language.
But as he gestured at the swing, the branch, and the river, shaking his head as if to say "Never again!" I gained a fairly good
idea of what he meant. He was trying to tell me that this job was
too dangerous for him to tackle. Somehow, in spite of the tense-
ness of that critical moment, I have never forgotten the word,
and it has come to my mind several times when I suddenly
found myself in a hazardous situation. *"Zanzabuku"* must mean
something like "perilous task" or "dangerous mission."

I took Meru to one side, got him to sit down, and offered
him a cigarette. We smoked quietly for a while. I wanted to give
him a chance to collect himself, and I knew that I had to handle
this delicate situation just right. If none of the other Pygmies
had volunteered to swing the first liana across the river before,
they certainly wouldn't now, after Meru's experience. And at
this moment, Meru himself was adamant against making another attempt. Somehow, I had to persuade him to try again.
Otherwise all our work up to this time would be fruitless and we
would not get our important Pygmy sequence.

Realizing that strong measures were called for, I got out a

bottle of the imported German beer which I'd bought at a *duka*
outside the forest. He enjoyed it, as he did the cigarette, and I
did not press him for a decision at this time. Instead, I called
off work for the day, thus postponing the need for an answer
from Meru. I talked to the young Pygmy about other things,
about his elephant hunting, about dancing, about his hunting
dog, and other pleasant subjects. I was searching for some basis
of appeal that might weigh heavily with him. I *had* to sell him
the idea of trying the swing once more, after it was properly
fixed.

Selling a Pygmy, however, is totally different from selling
anyone else. The appeals I might make to another American, or
to almost any civilized person, were ineffective with a Pygmy. I
could not use his vanity, telling him how movies of his great feat
would be shown in theatres all over the world and millions would
applaud his bravery and skill, for Meru did not know what pictures were and cared not a whit for the opinions of millions of
people far from the Ituri Forest. I could not even use to much
effect the argument that all the Pygmies would look up to him.
Pygmies lack almost all serious competitive spirit and they cannot understand the importance of being better than the next fellow except in games. There was not much more I could do in relation to his acquisitiveness, for the rewards already offered for
the man to take the first liana across the river seemed to him like
riches. At least, riches for a day or two, and beyond that Meru
was not interested.

In my talk with him, however, something came out that I
hoped I might use. When I asked him about his wife and children, he said with a rueful expression that he was not married. I
learned that there was a girl in a neighboring Pygmy group he
wanted for a wife, but he could not persuade his sister to marry
a young man in that group and thus make the head-for-head exchange of women.

There was only one thing for me to do—turn matchmaker.
I located the sister and talked to her. No, she did not have anything against the fellow in the other tribe. She was only thirteen

and didn't feel like getting married yet. Marriage meant a great deal of hard work, and she was having a good time as it was.

Now I had to do a selling job on Meru's sister. In other primitive tribes I would have found my task easier, for the appeal of mirrors, bright beads, scissors, safety pins, and such is very strong. Pygmies, however, do not care for personal ornaments, have no idea what a mirror is for, and have nothing to cut up or pin up. I had to rely on things to eat, plus two pottery jars with which she could start housekeeping.

In the end I won her over. She agreed to take the young man from the neighboring group right away, and that meant Meru could have the girl he wanted. He was overjoyed, the next day when all this was settled, and agreed to make one more effort to span the river. But first we had to find a branch that would not bend under the force of his swing.

About ten feet above the branch we had used was another, much thicker and stronger. This meant cutting off the first branch and also finding longer lianas for the swing itself. I was pleased, for it seemed to me that they would now be long enough to reach clear across the river, with a bit to spare.

By the next day, everything was ready. The branch was obviously sturdy enough and the swing long enough. Still, Meru looked as if he had made a mistake when he sat himself in the swing. He was quickly lashed to the seat, given his hook, and started on the backward pull. Higher and higher he rose until I gave the signal for him to be released. Down and out he flashed, and this time nothing went wrong. Meru arched out over the river and up toward the branch on the opposite shore. At the top of his swing, his arm darted out with the hook—and missed the branch by inches!

A groan went up from all the Pygmies—and from me too. Meru swung to a stop, and I walked up to him disconsolately, feeling sure that he would refuse vehemently to try again. But he was not frightened this time. The branch and the swing had held firm, so there was nothing to be afraid of. He was truly a courageous little Pygmy!

Meru explained that if the men who hauled him back to start the swing would pull just a few feet farther he felt sure he could then reach the tree across the river. I gave the necessary instructions, installed Meru in the swing again after a brief intermission for a cigarette, and started the procedure for the third —and, I felt sure, the last—time.

Some of the other Pygmies were no help, for they cried out *"Utanguka!* (You'll fall!)" as Meru was being hauled up in the air. But the young man was so determined that I don't think he heard them. I waited to give the "Cut!" signal until Meru was several feet higher than before, then watched him speed down and out, looping up gracefully toward the distant branch across the water. At exactly the right moment Meru lunged with his hook and caught the branch. His body jerked so violently that I felt sure he would lose his grip, but he pulled himself up slowly until he lay panting on his long-sought goal.

"Mukaramisu!" the Pygmies cried, deservedly calling Meru "fearless one."

Everything after that was anticlimax so far as spine-tingling excitement was concerned, although there were many fascinating shots for the cameras as the main supporting vines were placed lower down on both trees, arching down over the river like the cable of a suspension bridge. The Pygmies built ladder-like approaches up from the ground on either side and set quickly to work enlarging the bridge. More thick lianas passed across the water, a little higher than the first so that they could serve as handrails. Pygmies worked their way out from the tree making a narrow footpath, and more vines were woven in and out to form a kind of netting on either side between footpath and handrails. Finally the day came when I ascended the ladder at one end, stepped onto the bridge and made my way across. The bridge swayed and danced under my feet, and I looked with a good deal of trepidation at the rushing waters below. But the bridge was strong and would no doubt last a long time.

It had been a long and arduous task, but in the end it had turned out so well that I felt like celebrating. I gave Meru more than I had promised, and made sure that the essential marriages would take place. When I left the Ituri Forest the third time I felt happy. And somehow, I no longer felt that the Pygmies were strange or unusual human beings. We had been through too much together.

Although the bridge-building was the outstanding incident of my third visit with the Pygmies, there were other events that come back to my mind now. On this trip I finally learned, I believe, the secret of the Pygmy's uncanny ability to find his way through the forest. What has always baffled outsiders the most is not the Pygmy's marvellous tracking of animals, but rather the beeline route he follows, without a path, in going from any one spot in his jungle to another, even five or ten miles away. William Spees showed me that there is no mystery involved, no sixth sense. The Pygmy is very observant, yes, but above all, he is thoroughly familiar with his section of the forest—with every single part of it. There he has lived his entire life. He has lived a month here, and a month there, ranging throughout the whole territory, and has hunted through those woods daily. When he wants to make sure just where he is, he looks up and sees an ironwood or mahogany tree which has stood in this spot for longer than the Pygmy's grandfather can remember. To a forest-dweller's eyes, this particular tree is somewhat different from any other tree in the forest.

"It's just as if he looked up at the tree and read it as you would read a street sign, 'Park Avenue and 58th Street,'" Bill Spees said. It is as simple as that.

I think of the old white-haired Pygmy with all of his original teeth who remembered H. M. Stanley, the first white man to enter the Congo. "We fought him," the old man said, "and tried to kill him."

Another old man had been to *Bulaya*, the white man's country, he insisted. Mandiboka was the old fellow's name, and he told a convincing story. He said that the trip had occurred many many years before, when he was a young man—so young that he was not even married. He recalled incidents of the trip from the

Ituri Forest to the ocean—and it sounded like going down the navigable part of the Congo River. He told about a huge boat he traveled across the water in—and pointed out a distance of four hundred to five hundred feet as its length. The trip was long, he said, and terrible. He was sick for many days. Then he was in a country where there were nothing but white men, no forests, and so many strange things that he could not remember them all. Then he was brought back to his forest, and the white men gave him some papers to keep to prove he had been to Bulaya. These documents, according to the old man and the other villagers, had been given to the Bantu "owner" of Mandi-boka for safe-keeping. But the Bantu's house had burned down a few years before, with everything in it.

The village Bantu confirmed the tale. William Spees spoke a few words in English to the old Pygmy, who showed some signs of comprehending. He even mumbled a few English words himself, but obviously no longer associated any meaning with them.

At a World's Fair in St. Louis in the year 1900 a few Pyg-mies were exhibited. So far as I can figure out, the time is right, and although it can never be proved, I like to believe that I have met a Pygmy who has visited my own country. When I go to St. Louis now, I see it in a new light, trying to visualize it as the Pygmy Mandiboka must have seen it. I like the city and have good friends there, but I am forced to admit that Mandiboka must have been very happy to get back to the Ituri Forest.

It is difficult for me to believe that the Ituri Pygmies will ever be civilized. They reject civilization and everything that it offers, except for a few items. It is amazing that they have been in contact with the village Bantus for so many decades and have adopted so few of their ways. I believe that Pygmies pos-sess the intelligence to cope with civilization, if it is not thrown at them too rapidly. Converts who have grown up in and around some of the missions have learned to read and write readily, have shown themselves adept at learning new skills *if they want to*. Most Pygmies don't want to.

Once there were no roads through the Ituri. Now there are two or three. In time there may be dozens, with the forest cut up by them into smaller and smaller areas. Bantu will cut back the forest along the sides of the roads to make gardens and villages. The Pygmies will be confined to continually smaller areas. This is the inevitable course of civilization on the march in Africa. But if no one finds gold or oil or uranium in the Ituri, perhaps there will be a limit beyond which the constriction of Pygmy country will not go. I hope so. I hope that the Belgian government will create for these wonderful wild humans a sanctuary in the Ituri as it has set aside huge reserves for wild animals.

 *VII*

Giants in the Earth

WHEN you walk out of the steaming, dripping, stifling tropical forest of the Pygmies, you can drive one day and find yourself in an African Switzerland where the air is clear and dry, the temperature balmy by day and a little chilly by night—the homeland of the Watussi. On the way from tropics to mountains, in the course of a few hours, you will cross the equator and snow-covered mountain peaks. A little later you will see a row of volcanoes, the Virunga group, and nestled at their feet the most beautiful lake in the world, Kivu, whose waters contain no crocodiles or other dangers, whose shores are infested with no mosquitoes or tsetse flies.

On one of the routes to the country of the Watussi, you will drive over a narrow road which climbs up the side of the escarpment, making 844 sharp turns—or so I was told, for I did not count them—in rising close to four thousand feet. On some sections, where only a narrow shelf has been carved out of the precipice, you will encounter a barrier operated by a native perched on a high rock with a shiny, empty gasoline tin suspended from a pole and another on which to drum. When the one tin is raised and the other is loudly pounded, another native perched on another rock miles away knows that a car has entered this one-way traffic area. You will perhaps see him in fifteen or twenty minutes, after you twist around a dozen hairpin bends and climb a few hundred feet. At every turn you look down on a breathtaking sight—the blue gem that is Lake Kivu, with the smoking volcanoes at its upper end, one of which sends down a broad, imperceptibly moving avenue of lava to hiss in the water; at the lower tip of the lake the Ruzizi River noisily fights its way through rocky gorges on its way to Lake Tanganyika. You see vast plantations of coffee, cinchona, pyrethrum—some rising to great heights on terraced mountains.

On your way you will perhaps stop for a delicious meal at the Hotel des Volcans in Goma, or the excellent hostelry in Kisenyi run by a gracious Russian woman. While savoring the food and gazing at lovely Kivu, you will recall that just that same morning you watched Pygmies at their breakfast of caterpillar grubs and snakes.

With all these contrasts in the course of a day, you will not be surprised to see seven-foot aristocrats from a civilization far more ancient than our own. By this time you *expect* the unusual —and Africa never fails to give it to you in full measure. Just as it has preserved Paleolithic man in the Ituri Forest, so it has preserved at least some aspects of an ancient culture—Egyptian, Abyssinian?—in the mountains of Ruanda-Urundi. The bas-reliefs of sacred cattle on the walls of an old Egyptian temple come to life in the million cows owned by the Watussi—cows with graceful white horns of ten-foot span, cows whose heads are bejeweled, cows on whom the dignity of a great lineage rests as naturally as it does on their human masters.

Ruanda-Urundi is the heart of Africa, but a heart that seems to have been transplanted from another body because so many characteristics of this tiny area—only twenty thousand square miles—are strikingly different from the vast continent that surrounds it. It has the densest concentration of people of any area in Africa except Egypt, with two hundred humans to the square mile in comparison with the Congo's eight. In addition it contains and supports a million cows, a million goats, half a million sheep—animals for which there are not even names in some areas of the continent. In many ways the most civilized country, so far as the natives are concerned, it was just about the last part of the continent to be found by white men. The German Count von Götzen discovered Lake Kivu and the lovely lands on its eastern shore in 1894.

When you begin to think that Ruanda-Urundi is not typi-

cally African, you must ask yourself just what *is* typically Afri-
can. Nothing, of course. Tropical jungle, veldt, desert, gently
rolling hills, steaming malarial marshes—Africa has them all.
Ruanda-Urundi is just different from our stereotyped concept of
Africa, which actually applies to only a small part of the conti-
nent. You might as well try to believe that any one section of
America is typical of our nation—Florida, the Rockies, New
England, the Bad Lands, the Mojave Desert or Iowa.

Ruanda and Urundi—the words bring into focus on the
cinemascopic screen of my mind not only scenery of incom-
parable beauty but actors perfectly cast to occupy such a stage,
the patrician giants called the Watussi. But they are really only
a handful of the inhabitants of this land, about twenty thousand
out of a total of four million. Most of the balance are Bantus
called Bahutu, dark-skinned, docile people of average height,
apparently content to occupy a secondary role in the feudal caste
system of these twin kingdoms. In addition, Africa tossed a
touch of another race into the small pot—Pygmies. To be accurate, the Batwa are Pygmoids, for they are not a pure race like
the Bambuti of the Ituri Forest. Nor are they as diminutive. At
some point in history the Batwa interbred with some of the
Bantu tribes, from which they borrowed eight or ten inches in
height, so that they range from four and a half to five feet tall.
Although occupying the lowest rung on the social ladder, the
Batwa won some special positions for themselves in the old days
—as court executioners and jesters, for example.

The Watussi are a minority, but the country is unmistaka-
bly theirs. They have molded it in their image not only socially
but to some extent physically, for they caused thousands of
square miles of forest to be razed to provide grazing land for
their sacred cattle. The result, up to twenty-five or thirty years
ago, was recurrent famine, for the terraced farms did not provide enough food when a bad year came along. The people who
died, of course, were chiefly the inferior Bahutu and Batwa, so
the lordly Watussi did not mind too much. There was some
resistance when the governing Belgians started reforestation pro-

grams and commanded increased production of profitable crops, among them the most flavorful coffee in the world. Famines, however, seem to be a part of the glorious Watussi past, and the aristocrats cooperate intelligently, but with a hint of condescension, with the Belgian authorities.

When you watch and talk with the Watussi King and the chief princess of his court, you know you are not dealing with uncivilized men, despite their lack of hydroelectric plants, refrigerators, and other technological gadgets. Indeed, you may feel that *you* are the representative of a raw, new civilization inspecting a far older and more gracious culture. The Watussi *know* that they are aristocrats, and they have known it for centuries. There is no arrogance in them, as there might be in someone doubtful of his superiority and thus determined to prove it.

The great height of Watussi men—from six and a half to seven and a half or even eight feet—has a great deal to do with this effect, of course, but even more impressive is the way they carry that height, the noble air that surrounds them. Some unusually tall men are gangling; the Watussi move gracefully no matter what they are doing, even when they tuck their long robes up around their waists and jump over a crossbar eight feet high. These robes are designed, too, to aid the aura of dignity and grace—long flowing robes like a Roman Senator's toga, snowy white with sunbursts of gold or broad red stripes. They are simple and rich, draped just right on tall thin bodies. You never see a fat Watussi man or woman. On the other hand, all Watussi babies are fat, for they live on nothing but milk—sweet or curdled—until puberty. At that time the diet and the physique change. Milk in some form still occupies an important place in adult diet, but fermented honey is added, and bananas, occasionally some meat, and a few vegetables. It must be a perfect reducing diet, in any event, for after puberty the Watussi men stretch up and up until they are tall and thin but not bony. Their hands and fingers are long, slim, almost delicately feminine. A contributing factor here is the fact that those hands need never soil or toughen themselves with physical labor. All work in Ruanda is handled by Bahutu and Batwa. The Watussi manage their estates and see that their great herds of cattle are properly cared for; they go in for sports such as javelin-throwing, high-jumping, archery. A select group is trained from childhood as court dancers. Recently, under Belgian tutelage, they are being trained to become community and national leaders—leading in the direction the Belgians designate.

The grafting of western civilization on the sturdy tree of Watussi feudalism appears to be singularly successful. For one thing, the Belgians have gone about the task intelligently, tough of purpose but not of manner, determined but understanding. More important, a civilization existed in Ruanda-Urundi, with a stable government, a system of laws, a complex social structure, and a long tradition. Altering the nature of a civilization is easier than bringing a group of primitives quickly through the normally slow process of becoming civilized.

For me personally, the westernizing of Ruanda has been too rapid. Not that I have anything against civilization as compared with primitive life, for each has its merits and its faults aplenty. My private interest happens to be primitive people and the Watussi have not been that for many centuries. Still, they are picturesque, colorful, likable. But the change was so great between my 1937 trip and the 1946 journey that I did not care to return in 1954.

In 1937 the young king, Rudahigwa, lived in the traditional Watussi *inzu*, a large domed structure of poles and thatch, circular except for a rounded growth on one side which served as a foyer, the interior divided into sleeping, eating, cooking sections by fiber mats that made me think of Japanese screens between rooms. In 1946 King Rudahigwa had moved into a brick and concrete house with flush toilets, picture windows and broadloom carpeting. Some lion and leopard skin rugs lay on top of the broadloom, and a few Watussi baskets and other art objects were visible, but the King's own possessions of this sort were not as attractive or as expertly made as several things I had

brought home with me in 1937. When artistic ability and crafts-
manship deteriorate that much in nine years, you can be sure a
culture is dying, even if it does so gracefully.

Another significant change occurred between 1937 and 1946,
in the king's name. His name had been Rudahigwa, upon coming to the throne of Ruanda at the age of sixteen, when the
Belgians ousted his father, King Musinga, for lack of cooperation
and some cruel butchery. When Rudahigwa ascended the
throne, another name was added, as was always done with new
kings. A council of Watussi elders selected the name which was
chosen with great care so as to inform the new king what
direction his reign was supposed to take. In the distant past, at a
time of trouble between many Watussi clans, one king had been
named Mazimpaka, "the peace-maker." Another had been called
Lwabugiri, "the conquering hero," when new territory was
desired. Rudahigwa was designated Mutara, "the reformer" or
"the evolutionist," which was a plain instruction to abandon the
dictatorial methods of his father and lead the way to beneficent
collaboration with the Belgians and the new civilization.

In 1937, the king, or *Mwami*, I met and talked to was
called Mutara III Rudahigwa. But by 1946 he had become a
Christian and added several names to underline not only a
religious but a cultural conversion. He was Mwami Mutara III
Charles Léon Pierre Rudahigwa, no less, thirty-ninth ruler in a
dynasty that can trace its line clearly back about four hundred
years.

Many changes followed. Rudahigwa, for example, would
never collect thirty wives, as his father had done, or even the
two or three that were almost a minimum for any Watussi lord.
Nor would he find his bed warmed, on a chilly evening, by the
court virgins. The preceding thirty-eight rulers of Ruanda had
always chosen several comely maidens from among the daughters of Watussi princes for this honorable chore; they merely
occupied his bed for half an hour before he retired, to take the
chill off. I suppose that Rudahigwa has replaced them with an
electric blanket which is undoubtedly more efficient. Certain it

is that the Watussi tradition of incestuous relationships is almost dead, although there is some talk of occasional secret indulgence. According to the Watussi legend of the creation of the world, the first man descended from heaven and took his sister as his wife. Here is another feature of Watussi culture that reminds one of the ancient Egyptians.

Mwami Rudahigwa is a pleasant, unaffected, and intelligent young man who has worked hard at his role of ruler under the aegis of the Belgians. And for the son of a king with absolute life-and-death power, he has made the transition from autocracy to a kind of constitutional monarchy swiftly and smoothly. In his case, of course, the restrictions on his power are not from a people's constitution but from Belgian regents; from his point of view it makes little difference. He is primarily a symbol for his people, the one who, by example, must try to lead them into new ways. Ostensibly, he still owns all the land of the country, as the kings always have, but he would never dream of claiming it. He appoints local officials, promulgates new regulations, and administers the laws through native courts—but all of this is done with the constant but inconspicuous advice of the Belgian Resident and the Belgian Vice-Consul General in charge of Ruanda and Urundi. An important part of his job is to try to preserve those aspects of Watussi culture which are not tabu in western civilization while rejecting the rest. Retain the costumes, which have always been sufficiently modest to meet the approval of missionaries—except in the case of some women dancers. Reject polygamy and incest and summary executions. Retain the hierarchical caste system rigidly, for it is easily managed. Retain the colorful dances and pageants, the sports of high-jumping and javelin-throwing. Indeed—make a show of these aspects of Watussi life, for they attract tourists!

And tourists there will be, increasingly and inevitably. Ruanda is far away, but planes have cut long distances to one-tenth. The service to Leopoldville and Stanleyville, in the Congo, is excellent, and now that airfields have been made near Usumbura and other spots in Ruanda-Urundi, travelers with enough money will find it easy and pleasant to reach this land which will delight even the blasé tourists who have been everywhere. Scenery, climate, two thousand miles of acceptable roads, several good hotels—and more will be built as needed—plus personable, colorful and untroublesome tribesmen will bring in thousands of sightseers from Europe and America.

July will be one of the best times, for near the end of this month the Watussi stage one of their biggest and most attractive festivals. I fervently hope that some promoter will not try to make a production of it, for when it is honest and natural it is a memorable sight.

On my first trip I saw it from sheer luck, since I happened to arrive in Ruanda just a few days before it began. After driving over the spectacular Kabasha escarpment road with Cézaire in his old Chevvy, we headed for the town of Kigali, not far from the small capital of Ruanda, called Nyanza. We knew that in Kigali we would find a mission of the White Fathers who were always hospitable and helpful. Not far from the mission, just as it was getting dark, I saw my first Mutussi (singular of Watussi). Despite all I had read and heard about these giants, I was strongly impressed, for he was almost eight feet tall and his robe was resplendent. His triangular face with small black goatee, large soft eyes, his satiny bronze skin, tapering fingers, high-bridged straight nose, and strange hair-do calculated to increase the impression of great height—everything about him was striking. His grave courtesy, when Cézaire asked him the way to the mission, spoke at the same time of warmth and reserve, friendliness and dignity.

Father de Bekker, a sturdy, blue-eyed Hollander, welcomed us at the mission and introduced us to the rest of the brethren, bearded and impressive in their white robes. I could see why they and the Watussi had managed to get along well together, even though it had taken the White Fathers several decades to make much headway in their missionary work. They were patient but vigorous men, who used medicine as an entering wedge, followed by education of children. Religion, they felt, would follow.

We shared an excellent meal with the Fathers, then looked forward to a good night's sleep, for Cézaire and I had covered much territory that day. Our good hosts, however, were hungry for human companionship from their own world, and wanted to talk.

I found among my things a box of good cigars and passed them around. The brethren happily and gratefully took them, lighted up, and relaxed for a couple of hours of conversation, ignoring the irrepressible yawns which emanated from Cézaire and me.

In spite of my fatigue, I found the talk fascinating, for the Fathers were extremely well informed about the Watussi and their country. The big task, as they saw it, was education and education of a different nature from that needed among really primitive peoples. It would be a long time before the Watussi changed their views about their cattle, but such a change had to come. The first purpose of the land, in Watussi eyes, was to support the sacred cattle, even if it could not support human beings. If the cattle contributed something to the country's economy, that might be all right, but no one slaughtered these sacred animals. Even the first of the milk went to the calves to make certain they grew up strong and beautiful. Humans came next.

Once rinderpest had periodically reduced the cattle population, but under the Belgians and the White Fathers this plague had been almost eliminated. So now there were more cattle than ever. Cows were not only sacred, as in ancient times in the Egyptian cult of Apis, but they were the measure of wealth and social prestige.

Father de Bekker felt certain that the old tradition of Watussi migration from Egypt many centuries ago was true. In some time of terrible drought, a noble clan with great herds of fine cattle sought better pasture lands to the south, walking across deserts and through heavy bush country until they finally reached Ruanda. The nomadic Bahutu and the few Pygmies who inhabited the region were easily brought under Watussi control despite their greater numbers.

Like the Egyptians, the Watussi studied the entrails of chickens for omens of the future; they believed in the transmigration of souls and used animals as clan totems. One claimed the chameleon, another the toad, while the totem of the royal family was the crested crane. The Watussi held the monkey in great reverence, as the Egyptians had Anubis. According to legend—all legends were passed down by a special court group called "the makers of intelligence"—an early Watussi king, trapped by enemies in a cave, had been led to safety by a monkey. Another special group appointed by the king, called "the men of the cavern," had the duty of protecting and safeguarding monkeys. Still another clan had charge of an eternal fire, since fire had been given to an early Mutussi Prometheus by the gods.

After chapel and breakfast the next morning, Cézaire and I inspected the workshop of the White Sisters, who were overseeing the making of rugs—a fine Watussi craft in danger of disappearing, just as calico was threatening the superb cloth made by Watussi. Only the beautiful, conical baskets with their modernistic designs were still being made as much as ever. Nine years later, I was to see that even that art had waned somewhat.

Near the main mission house, we encountered four Bahutu carrying on their cushioned heads a *matshela*, or palanquin made of woven fibers in the shape of a long basket. When the Bantus set it down, a tall woman stepped from it, and I met Kangazi, one of the thirty wives of the deposed King Musinga, who had been exiled only a few miles away, in Kamembe. Although Watussi women are not nearly as tall as the men, I would guess that their average height is considerably above that of American women. Kangazi wore a traditional crescent headdress and plaited fiber rings from ankle to knee—an old custom that seems to be dying out. They certainly add nothing to the grace or attractiveness of the women.

It was rather unusual for me to meet a Mutussi woman in this way. They generally live in almost Moslem seclusion and in public are extremely shy, trying to efface themselves and saying nothing. Being a wife of a deposed king must have made some difference, for Kangazi was at ease, forthright and pleasant. She willingly posed for me and then agreed to accompany me the short distance to Nyanza, where Mwami Rudahigwa lived and held court.

In 1946, it was necessary for me to arrange my meeting with the king through the Belgian resident, and nowadays mere tourists do not gain an audience with Watussi royalty. In a way, he is a showpiece, but he is also much more than that. Back in 1937, however, there were not many visitors, and they were always welcomed warmly—which usually meant a visit with the king. He still lived in his domed *inzu* and, although surrounded by numerous princely attendants, he was accessible. On this occasion, when Kangazi and I arrived before his home—she traveling in style in her basket-litter and I walking by her side, King Rudahigwa came from his house and greeted me with a handshake. Over seven feet tall, dressed in robes that were resplendent but not more so than others of his court, he was imposing but set me at ease immediately. Not a handsome man, chiefly because of teeth that protrude slightly, he looked alert, intelligent, and every inch a leader.

We talked for a while in French—Rudahigwa's command of the language being perfect and mine quite halting—and then I presented him with a black silk umbrella and a small silk American flag. He seemed pleased, and fondled the flag gently, almost as a woman might a lovely handkerchief. I did not know if he was just being polite or if he really liked my gifts, for it is not an easy task to choose a present for a king, even an African king. People who are accustomed to giving shiny trinkets to Africans must not include the Watussi aristocrats in that classification. I

heard of a traveler who visited Nyanza shortly after Rudahigwa
ascended the throne. After an interview with the king, the
European produced some miserable dime-store jewelry, which
he distributed to the king and his royal entourage. Rudahigwa
thanked him as politely as he would if the baubles had been
priceless gems, but after the visitor left the Watussi, with expressions of contempt, tossed the trinkets to their Bahutu servants.

Mwami Rudahigwa showed me the great ceremonial drums,
most sacred possessions of the race, which are supposed to
accompany him wherever he goes. Drums are the heartbeats of
Africa—big drums, little drums, slit drums made from hollow
logs that boom high when struck at one end and boom low at
the other, drums that are beaten with sticks, drums that are
pounded, drums that are rubbed. They play for dances, play for
feasts, summon the men to council and to war, announce the
arrival of the chief, and send out long messages. In Ruanda, the
royal drums have names. Three of them—Ishakwe, Inyahura and
Inumvu—are beaten each morning to announce that the King
has awakened and all the Watussi must wake. They announce
his retirement, even though he has usually not gone to bed, and
nobody else goes to bed then. But it is tradition, and Rudahigwa
insists upon preserving the good traditions of his race.

The most sacred of all Watussi drums is the *Kalinga*, symbol of authority of the king. It is the equivalent of crown,
sceptre, and seal. When the Belgian authorities finally had to
rid themselves and the country of Musinga, they took away the
Kalinga and kept it safely guarded. Without the drum, Musinga
lacked all power, all prestige, all authority over the Watussi,
and he knew it. He gave up without a fight. In a short time,
when Rudahigwa was made king, the *Kalinga* was produced and
given to him. With this, he and his followers both knew that he
was truly the *mwami*.

At the end of my visit with King Rudahigwa, he invited me
to attend the great festival involving the presentation of the
sacred cattle, dancing, high-jumping, and other celebrations that

would take place in three days. Only two or three times yearly
are such ceremonies held, and I had luckily arrived in Ruanda
just in time.

During those few days I observed, talked, traveled, took
pictures. Among other short trips about the country, I went to
call upon the deposed king, Musinga, who lives in an unpre-
tentious *inzu*, comfortably but not lavishly provided for through
an allowance from his successor-son. Even taller than his son,
and much homelier, Musinga seemed to be a sour, embittered
man, but he greeted me warmly, then asked, "Have you any
medicine for my eyes?" Cataracts contributed largely, I decided,
to the unpleasant expression he always wore, and he looked
quite disappointed when I told him I had no medicine for his
condition. He tried to show off, then, by reciting a few fumbling
sentences in German, a language which no doubt recalled for
him his days of power and glory. Ruanda and Urundi had been
part of German East Africa until World War I, during which
Belgian forces from the Congo had helped defeat German
forces in Africa. Ruanda-Urundi had been given to Belgium
as a mandated territory under the League of Nations, continued
by the United Nations. I found remarkably few evidences of the
long German occupation of Ruanda and Urundi; all I can recall
right now, in fact, are those feeble and futile efforts of Musinga
to speak the foreign sounds associated with more than twenty of
his thirty-six years of kingship. By the time I left, I found myself feeling a little sorry for the lonely old dictator, who must
have sensed my thoughts, for he presented me with a particularly
fine example of Watussi basketry.

The royal ceremonies at Nyanza were even more spectacular
than I had anticipated. Mwami Rudahigwa, in the first place,
was more resplendent than ever, in magnificent white robe and a
beautiful headdress with dangling pearl strands and crest of
white monkey fur and feathers. Beside him were ranged about
seventy-five of the chief Watussi nobles. Among them I saw a
few men who stood out because of their normal height and I
learned that for unusual services in the past some Bahutu and

even Batwa families had been admitted to the Watussi aristocracy.

This line-up was a sort of reviewing stand at one side of a
huge field, awaiting the presentation of the long-horned cattle—
some of those belonging to the king himself, called Inyambo,
and others belonging to other Watussi, called Insanga. On the
sidelines were hundreds of Bahutu and Batwa tribesmen, some
to act their parts in the state ceremony, others to watch the
magnificent show. Even the trees not far from the field were
filled with clusters of Bahutu who had scrambled up for a good
view.

Before I started taking pictures, I saw that the king held in
his hand the small silk flag I had given him several days before.
Behind him stood a servant with the black umbrella.

The opening event of the spectacle was the high jump.
Two slender straight reeds were stuck in the ground and a thin
rod placed horizontally between them. On the ground in front
of the jumping standard was placed the top of a hard anthill, a
few inches high. Then a Watussi youth tucked his toga up
around his waist and raced about twenty steps—unbelievably
long strides—toward the standard. On the last stride his foot
reached the anthill, which served as a kind of hard springboard,
and he leaped upwards over the bar, using the technique that had
come into American sports only a couple of decades before. The
bar was first set, I guessed, at about five and a half feet, and all
the jumpers—there were five or six—cleared it by at least a foot.
It was elevated rapidly, and in sizable moves, until it rested at
more than eight feet. All jumpers sailed over the bar just as
easily as before.

I thought, as has every traveler witnessing the Watussi
high-jumping, that a team should go to the Olympic Games
some time. They would not be allowed to use the little mound
to leap from in international competition, but I imagine they
could get accustomed to its absence with a little training. And I
have no doubt they could break all records by several inches.

The next track and field event of the day was archery, in

which some Bahutu and Batwa took part as well as Watussi. I was not nearly so impressed, for I have friends at home who could have beaten these Africans in a sport that they should have excelled in. The bows of the Watussi were very large, but their accuracy in hitting the target was nothing special and not up to that of the Batwa Pygmies, with their tiny bows and arrows.

They must have sensed that they really were not superior in this field of sport, for before and during the archery there was exhortation on the part of the spectators, including the king, and prayerful self-stimulation on the part of the contestants. They petted their bows, stroked their arrows, talking soothingly to them as a gambler might to his dice before the throw. And after all this, few arrows hit the bull's-eye. Near the end of the archery contests, one of the White Fathers was invited to join in. He did, and hit the bull's-eye—to the cheers of all the assembled Watussi, Bahutu, and Batwa.

Finally came the most important ceremony of the afternoon, from the Watussi point of view—the presentation of the sacred cattle. The impressive creatures had gathered in a clearing not far from the exhibition field, and when I looked there I saw a forest of white horns. The cows were even on this occasion dignified and quiet, lowing gently occasionally but never making a spectacle of themselves. They reminded me of elderly aristocratic ladies or dowager queens, conscious of their importance and all the proprieties that must be observed on this state occasion. I suppose they are well behaved at all times, but they apparently sensed that they were part of something special.

Each cow had its own attendant, or groom, who led it before the king and his court, talking to it soothingly all the time, waving away flies that might annoy it. These grooms, as special favors for performing such an important task, are permitted to drink the cow's milk, but no one else may drink the milk of the king's cows, the *Inyambo*. The grooms had certainly done an exacting job in preparing the cows for this occasion. Their coats glistened in the sun, the result of careful rubbing with butter.

Their long curving horns looked like the finest ivory, due in part to the painstaking polishing with fine sand. Each cow's forehead was decorated with a head-dress of pearls and fine embroidery and the tips of horns were gay with colored tufts of fibre.

The cows were not uniform in color, some being red and white, some black and white, others red and light gray. They were all big animals, with surprisingly thin legs, straight backs, and long dewlaps, but one scarcely noticed features other than the startling horns. Some had a span of close to twelve feet, but in spite of their great size the cows carried them as if they were ornaments.

As each animal was presented, its groom cried out its qualities, gesticulating, jumping up and down, beating the ground with his staff. Soon all were jabbering at once in high, shrill voices, extolling the length of the horns, the progeny, the sires, the sleekness of the coat. The ruler and his assembled nobles discussed each animal thoughtfully and carefully. The vocabulary of the Watussi is rich in words of many subtle shadings, used only to describe cows.

The presentation of the cattle took a long time. I began to find it rather tiresome, and was eager to see the dancing which I knew would follow.

I've watched dancing in most of the countries I've visited, for dancing is often more truly revealing of a group's feelings and heritage than any other activity. The barrier of language does not exist when a "foreigner" looks at people dancing. Like music, art and mathematics, the dance is a universal language.

Actually, much dancing by primitives is disappointingly awkward, even tame. Many times have I looked forward to a dance when I heard the first rhythmic beats of drums and perhaps the piping of strange horns, only to witness a half-hearted shuffling of the feet, with a few steps forward, a few steps back. Half of the Indian tribes of South America danced this way, and even the head-hunting Jivaros were not exciting except in their

dramatic ceremony, the *tsantsa*, celebrating the capture and
shrinking of an enemy head. The Bororos of the Mato Grosso
were thrilling chiefly because of their magnificent head-dresses,
costumes, and body decorations. The Pygmies of the Ituri Forest had been electrifying in their pantomime dance re-enacting
the killing of the elephant; their general dances in the evening
were full of verve and abandon, plenty of joy and noise, but
they were not really graceful and carried no meaning beyond a
happy release of emotions.

But the Watussi—they are real dancers! Jivaros, Bororos,
Pygmies and all primitives would gasp with amazement and
admiration if they could watch the Watussi dance. And they
would bring down the house in Paris, London, New York, Co-
penhagen or Moscow. One secret is the tall elegance of all
Watussi, another the beautiful costuming which is designed to
enhance and accentuate the movements of the dancers. But the
primary reason for their superiority is that they are professional
dancers, trained from childhood to dance for the entertainment
of the king and his court. Such cultural achievements seem to
occur only in societies in which there is an aristocracy, a court
rich enough to pay for the special terpsichorean training of a
certain class of young men. The result is ballet—with all the
controlled grace of that highly developed art, plus the dynamic
fire of elementary savagery, of war, of the hunt. And all this on
an open-air stage of several acres, at an altitude of six thousand
feet, against a backdrop of far-ranging mountains and equatorial
sky.

At the outset, I was somewhat disappointed, for the
Indashyikuwa, or Insurpassable Ones, consisting solely of
Watussi dancers, did not open the dancing program. The first
were a group of Bahutu women, who filed slowly onto the field
to the accompaniment of drums, cymbals, some reed instruments with a nasal whine, and low mellow woodwinds made of
gaily decorated ox horns. Most of the musicians were Batwa
Pygmies, with some Bahutu beating drums so tall that Pygmies

could barely have reached them. Like the dancing, the music was somewhat more elaborate, with a greater variety of instruments, than that of most primitive groups.

The Bahutu women were dressed in calico sarongs which I felt sure were a recent addition to the festival, introduced no doubt by the White Fathers who had not, happily, been able to cover the beautiful bodies of the Watussi women who followed. The dances of both groups were little more than a rhythmic stepping and—so far as the Bahutu were concerned—bouncing. But the tall, slender yet rounded figures of the Watussi women were so lovely and every movement was so much the embodiment of dignified grace that watching them was a pleasure. Narrow bands of antelope hide hugged the girls' slender hips so low that I wondered how they stayed up; from them dangled a skimpy fringe of twisted strips of fur. A single strand of pearls around the neck completed the costume.

The women dancers were followed by some solos performed by Batwa Pygmies, the most striking of which was a pantomime of simplicity and dramatic power. A long strip of papyrus was placed on the ground to represent a snake, then onto the scene staggered a Batwa, clutching his short spear in one hand and bent over as if carrying a heavy burden. Suddenly he saw the snake and jumped back in fear and surprise. Putting down his load, he decided to kill the snake and approached it cautiously. As he was about to thrust with his spear he leaped backward, as if the snake had struck, and his stomach muscles twitched with fright. Again he moved forward, stabbed at the snake and missed, leaped back and circled around. Finally as the drums built to a climax, the Pygmy impaled the snake triumphantly and danced around it.

A group of Bahutu dancers led by a Mutussi were good, but their dance was erased from my mind by the breathtaking spectacle that followed. Fifty or more tall and lithe Watussi dancers rushed onto the field to the equivalent of a rolling fanfare from the orchestra and their own war whoops. The dancers were dressed in rich costumes—crossed bands over the chest of embroidery and pearls, leopard-skin bands about the waist from which dangled thin strands of fur, leather anklets with small bells attached, a collar of more beaded embroidery and a ring of white monkey fur, and a plumed head-dress like a lion's mane that tossed gracefully with each movement of the head.

As the dancers ranged themselves in rows, each man about ten feet from his neighbor on either side, the leader leapt into place before them. He was Butare, son of one of the highest Watussi princes and a minister at the king's court, one of the *Biru,* or council of elders. He was clad much like the others except that he wore a toga of flaming red cloth of very fine texture. When it swirled about his legs, it looked like the leaping flames of a fire. Butare's white teeth flashed in a happy smile as he led his dancers, and part of the beauty of the spectacle came from the joy that animated the performers.

I have no hesitancy in saying that, in his prime, Butare was the outstanding dancer of Africa. He made leaps of astounding length and grace, leaps in which he floated through the air in defiance of the law of gravity. Every muscle of his body contributed to each gesture, each movement; the toes, the fingers, the arch of the supple neck, the flashing eyes all spoke the same message. The skirt, the streaming head-dress, the long staff in his hand—each item became an extension of the dancer's body as he advanced to the charge, swerved and retreated, whirled and thrust again in an increasing frenzy of combat climaxed, of course, by victory over the enemy and an exultant pirouette of triumph.

While they rested briefly the dancers sang a song of praise of their king, then took their places for a dance of an entirely different quality and flavor—one that pantomimed the motions of the crested crane, symbol of the ruling family. Here there was much delicate, graceful stepping in which the long-legged cranes should have felt flattered by the actions of the more attractive long-legged Watussi, whose flowing head-dresses became for the moment the crests of the noble birds. In another dance they were the manes of pouncing lions. In the final dance,

called "the thundering legion" the dancers became an advancing army, proud, irresistible, sweeping all before it. Their feet
stamped the earth so hard that clouds of dust arose from the
field, and I felt the ground shake beneath me. They chanted as
they danced, and so did all the musicians and the Batwa and
Bahutu dancers. Throughout the entire series of dances, a
special group on the sidelines whose duty was to act as cheer-
leaders, had urged the dancers on to greater and greater efforts,
but for the final dance they screamed for the display of the last
ounce of energy by the terpsichorean chorus. And they gave it
everything, until I was limp and exhausted when the festival
suddenly ended. The dancers trouped off, panting but smiling
with pleasure, and the dust slowly settled back to earth under
the hot sun. I looked happily down at my camera, for in it lay
the first colored pictures ever taken of the Watussi dancers.

After such a spectacle, it is not surprising that in 1946,
when I was taking pictures for "Savage Splendor," Ruanda was
the first objective on my long itinerary. Actually, it was planned
for the second, for I had intended to drive from Stanleyville
down to the Kasai, where I would film the artistic Bakuba. But a
truck delayed in its journey up the river, difficulties with a
cameraman, and other troubles which I like to forget inter-
vened, and the Bakuba were postponed. Memory is a wonderful
thing; it can so easily—given a little time—wipe out two weeks of
worry, problems, frustration and no film, in order to concentrate
on a few days of pleasure and accomplishment.

The point was that I had to be in Ruanda by July twenty-
first, when the big ceremonies would be held. When my depar-
ture for the Kasai was delayed, I had to pass it up entirely in
order to make certain of filming the Watussi. So I flew one
thousand miles up the Congo River to Stanleyville, rented a
truck, and arrived in time. Mwami Rudahigwa was just getting
over a bout of malaria, but he greeted me with warmth and
recalled several incidents of my first visit. The Belgian resident
was most helpful, and I obtained good films of all the ceremonies. Actually, the first shots of the cattle and of the Watussi

dancers were somewhat disappointing, because we could not get up high enough to show the whole scene well. When I mentioned this to the territorial administrator after the first day of shooting, he consulted with Rudahigwa, had a platform built, and called the dancers and cattle-tenders to repeat their performances, which they did gladly and with even more spirit, I thought, than on the first day.

I was most pleased, during my 1946 trip, about my "success" with Watussi women. These pleasant creatures are rarely seen by outsiders. They are reserved, aloof and never filmed. Except for my chance meeting with Kangazi and my pictures of women dancers, I had enjoyed nothing but a formal introduction to any Watussi lady. Yet I knew that they occupied very important positions in the world of Ruanda. Watussi women are not the beasts of burden and the drudges of all work that women of other African tribes are. They are never forced to marry against their will, for example, and they have the right of divorce. Husbands treat their wives as companions, as equals, as persons of intelligence to be consulted on all affairs pertaining to the family. They weave beautiful basketware, some of it so fine that baskets may be used to contain liquids. They weave lovely cloth and oversee the management of the home and the bringing up of the children. But they do no menial tasks.

The coming of civilization has produced a strange effect on this relationship between Watussi men and women. Usually one of the most praiseworthy efforts of missionaries and European colonial administrators in Africa is to attempt to improve the lot of women, who in most tribes are chattels, just so much property. But in Ruanda, where women already occupied a favored position, just the reverse is happening. Many Watussi young men are being educated in fine schools, trained to become leaders of their communities. They learn French, many skills, and the sort of thing that one gets in a liberal arts college. But their daughters and their wives have no Belgian schools. They cannot understand or speak when French is spoken in their homes, as it is increasingly. They have less in common with

their husbands than before the Belgians came. The Watussi
men do not like it, and they are beginning to say so. The
Belgians have in general been so alert to situations like this that
I have no doubt they will soon find ways to bring the Watussi
women along the road to civilization in company with their
husbands.

It was the Belgian administrator in Ruanda, who, after
consulting with Rudahigwa, made it possible for me to visit
with several Watussi ladies and to take motion pictures of
them. Even with his help and Rudahigwa's permission, it was
not an easy task for me to gain their cooperation. I could not
pay them or give them gifts as an incentive. I had to ask them to
inconvenience themselves and go through something no Watussi
women ever had, merely to be kind, to help me show the outside world what Watussi women are and what they do. At first
they agreed, but with reluctance. As the filming of scenes over a
period of several days continued, however, they became more
and more friendly, though always reserved. In the end, I was
able to get pictures of them being carried in their palanquins by
their Bahutu servants, as if on a trip to visit friends; then the
meeting with friends and gathering together in the compound
of one of their houses. I took pictures of several of them weaving
baskets, another of them playing games, another of servants
bringing them food. They understood through all this that I
wanted them to re-create normal scenes, and they acted quite
natural. When I asked them to pose having a talk with me,
they agreed but pointed out that it was *not* a normal scene.

My admiration for them grew the more I saw them, worked
with them, and talked to them. Rarely have I seen such poise,
natural and without affectation.

When I was leaving and trying ineffectually to express my
gratitude to the ladies, they thanked me instead, and one of
them presented me with a gift—a low, hand-carved stool which
I had admired. It was really a touching gesture. I had come to
Africa in search of the primitive and here had encountered
such good manners and generosity as are rarely surpassed.

The irony of it is that when the time came to cut the thousands of feet of movie film down for "Savage Splendor," almost all of my rare pictures of the Watussi ladies were omitted. Not enough action, Hollywood said, and Hollywood must have exciting action. But I still retain my satisfaction in the memory of the rewarding hours spent with my charming Watussi princesses.

VIII

Fishermen, Artists, and Femmes à Plateau

THERE is no place like Africa for a study of the human race in all its diversity of shape, color, size and features and in the infinite variety of dress, decoration, architecture, art, religion, morals and manners. Africa was the home of perhaps the greatest of ancient civilizations, and it is still the home of men of the Old Stone Age. It contains more different racial groups and languages than any other continent—perhaps more than all other continents combined. If you were to spend just one week with each distinct tribe in Africa, you would be visiting for more than eight years. Obviously, all generalizations about Africans are bound to contain more error than truth. No one person has even seen more than a small fraction of the hundreds of different kinds of tribesmen.

We Americans think of our country as containing many different racial stocks, but we haven't a tenth of Africa's human ingredients. Some of these have apparently remained fairly pure, but most have intermingled in an uncountable number of blends. Except for the desert areas, the continent presents few barriers to human movement; the races of Africa have been moving back and forth for centuries, conquering, being conquered, intermarrying or running away. There were Bushmen, Pygmies, West African Negroes, Bantu, Sudanese and Nilotic Negroes, Hamites, Semites and the perhaps-White Berbers of the north. There are countless mixtures of all these, such as the Hottentots who are probably a blend of Bushman, Negro, and Hamite; the

Masai who are Hamite and Negro; the Batwa who are Pygmy and Bantu; Ethiopians who are Hamite and Semite, with some Negro; the Tibbu who are Berber and Negro; the Luo who are Nilotic and Bantu. The Azande and the Mangbetu are usually called Sudanese, but they probably intermingled with the Fula who were in all likelihood a mixture of Berber and Negro. The aristocratic Watussi are pure Hamite surrounded by Bantu and Pygmy and blends of those two.

As if a continent with four or five hundred tribes was not varied enough, Africa has welcomed Arabs, Persians, Turks, Indonesians, Indians, Chinese, plus French, English, Dutch, Spanish, Italian, German, Belgian, and Danish traders, missionaries, conquerors and settlers, some of whom added their bloodstreams to the racial rivers of Africa.

Languages? There are over three hundred—not counting dialects. A few trade languages have in the past century spread over large areas, although there are variations in dialects of these tongues. On the other hand, one can find small areas with half a dozen villages within fifty square miles where four or five different basic languages are spoken.

Most of Africa has no recorded history, in contrast to one part of it—Egypt—which has just about the longest history possessed by the human race. There was ancient Carthage, too, and the later Roman encirclement of the Mediterranean, followed in the Middle Ages by a thriving Arab civilization which even invaded Europe. But all of these were along the northernmost edge of the continent and may not even be considered as characteristically African.

From central and southern Africa we have no records. The British found a strong and well-organized kingdom in Uganda when they first went there, but it was not an advanced civilization by our standards. Other tribes, such as the Zulu and the Basuto, organized themselves into strong confederations, chiefly to oppose white men's encroachments. Almost every tribe has its legends which may well be founded in history, but it is difficult to tell how far back they go. The Pygmies of the Ituri Forest, for instance, say that their people originally came "from the North," but when and how far north no one has the faintest idea. Ethnologists and anthropologists can figure out many answers as to which group is related to which and who intermarried with whom; they can even make pretty good guesses as to the movements of some groups. And that is probably all the history we shall ever have for most of Africa and its peoples.

In some ways, the lack of known history makes visiting African tribes more interesting. You have no preconceptions such as you might get from reading a history of a people before seeing them. Most of us, however, have other preconceptions so firmly rooted that we cannot eradicate them easily. We have a mental picture of a "typical African native"—with dark skin, kinky hair, flat broad nose, big mouth, prognathous jaw, few clothes, many superstitions, a dislike of work or responsibility, a wonderful sense of rhythm, a childlike gaiety. A few Africans are like that, some are totally unlike that, others have some of these traits. If you can manage to wipe the preconceptions from your mind, you will find the tribes of Africa fascinating, continually surprising, always different from each other and from everything else you've known.

Even if you confine your visiting to a small area, you will find amazing variety. Although I have traveled widely in North Africa and South Africa, I have concentrated on the central belt made up chiefly of the Belgian Congo, Ruanda-Urundi, Uganda, Kenya and Tanganyika. Even here I found every kind of terrain and climate and almost every kind of human being. There are hundreds of different tribes drawn from four basic human stocks and scores of combinations of these stocks. Let's restrict the territory even more and look only at the Belgian Congo, where there are Bantu, Nilotic and Sudanese Negroes, plus Hamites, Semites, and Pygmies—with blends. There are Baluba, Bakuba, Balunda, Babali, Bambole, Babira, Bahavu, Bambuba, Bakele, Bakusu, Basonge, and a dozen more beginning with *Ba*, which is a common prefix meaning "people." There are the hot-tempered Walendu, who are tall and long-legged like most Nilotics but not as tall as the Hamitic Watussi. Other Nilotics are the Alur, the Logo, the Lugware and the Kakwa. Then there are the Sudanese, among whom the Azande and the Mangbetu are the best-known tribes—and these are quite different from each other in language and costume and culture.

There are Walese, Wanande, Warega, Wazimba, Wasongola, Walengola, Wanianda, Wagenia and others whose tribal names begin with a second prefix, *Wa*, meaning "people" or "tribe." This great profusion of names is confusing enough for the outsider wondering where to go and whom to visit, and at first the confusion is doubled by the nature of the languages, which makes singulars out of plurals by changing prefixes. A man of the Babira tribe is a Mubira, and one of the Bambuti Pygmies is a Mambuti. A Walendu woman is a Mulendu, just as a Watussi princess is a Mutussi.

For additional confusion there are the Bangwana, or Arabized natives found in the Eastern Congo. It is a little startling to come upon a community of dark-skinned men—the women are rarely seen—who are indistinguishable physically from most Bantu tribes but who wear flowing white robes and fezzes. They are devout Moslems with their own schools for teaching their children the Koran—a peaceful people who were once the scourge of this whole region. Their houses are easily recognized, for they are whitewashed plaster, suggesting something from Morocco or other thoroughly Arab countries.

How does one happen to find Moslem Bantus in such a place? Well, many centuries ago, Arabs from Muscat and Oman, in the southeastern corner of the Arabian peninsula, traveled to the island of Zanzibar, off the eastern coast of Africa. These Arabs began to trade on the mainland, penetrating deeper and deeper in search of ivory and other valuables. By force of arms they made some of the Africans carry the ivory back to the coast, where they sold the black men along with the white ivory. It did not take the Arabs long to discover that they had found a human gold mine more valuable than any normal trade goods. The slave trade began in earnest.

By the 1840s, Arab slave traders had reached Lake Tanganyika in the course of their bloody raids in search of slaves. Forty years later they controlled most of the eastern half of the Congo, but their armies consisted primarily of natives led by Arabs. Bantu warriors by the thousands were converted to Islam, supplied with arms, and enlisted in the service of the Arab slave-traders.

Many Arabs intermarried with Bantu women, so among the Arabized natives were numerous blends of Arab and Bantu—and these were natural leaders.

The Arabized armies attacked Falls Station, now Stanleyville, in 1886, and the young new Free State of the Congo, founded by King Leopold of Belgium, decided that it had to wipe out Arab control and influence—and also the institution of slavery—or be wiped out in time. A bloody and costly eight-year campaign did the job, and Belgian authorities ruled unchallenged. But here and there in the eastern Congo were groups of Arabized Africans, far from their original homes. Most of them settled down, but they retained their religion, their Arab dress and customs and much of the Arab cleverness in trade and barter. Stanleyville is the largest settlement of *Arabisés*, although there are many others. They have their own Sultan, who is recognized by the Belgian authorities as other native chiefs are.

The *Arabisés* are scarcely to be considered a primitive tribe, or group, since they lived for some time under the "civilizing" influence of slave-trading warriors, but they are interesting as evidence of the native African's ability to adopt new dress, customs, skills, and religion. And there are few tribes that are not changing today—and changing fast. The big push into Africa— a last gigantic frontier for modern civilization—which had for several decades touched the edges and easiest lines of interior communication, picked up speed in the twenties, gained momentum in the thirties. The Second World War delayed the invasion of calico and khaki—although in a few spots it speeded things up. The Congo moved ahead in the mining areas because the Allies needed certain materials badly. And in the Northeastern Congo a staggeringly difficult transportation operation was carried out. The little town of Paulis was a main terminal with more than three thousand trucks rolling out of it during the crucial months of the North African campaign. It had for some time been a center for Vicicongo—the big company handling most of the trucking throughout the Congo. There was a repair shop in Paulis, and a hotel—The Mangbetu—maintained by Vicicongo. But before the war, only a few trucks a day went in or out of Paulis.

The war brought to Paulis road-builders, mechanics, technicians, drivers, and three thousand trucks—plus tons of essential war materials which the trucks carried northeastward through the Belgian Congo, the Sudan and Egypt to the armies trying to drive back Rommel. The Axis forces had made the Mediterranean a precarious route at best, so it was essential to find alternate supply lines. Even the long, long one by ship to the mouth of the Congo, by rail and steamer up to Stanleyville, and by truck to Paulis and on to Egypt was worth trying. In 1946 I found the truck roads to and out of Paulis quite good, with some pontoon bridges replacing the native ferries. On the other hand, the roads around Beni and Irumu, being off the lines of military communication, were far worse in 1946 than they had been in 1937. They had been neglected—as almost everything was neglected—for the war effort. But with the fighting ended, the roads were soon repaired, new roads built, and the Belgian Congo raced ahead with the civilizing and mechanizing process at an incredible pace. The Congo is, of course, still strange, colorful and, in many areas, primitive and wild, but it is significant, I think, that on my last trip the only tribe I visited in the Congo was the Pygmies of the Ituri Forest.

Even on my first two trips, or between them, I saw the first evidences of change. The younger mothers among the Mangbetu no longer bound their babies' heads, and the teen-age Babira

girls wore no lip disks—at least in those villages in closest and
most regular contact with missionaries, doctors, officials and
travelers.

I visited some of the Babira tribe, near Bunia in the eastern Congo, in 1937 and again in 1946 to take pictures for "Savage Splendor." Most of us think of the Ubangi when we think of
plate-lipped women, but the practice has been found among
other tribes. The Babira "femmes à plateau" were friendly and
delighted to have their pictures taken, proudly displaying their
upper lips with three and four-inch disks inserted in them. I
learned how the lips are made to accommodate the thin wooden
saucers, but by 1946 there were no little girls wearing the small
sticks which are first inserted in holes pierced in the lips, as
many other people pierce their ear lobes. Sticks of larger and
larger diameter are fitted into the lip hole, stretching the skin.
By the time a girl approached puberty the hole was large enough
to accommodate a wooden disk about two inches across. I saw
only one or two of this size, on my second trip, and by now I
feel sure that only the old women will be found with plate
lips.

One older woman had a rather small disk and a strange
looking bump on the skin around it. The skin had been stretched
so far and had become so thin and lifeless that it finally broke.
She tied the two loose ends together, which made her take a
smaller disk, of course. I touched the lip of one woman with a
particularly large disk and found it as cold as if it were dead.
Then I asked how the disk was held in place so that it stood out
instead of hanging down in front of the mouth. The lady replied
by removing the disk—and I almost wished I was not so curious.
The long loop of outer lip hung down to her chin, and through
the big hole made by the disk I saw that the top four teeth had
been pulled out. The disk was held in place by the lip's pressing
it firmly against the recess created between the two canine teeth.
It was as ugly a sight as one might find on a human face, and I
felt that the theory as to the origin of this practice must be true.

The story is that back in the days of the Arab slave-raiding, the men of the Babira tribe decided to make their women so unattractive that no slaver would want to steal them. The duck-billed lip was the solution, and by the time the slave raids had ended the custom was so firmly established—and custom is everything to primitives—that it was continued. By that time, perhaps the Babira men thought *undusuma*, or duck-billed women, were the only attractive females in the world.

The trouble with this widely held theory is that such mutilations as stretching the lips usually go back in time far beyond the period of Arab slave raids. Furthermore, many African tribes perform some kind of physical mutilation not essentially different from this one, which just happens to strike us as particularly ugly. On my third trip, I found a tribe in Tanganyika in which the men enlarged the lobes of their ears in this same way, eventually making the opening far larger that that in a Babira woman's lip. Only a few miles from the Babira village I saw Walese women with both lips pierced, and also the septum of the nose. They didn't bother to enlarge the openings to take big disks but inserted sizable ornaments of iron or other metal. I am inclined to think that, human vanity being what it is, some Babira woman in the dim past decided that if a little stick in the lip was a fine thing, a big stick would be even finer. Her neighbor decided to go her one better and stretched her lip even further, so it took a thicker stick, and so on until four-inch disks became the one item without which no self-respecting Babira woman would be seen.

Few visitors notice the men of the Babira tribe, so busy are they looking at plate lips. There is nothing physically distinctive about the men, but I talked to some of them after taking pictures of a group and learned that some of the old men had fought Stanley when he first explored the Congo. Later they were won over by him and served as his bearers.

I visited dozens of tribes, of course, too briefly to say anything about them except what I happened to see. One of these was the Banyali, near the Semliki River north of Lake Edward. In one village I happened to see two albino children—a girl of fourteen and her younger brother—and I was reminded at once of the numerous albinos I had seen and photographed among the San Blas Indians off the coast of Panama. Inbreeding was supposed to have caused the white skin, almost white blond hair, and pinkish eyes among the Indians, and I assumed that the same reason held here among the dark-skinned Bantu Negroes. I located the parents and talked to them, learning that they had had four albino children in succession, then a normal dark-skinned child. Two of the albinos had died. While I was talking about this strange phenomenon—extremely rare in Africa, so far as my observation is concerned—I saw a young albino man walk into the village, to be welcomed in friendly fashion by everyone. He came from a neighboring Banyali village, and was courting the fourteen-year-old girl I had first seen. As with the San Blas Indians, most albinos can find happiness only with other albinos. They have difficult problems, sensitivity to sunlight and, above all, the stigma of being "different."

Being different from the people of another tribe is, of course, all right and serves usually to give anyone a feeling of superiority. What we do is right and good and has been done for hundreds of years; what other people do is different and therefore bad or at least not as good; therefore we are better than they are. It is a bit of unconscious rationalization that seems to work among moderns as well as primitives.

We envoys from civilization look at all the different tribes and decide that one is better than another, but we are judging by our standards and our judgments have no validity for anyone but ourselves. I liked some tribes far more than others, found some more interesting than others, and by my standards thought some more intelligent and cultured than others. But I would not expect many Africans to agree with me.

I like the Wagenia, for example, because the men have just about the most magnificent physiques I have ever seen, because they display such skill, courage and joy in their unique method of fishing, and because I obtained some good shots for "Savage Splendor" among them.

The Wagenia village I visited is just outside Stanleyville, on the shore near the cataracts of the Congo. It was startling to find a primitive tribe living in its age-old fashion so near a thriving, modern city. But the Wagenia are proud people, fond of fish, fishing, swimming, canoeing, and wearing few clothes. They too fought Stanley, the raiding Arabs, and almost anyone who sought to interfere with their way of life. They just ignore Christian missionaries. The Belgian authorities, when they took over the Congo, were smart enough not to try to change them. This technique has finally succeeded where outright opposition could not, for the Wagenias are finally changing. When I took pictures in 1946, only a few young men in the village wore some articles of European clothing. Nowadays a good proportion of the men in the village wear pants and/or shirt, taking them off for picture-taking—and for a fee.

On my 1946 visit, I made arrangements for accompanying the men in their daily visit to the fish traps at the cataract. Incidentally, the fish the Wagenia catch make delicious eating. The chief kind is the *capitaine*, or Kisangala, which is really a form of the Nile perch. They grow quite large, the record being about five hundred eighty pounds in weight. Catfish are also commonly snagged in the Wagenia traps, and these may run five feet long and weigh as much as two hundred pounds.

On the morning I appeared, about one hundred fifty men and sixty boys showed up for my movies—actually more than I could handle. But we all set out for the long, high-sided dugout canoes in high spirits. From the shore I could see the white foam at the cataract upstream. The Congo narrows somewhat at this point, but it is still a mighty, broad river with a tremendous quantity of water roaring over the ten-foot drop formed by a shelf of rocks and stony islands. The network of poles could be seen, too, and I wondered how the Wagenia fishermen ever managed to fix them in position in the midst of that torrent.

During the dry season, I was told, the river drops considerably and the water ambles mildly among the rocks of the ledge. The fishermen go out and repair broken poles, fix new ones deep in the river bed and wedge them between the rocks. Smaller poles brace the main supports and lianas tie the whole thing together in a strongly anchored set of fixtures to hold the traps. The traps themselves vary in size; some are ten or twelve feet in diameter at the open end; they taper down like a cone, where the fish are trapped. Made of saplings and lianas, they are tough and resilient. They are placed just below the surface of the water and are held in place by lianas tied to the poles. When the river rises and the water pours over the rocky cataract, it races with great force through the lattice-like traps. Fish are carried into the traps by the swift current and are held pressed against the small closed end.

The network of poles and traps extends from each bank of the river about two hundred yards toward the center, leaving an open stretch in the center of about a hundred yards. The Wagenias approach from below, paddling against the current to reach the traps, from twelve to eighteen men in each dugout. I climbed into a dugout, sitting on the thin gunwale near the stern, with one sturdy Wagenia specially delegated to hold onto me and keep me from falling overboard. I needed holding, too, for I held my camera in both hands, wondering if I could possibly get steady pictures in such a position in such a craft.

As we pushed away from the shore, it was easy. The current was strong but smooth, and the men paddled with perfect rhythm that shot the dugout ahead steadily. I got one fine shot with the camera pointed straight ahead toward the bow, and the film, as seen in "Savage Splendor," shows the glistening dark-skinned backs of two rows of paddlers, their muscles growing taut and relaxing in regular tempo as the canoe moves toward the cataract.

A quarter of a mile below the ledge of rocks the water was more turbulent, rushing here, swirling in a small eddy there, catching the dugout a sideswipe a few yards farther along. My protector wrapped both arms tightly about my waist and held on, but I felt as if we both might get tossed out at any moment. I was in far greater danger, I'm sure, as we came within a few hundred feet of the cataract but by that time I was so excited by the roar of the waters, the boiling foam of the falls, and the increasing efforts of the paddlers that I forgot to be frightened. It seemed that we scarcely moved ahead, despite the grunting lunges of eighteen strong men against the paddles. But we crept up to the traps until the first paddler grabbed a pole, looped a tough liana around it to hold the dugout, and yelled back to the others to relax. They did this for about half a minute, then piled out into the cataract to search the traps for fish. They held on to poles, lianas, the traps themselves, of course, but the rushing waters tugged at them with fury. One man within ten feet of me slipped, and his head disappeared. I caught a glimpse of his body hurtling past me and cried out. But he grabbed the side of the next dugout, pulled himself up to the traps again and went back to work.

I saw two or three others go under in the course of my half hour at the falls, but all saved themselves and kept on working. Never have I seen men swim so well or handle themselves in water so expertly against such great odds. Occasionally, I hear, a fisherman loses his grip and can't find another handhold. He goes tearing down the river about forty miles an hour, darting around boulders and rocky islands. He doubles himself in a ball for the worst waterfalls, then straightens out and finally swims to shore a couple of miles below. Almost never does a Wagenia fisherman lose his life in the river.

The man at the bow of the dugout, my holder, and I were the only ones left in our craft, which swung this way and that with the water. I tried to take pictures of the men in the water pulling up the big traps and extracting the fish, which they tossed into the dugouts, but only a few feet of my shots here were steady enough to show anything clearly. On top of that difficulty, I realized that, at the stern of the dugout, I was a little too far below the main traps to get the best shots. I saw a small rock, about four feet across, near the bow of the canoe. It was a foot or so above the water most of the time, and although wet with spray seemed never to be completely submerged.

Shouting above the roar and gesturing as well as I could, I finally made the men understand that I wanted to get out on the rock. They agreed, helped me to the bow of the dugout and over the side onto the rock. The spray stung my face, the water sloshed over my feet and threatened to trip me up, but I crouched and felt reasonably safe, especially after one of the men followed and held onto me. It was a perfect spot for shooting pictures of the Wagenia fishermen pulling up the huge traps, taking out three- and four-foot *capitaines,* fighting all the time against the torrents of water.

After shooting for a while I looked toward the shore. I had stationed my cameraman at a good spot there and told him to take whatever he could with his telephoto lens. I was pleased to see that my rock was in line with his position, and I felt sure that he must have taken some footage of me in the dugout, then clambering onto the tiny rock in the middle of the cataract. The telephoto lens would have shown me clearly enough. I could just visualize the finished sequence in the picture—showing me starting out with the fishermen from their village, then my shots of the paddlers in the canoe and our approach to the cataract. Then the scene would shift to the shots taken by my cameraman, showing the canoes from a distance, their nearing the poles and traps, and finally my climbing out on the rock to take pictures. Cut next to my shots from the rock. It would be wonderful, and I already felt fully repaid for the risk.

You can imagine, perhaps, how I felt when I returned to the Wagenia village an hour later, wet and completely exhausted, only to have my cameraman say that he had not bothered to shoot me getting on the rock. He had not thought it would be interesting.

He got some other excellent shots of the dugouts going up the river, of me photographing from the dugout while one Wagenia husky held onto me. Whenever I have looked at "Savage

Splendor" I realize that one of the most dramatic shots of the Wagenia sequence is missing. But then so are dozens of other shots of even greater impact from other sequences. It seems to be an inevitable part of the business of making this kind of movie. There are no retakes, especially of the most dangerous and exciting events. You can't get a wild leopard, for instance, to make that ferocious charge just once more. For one thing, if it was a really ferocious charge, he is now dead. Nor do you ask a big herd of giraffes to come back and stampede once more, across the same plain where the light is just right.

Picture-making is less difficult among the tribes whose chief occupations are not quite so active or hazardous—especially when they live in areas with good light a few hours a day. African groups famous for their art can be classed in the easy-picture category, and the outstanding among these are the Mangbetu, of Sudanese origin, and the Bakuba, a Bantu tribe living in the Kasai region of south central Congo Belge.

Negro art, like Negro music, has wielded great influence in America and in Europe. Decades ago the continent was rather thoroughly scoured for portable art objects, but the best can seldom be carried off. Houses, council halls and furniture—used and useful articles—generally show a group's artistic soul more truly than *objets d'art*, and there are still plenty in Africa. One striking sign of the times, however, is the projected establishment—perhaps it has come about by this time—of a museum by the Bakuba, with the encouragement of the Belgian authorities. The ruler of that tribe has a most valuable collection which traders have not picked up, and it is a good idea that they will be preserved in the first thoroughly "native" museum in Africa, or at least Central Africa.

The architecture and metalwork of the Mangbetu are beautiful but I was more attracted by their women. Just why they are so attractive is difficult to determine, but they undoubtedly have more sex appeal—without being obviously erotic—than any women of primitive tribes I've seen. Perhaps they keep their figures longer. At any rate, the proportion of young women with slim hips, firm breasts, and lithe bodies is greater among the Mangbetu than among other tribes, where only women between about fourteen and twenty-three look attractive by our standards. Perhaps part of the appeal comes from the *nekbwe*, an oversize fan or undersize chair-seat worn like a bustle on the buttocks. When Mangbetu women dance—actually a rather sedate and quiet dance except for soloists—the *nekbwe* twitches and shifts slightly with every movement, with a most alluring effect. This is enhanced by the fact that the *nekbwe* itself is usually very pretty, being made of woven fibres somewhat like raffia in geometric or other designs in various colors.

But it cannot be the *nekbwe* alone or its movements that make Mangbetu women so attractive, for I saw many of them without this ornament and they were very appealing, too. They have a great deal of dignity, as do the women of the Watussi aristocracy, but there is warmth beneath it—and not buried too deeply. The Watussi women are gracious, dignified, friendly and far, far away. The Mangbetu women are gracious, dignified, friendly, and—one feels—they might also be very close. The Watussi arouse admiration; the Mangbetu arouse more fundamental emotions.

Don't misunderstand me. The Mangbetu women are not lecherous, promiscuous or preoccupied with matters of a sexual nature. They show no particular interest—as do some native women—in male visitors. Most of them would certainly resent any untoward suggestion or action from such visitors. They do not invite; they stimulate. Certainly their elongated heads are not particularly attractive by our standards, although when these heads are crowned by the elaborate and unusual hairdos of Mangbetu women they are quite stunning.

Perhaps Mangbetu men find the women of their tribe as attractive as I did, for polygamy is practiced by those who can possibly afford it. The tribal chiefs have anywhere from thirty to four hundred wives, and other important men enjoy a sizable assortment. But the plebeians usually have only one.

Although the Mangbetu seem to us artistic, cultured, and

interesting to the degree that they are now becoming first-rate tourist attractions, they once enjoyed a most unsavory reputation for cannibalism. There has been considerable loose talk by hit-and-run travelers about cannibalism in Africa and there undoubtedly was a good deal of it among many tribes. Such customs are hard to kill. In the case of the Mangbetu, there was definitely much more than talk and reputation—there was proven fact. The distinguished German ethnologist, G. A. Schweinfurth, who revealed so many truths about equatorial Africa, lived with and studied the Mangbetu during the 1870s and 1880s, when that tribe was still living as it had lived for centuries, without the slightest influence of European civilization. The scientist, wanting to take back to Europe bones and skulls for his studies, offered the tribesmen copper—which they valued highly—for human bones left over from their feasts. In a very short time he had accumulated a great pile, although he was disappointed to find that most of the skulls had been shattered so that the Mangbetu gourmands could get at the brains —a great delicacy. Still, he came home with forty excellent skulls out of about two hundred he collected.

Another German who knew Africa in the early days, the fabulous leader who took an Arabic name, Emin Pasha, reported that the Mangbetu delighted in meals of human flesh. He could not find a grave in their country, he said. The humans served up at banquets were, of course, captives from surrounding tribes. People were thus not a regular part of the diet but a special treat enjoyed on rare occasions.

In an effort to explain why some tribes are cannibalistic, others vegetarian, and so on, some authorities have claimed that the Mangbetu ate human flesh because they raised no cattle. The Zulu and the Masai, they pointed out, never indulged in cannibalism—and they were cattle-growers. On the other hand, the Mangbetu have always raised poultry, so any possible craving for meat was satisfied.

No doubt all eating of human flesh among the Mangbetu has ceased by this time, but on my first trip I received some vague and confusing answers to my many questions about it. One missionary, who knew the country and people very well, told me, with a not-to-be-taken-too-seriously look in his eye, of the Mangbetu wife whose husband died. Instead of burying him, she made a stew of him and invited all her friends to the feast. Turning to a guest, she said, "You know, this is the first time I've really appreciated my husband."

From others I heard more serious answers to my questions about cannibalism, but all inconclusive. One honest explorer told me that, tiring of roundabout investigations, he asked an old Mangbetu, "Do you eat human meat?" The ancient one was silently thoughtful for a moment and then, looking down his nose, said, "It is very hard to stop old habits."

The point is, of course, that the chance to eat human beings rarely if ever presents itself any more. For decades there have been no tribal wars, no raids, and no captives. But when Schweinfurth first discovered the Mangbetu, their king, Munza, treated himself almost daily to a meal of a tender child. Along with this habit has disappeared also the Mangbetu greeting which Schweinfurth reported. They held out their right hands, said *"Gasiggy,"* and cracked the joints of their middle fingers. Being something of a collector of the multitude of ways which the human race has found to say hello, I looked hopefully but in vain for this novel method.

On my first two trips, however, I found plenty of examples of the characteristic by which the Mangbetu are best known— long heads. I was even permitted to photograph a mother binding her baby's head with long strands of raffia to give it this shape. During the first years of life, when a child's skull is still pliable, the raffia bindings are worn almost all the time, forcing the skull to grow up and back into a not unattractive extended oval. Doctors say that this alteration of nature's intentions has no bad effect on the brain or intelligence, but it does give the eyes an oriental slant and make them pop slightly. Mangbetu women accentuate the length of their heads by building out even further elaborate hair-dos, with their own and false black hair arranged in a kind of halo or crown fixed with small ivory or silver pins. It is the most dramatic coiffure I've ever seen, and takes at least three days to prepare.

For some reason, despite the fact that medical men say the head-binding is harmless, the Belgian authorities have been discouraging, but not prohibiting, the practice. A friend who has visited the Mangbetu recently informs me that many children are growing up with normally shaped heads. I approve heartily of the ending of intertribal wars, of cannibalism, and certain other primitive habits, but I wish the representatives of western civilization would not interfere with colorful and harmless customs of the different tribes. We'll eventually cast all the natives of Africa into one mold, and a great deal of beauty will be lost to the world.

The Mangbetu are fine artists, musicians and dancers. The house of Chief Ekibondo, in the village not far from Paulis, has walls of plaster, and even the poles supporting the roof have been covered with plaster to make them into square pillars, upon which have been painted in black and red various designs suggested by animals—crocodiles, snakes and fish. Geometric patterns, complicated and yet not cluttered, cover the plaster walls. Even the smaller houses were attractive, round with conical thatched roofs, their plaster walls decorated almost as beautifully as the chief's.

Ekibondo himself was pleasant, cooperative, and almost too eager to see that his musicians performed, his dancers danced and every native acted as he should for the movies. In 1937, I was pleased by this treatment but by 1946 the eagerness to help had gone so far that everything seemed a little staged. The chief was dressed in European trousers; he wore a wrist watch. He was happy to change into his native and regal attire, with woven fibre cap decorated with brilliant feathers, and the voluminous bloomer-like loin cloth made of pounded bark. He gathered his court around him, including several of his seventy wives, brought in the orchestra and the dancers. Altogether he put on a very good show and I obtained some excellent shots.

Another Mangbetu chief, Tongolo, even lived in a new brick house and sat in a Morris chair of which he was particularly proud, while I talked to him sitting on a beautifully carved stool made from one big piece of wood by the native woodworkers, who are almost as expert as the Mangbetu metal workers and ivory carvers. Tongolo had a good orchestra, and his dancers were accomplished, particularly his daughter, the most attractive of all the attractive Mangbetu women I saw.

A third village I visited possessed a dull, fat potentate who offered neither spontaneity nor much cooperation, so I stayed there a very brief spell. Finally I drove an extra two and a half hours to the little village of Gata, far enough from the centers of civilization to have remained more or less unspoiled. Here I saw dancing and heard music I'll never forget.

The Mangbetu are accomplished choral singers—a rare talent among primitive tribes. Their orchestras boast far more instruments than most African tribes—drums of many shapes, including some that are triangular, others square, and all covered with antelope skin. There are even a few stringed instruments, crude violins, I suppose they might be considered. Horns and trumpets of elephant tusks, some as long as five feet, were decorated with leopard skins and parrot feathers; the biggest horn gave out a throaty blast that sounded like some stalking wild animal of the forest. The rhythm section included some wooden clappers, rattles made of closely woven fibres with pebbles inside, and a long stick with a cluster of bells on one end.

The music produced by this assembly of instruments was loud, exciting, feverish and infectious. Certainly the Mangbetu dancers grew more and more aroused, more and more spirited, as the music went on. Men and women both danced, but not together. First the men formed a circle with the women inside, shuffling at first in a subtly erotic movement which made their *nekbwe* bustles go through strange gyrations. Then the women opened a small circle into which leaped two of their number, who gave special performances, leaping, twisting, jerking, kicking.

Suddenly the soloists retired into the shuffling, hand-clapping circle. The women then moved back to allow the men to come into the center. The music quickened its pace as three men with raffia shields and sticks simulating spears went into a war dance with leaps, thrusts, parries and crouches. The encircling men and women shuffled around more swiftly, shouting, clapping hands, and finally singing together in a fervor that seemed half religious, half lascivious.

The male soloists retired to the outer ring and for a minute the circle was empty. Suddenly a very fat man who had been watching—he weighed four hundred pounds at least—broke into the circle and with surprising agility danced for several minutes, his huge stomach and breasts shaking up and down like jelly. In spite of the ludicrousness of the spectacle, there was something graceful and impassioned even in this human hippo's dancing.

The king or *Nyimi* of the famous Bakuba tribe was almost as fat as my Mangbetu dancer, and not nearly so happy. The Bakuba are a Bantu tribe living in the south central part of the Congo, in the Kasai region. They are so well-known because more of their artwork has been collected by museums and connoisseurs of Europe and America than that of any other tribe. Their sculpture and wood-carving are astonishingly beautiful; the designs in their cloth woven of raffia, their mats and even the raffia walls of their houses are colorful, imaginative and quite "modern" in feeling; their embroidery—a rare art among African tribes—is intricate and beautiful. One of the loveliest pieces of art I have ever seen is a Bakuba mask carved in wood and decorated with colored beadwork.

The importance of art to the Bakuba themselves is illustrated by the fact that among the king's council are representatives of various arts and crafts, including sculptors and legend-keepers, or historians. Bakuba legends, which are memorized and passed on from generation to generation, go back much further than those of most tribes and here and there can be tied to known historical events so that we have an inkling of their history. Among the legends is one of the creation—the Nyimi, of course, came down to earth from the creator of earth and heaven and all things—which has some striking resemblances to the creation stories of many other religions. There is even a Flood legend among the Bakuba similar to our own.

The Bakuba love beautiful ornaments—beads, feathers, metal pins, rings, and bracelets. The king wears more than anyone else on his capacious body, but he also wears, most of the time, an expression of great weariness and boredom. He is so restricted by custom and tradition that he can scarcely move. When he sits down, for instance, he must sit on the back of a kneeling slave. His feet are not supposed to touch the earth, so he walks on mats strewn before him, or is carried in a litter. As a sign of his royalty and divinity he must wear two metal rings on his right big toe.

It is this king who is building the first native museum, to house his own priceless collection of Bakuba art objects. In the coming years, I believe the museum will be one of the "must" visits for travelers in the Congo. It will be as rewarding as many museums in the great cities of the western world. But I have another prediction, unfortunately. In twenty-five years there will be no first-rate artists among the Bakuba people. They will be trying to paint in oil on canvas, in imitation of European artists. Reproductions of Bakuba figurines may be readily available, however—made of plaster of Paris in Japan.

In filming the capture of elephants, one of my cameramen lashed himself to the back of a jolting truck to free both hands for his camera.
An irate elephant turned and chased the truck instead of running
away. He was uncomfortably close when the truck driver, intent on
the herd ahead, learned of the danger and sped away.

The largest African beast is the favorite prey of Africa's smallest people, the
Pygmies of the Ituri Forest, who smear themselves with elephant dung,
stalk the animal in uncanny silence, and bring it to earth by hamstringing.
Then it is an easy victim of their spears and carving knives.

Ituri Forest Pygmies celebrate an elephant kill—or almost anything—with high spirits and vigorous dancing that may continue all night. Below, they enjoy a tug of war between men and women; dances and games are always so arranged because Pygmies avoid physical contact between the sexes in public.

Pygmies gather round for their precious *matabishi* of salt, prized above most other gifts. For salt and palm oil they performed prodigious feats for our cameras, such as bridging the Ituri River with lianas, as shown below. This is the easy stage, following the dangerous crossing with the first long vine.

I make my first cautious passage over the swaying Pygmy bridge.
Actually, it is strong enough to hold a score of men with heavy
loads, although constructed solely of forest vines.

Pygmy women can build a house in less than an hour from saplings bent into a dome and overlapping phrynium leaves.

Pygmies are not the only strange inhabitants of the Ituri Forest. Here I feed some okapi, shy relative of the giraffe, long believed to be only a Pygmy tall tale.

The most dramatic feminine hairdo is that of the Mangbetu women, which is an accentuation of the elongated skull caused by binding the heads of babies. Although doctors have said the practice causes no harm, it is dying out as tribes have increased contact with civilization.

Mangbetu women beautify not only their heads but their rears. These beautifully woven *nekbwe* move in a subtly erotic fashion during tribal dances.

I admire the long earlobes of the tall witch doctor of the Kuria tribe. Later, a woman passed her newborn baby through one of the loops of skin in a ceremony calculated to bring good fortune.

When we could not get milk for a nursing bottle, this Turkana mother came to the rescue of a baby lion we had found.

The aristocratic Watussi live in the mountain region of Ruanda with Bahutu servants, Batwa slaves, and sacred long-horned cattle. Below, during a rare visit with four Watussi princesses, I watch them play a game while one plays a musical instrument similar to a lute.

The Masai of southern Kenya and Tanganyika, once great warriors, are cattlemen who eat not the flesh but the milk and blood of their herds. These "bravest of the brave" hunt lions with spear and shield. The pair of beasts below, however, have killed a zebra instead of a Masai cow.

A vindictive rhino charges the jeep, but cameraman Johnny Coquillon keeps filming even when the long horn plunges within a few inches of him.

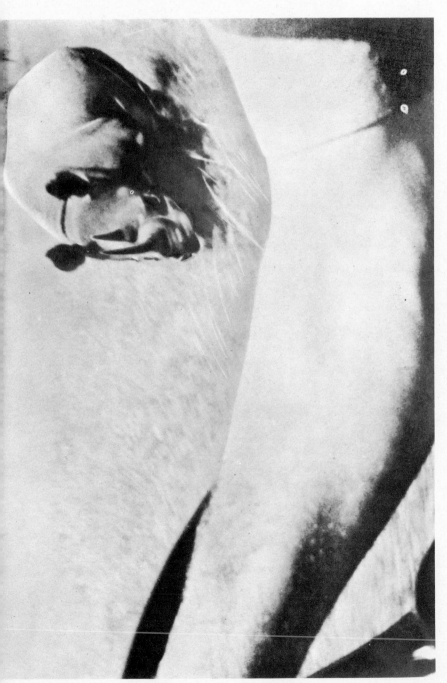

This is what Johnny filmed as the two-ton monster, puffing like a locomotive, attacked repeatedly. The arm belongs to Ace DuPreez, who maneuvered the jeep skillfully until a particularly vicious blow disabled it.

Some of the "actors" and staff on my third expedition. Carr Hartley and his son Mike sit in front of the Power Wagon, cameraman Freddie Ford Sr. at the left, myself and cameraman Dave Mason on the right, assistant Geddes in the cab, and Turkana tribesmen on either side. Cameramen Johnny Coquillon and Freddie Ford Jr. were on another mission when this picture was taken.

Leaving the truck for close-ups of the rhino charging the jeep, I feel relatively safe because the enraged beast is concentrating on the two men in the open vehicle. Suddenly the always unpredictable rhino turns and comes for me. I run for the truck and, as the second picture shows, the jeep cuts in front of the animal to divert him. But he keeps coming. As the last picture shows, the rhino was gaining on me as I reached the truck, which then raced away safely.

Animal capturer Pellegrini ties a cow rhino temporarily to the truck while he prepares the crate. He is interrupted by the rhino's mate, which charges the truck and rouses the female to attempt escape. After a series of fruitless attacks, the male retires in angry confusion, and the crating of the captured animal proceeds.

Chief Kasciula of the Pygmies living on Mt. Bugalamisa takes a cigarette before we start the gorilla hunt. The greybeard on the left is the one whose thin arm helped me clamber up the ledge when the gorilla was after me.

We found gorillas on the mountaintop. As I snapped this picture in poor light, the gorilla became annoyed at my intrusion and, opening its mouth in a chilling scream, headed for me.

The desire for close-ups of wild animals leads one frequently into dangerous situations. Above, the buffalo dislike my approach and debate the idea of charging me. Below, Ace DuPreez drifts into a herd of hippos, one of which could easily turn over his little boat and finish him with one crunch of its mighty jaws.

Beauty, danger, and humor on a giraffe hunt. At our approach, the herd runs with a rocking gait that is somehow graceful. After we lasso one giraffe, a helper grabs the animal's tail—almost universal procedure for throwing a beast off balance. But one kick can be fatal. The crated giraffe below has calmed down and shows only curiosity as it nibbles the hat from its captor's head.

Life and death in Africa. The hippos above were enjoying their mud bath so much they allowed me to approach quite close before one heaved itself up and chased me away. Below, some months later and hundreds of miles away, we saw scores of hippos trapped in hardening mud and broiled alive by the sun as the waters of the Rungwa River receded during a severe drought.

IX

Animals for Tea

ONLY in Africa, I'm sure, can one have tea with a kudu, an eland, a baboon, a zebra, a hyena—and an attractive woman. All at the same time. And not only that, but with two white owls looking on and making apparently acidulous comments.

There is probably only one place in Africa where such a scene might occur—Carr Hartley's big animal farm near the slopes of Mount Kenya. It is an amazing place, with normally wild animals wandering about like pet dogs, some of them in the houses as well as outside, and still-wild wild animals in strong pens awaiting shipment to zoos all over the world. If a particular species you want happens to be missing, Hartley will rustle one up for you. He will capture it without hurting it; he can take baby animals from their mothers without killing the mothers, which was previously considered essential.

Several movie companies have used both the animals and services of Carr Hartley. As a result of his work on such films he has acquired several valuable things, including a very large fenced arena in which animals can move about as in their natural environment. This can sometimes be of great value to producers of factual pictures; if you put an animal inside the arena you at least know where it is and can perhaps get some good shots of it. Otherwise you might have to track for days, wait patiently for more days, and then find the light wrong when you finally locate your camera's prey. When I think that during my three long visits I never saw one lion in the Congo—although I filmed many in East Africa—I know how frustrating

183

the filming of wild animals can be, and thus how helpful a natural-looking enclosure can be.

The arena, however, was not the chief reason for my visit to Hartley's on my 1954-55 trip. I hoped to obtain some amusing sequences involving the more or less tame animals around his place, and I knew that some exciting shots could be taken of Hartley going about his regular business of catching wild animals alive. For "Savage Splendor" Armand Denis had made some thrilling footage of Hartley lassoing animals from a fast-moving Power Wagon. But there was another short bit from that picture which served as the main lure drawing me to Hartley's. This was a sequence showing Mike Hartley, Carr's six-year-old son, riding on the back of a huge turtle and feeding some of the animals. The boy had a winning smile and an appealing way about him that came through on film. I figured Mike as being thirteen now and undoubtedly helping his father with the animals and the capturing during his vacations from school.

This fact, I hoped, would serve as the theme of my new motion picture for Republic, a thread upon which I could string many of the animal shots I might take. A theme of some kind is essential in such pictures, and they are not easy to find. The public enjoys good pictures of wild animals and tribesmen, but you cannot just put together seventy minutes of such sequences and wind up with a good feature film. Something must tie them together, some theme lead naturally from one subject to another. My picture had to compete in the theatre with multimillion-dollar films starring famous actors and actresses, with absorbing plots full of suspense and drama. My stars must be the animals and Africans themselves and my "story" necessarily plotless. Some suggestion of a story line, no matter how thin, was required, however.

During the months of preparation for my 1954-55 trip, I kept trying to find a theme, a framework within which I could fit at least a fair amount of the footage I would shoot. Then I thought of young Mike Hartley. How about a story line built around young Mike learning the art of capturing wild animals, like his father? It was not much but it *was* a theme, a thread on which any number of animal sequences might credibly be strung. And since a good deal of animal hunting involved Africans, different tribes could be brought in without undue strain, too. Not all animal sequences and certainly not all tribal shots could be worked in around the character of young Hartley, but with careful planning and good editing he could serve as the unifying element for a fair amount of the film.

A long distance call from New York to Carr Hartley in Kenya took some hours to go through but soon I was talking about my idea. Carr agreed that we could work something out, that many good animal sequences could be filmed at his place, and he thought Mike would enjoy the role I had in mind for him. He would be home from boarding school in about three weeks and would be at the farm just two months. I would have to fit in everything concerning Mike during that period.

This was good news, but it meant rushing things faster than I had anticipated. What had begun as a leisurely trip to Africa for pleasure and some 16-millimeter films for my own purposes had, through an unforeseen series of events, developed into a much larger and more urgent project. First, while planning my private trip with one cameraman, I had run into an old friend, Harry C. Mills, a director of Republic Pictures, and mentioned my journey. He asked me to see Herbert J. Yates, head of Republic, and his son Douglas Yates. After relatively little discussion, we decided that I should produce a full-length picture in color, using professional 35-millimeter equipment. So far as Republic was concerned, it was to be an English quota picture, which meant that the expedition would be financed by its subsidiary, Republic Pictures of Great Britain. This also meant that my staff had to be British citizens. Fortunately, the cameraman I had already made connections with, Johnny Coquillon, was a Canadian and thus acceptable as part of the staff. The budget was a modest one by Hollywood standards, but allowed me more leeway than on previous trips.

Since the Chrysler Corportion had helped on the "Savage Splendor" expedition I naturally turned to them. They were immediately cooperative, offering me a Dodge Power Wagon and a 2½-ton stake truck. This time, however, in view of the necessity of reaching Africa in time to catch Mike Hartley while he was on vacation, I was forced to ask for speed. The trucks, equipped and ready to roll, had to be on a ship sailing for Africa in just ten days. Somehow, Chrysler managed to get both trucks on that ship.

But it's a long trip, and the ship took forever. I could not wait for it, so completed my arrangements in New York, leaving my insurance business in the capable hands of my secretary, Louise Smith. Then I flew to London for conferences with the Republic people there, and learned that union regulations made it necessary for me to have an assistant director and four cameramen, so my staff was immediately larger than I had planned.

We flew to Nairobi, Kenya, a bustling city of over one hundred thousand which only a few decades ago was a little village through whose streets herds of zebra and antelope occasionally ran. The airport still must be fenced in to keep wild animals off the runways. Many species of East African animals live in the near-by park—readily accessible and most interesting—but it was not right for our purposes, as the animals had become rather accustomed to visitors and restrictions were rigid. Anyway, it was essential for us to get to Hartley's farm, about 145 miles north of Nairobi, as soon as possible.

In Nairobi, whenever we mentioned that we were going to Carr Hartley's place at Rumuruti, people looked askance at us. Finally someone said what was obviously on all minds. "The Mau Mau situation is pretty bad, you know."

I knew about the Mau Mau killings, of course. I had read the newspapers. A secret society of Kikuyu tribesmen, in a surge of strong nationalist, anti-white feeling, had brutally murdered many white settlers, chiefly on outlying and isolated farms. On my earlier trips I had seen evidences of the ferment between Africans and white farmers out of which the terroristic movement had grown. Knowing as many Africans as I did, I understood why the British authorities were having such difficulties in coping with this secret, ritualistic band that struck without warning in the dark of the night. I knew, too, that at the time of my trip the killings had been on the increase, that the Mau Mau movement was growing in power, and that officials and individual white settlers were taking strong steps to combat the most serious threat to European lives and property that had arisen in Central Africa in decades. I was concerned and interested, but not deterred in my plans to do a good deal of filming in Kenya. It just did not occur to me that the Mau Mau situation might endanger or even interfere with my expedition.

Then in Nairobi the British authorities told me that I and my staff must carry guns at all times. When I protested that I had traveled thousands of miles through Africa unarmed, I was told that this was not a suggestion—it was an order. All whites were required to carry revolvers everywhere, and this meant literally everywhere—to meals, bathroom, and bed. The weapons were intended primarily for protection, of course, and also to demonstrate to all Africans that the whites were prepared to defend themselves. The fact that I was an American owning not one square foot of Kenya land which the tribesmen might think belonged to them would make no difference in the event I put myself in the position of easy target for the Mau Mau. There was no plan in their killings. They just killed whites who could be reached with the least danger. If I should go about unarmed I would be inviting ambush and attack.

The reason for carrying the weapon even in safe circumstances was to forestall theft. The Mau Mau had few guns and desperately wanted more. The one sure way to prevent theft was to wear one's gun and keep it at hand every minute of the day and night. Thus housewives went shopping in perfectly safe Nairobi with guns on their hips and in their pocketbooks, not because they expected attacks there but because they did not dare leave the guns at home. Even long-trusted servants had too often turned out to be Mau Mau members or sympathizers—or, in some cases, slaves of fear. The Mau Mau had killed hundreds of Kikuyu—far more than whites—because they refused to take the Mau Mau oath and cooperated with white masters and authorities.

We equipped ourselves with guns and then made preparations for our trip to Carr Hartley's farm. Since our trucks would not arrive for several weeks, I bought a Volkswagen bus, loaded some of my men and equipment into it, and headed north for Rumuruti in spite of warnings that we were driving right into the heart of the Mau Mau country, near Mt. Kenya and the Aberdare Mountains, where Carr Hartley's farm lay.

Housing was one difficulty. While Carr Hartley's place was a big establishment, consisting of a main building, barns, pens, animal compounds, and several small mud-and-wattle thatch-roofed *rondavels*, there was not enough room for all of us. Hartley put me in a small *rondavel* near the main house, and found quarters for the rest of the men at a kind of local farmers' club about ten miles away. We were somewhat taken aback to find this building completely surrounded by thick barbed-wire fencing designed to keep out or at least hamper Mau Mau attackers. We were reassuringly told that the nearby building, which was similarly protected, had been set up as the police headquarters for battling the Mau Mau menace in one of the worst Mau Mau areas.

Although we were sobered by these evidences of the immediate presence of serious danger, we were not really frightened because we could not believe that anyone would attack us. I talked the situation over with my assistant and the four cameramen, and they all agreed that we should proceed with our work as planned. They would drive the Volkswagen bus to and from Hartley's place every day, and we would depend primarily on Hartley's trucks for work in filming the capturing of animals.

Hartley himself did not seem very perturbed by the Mau Mau threat, although he did not minimize the seriousness of

the situation. I learned that he was high on the Mau Mau list of
whites they would like to eliminate, and they had actually am-
bushed him twice as he drove his truck along the twisting road
to his farm—both times at the same place, where he had to
slow down for a curve and could not see ahead. They had missed
him because they were such poor shots and because he just
stepped on the accelerator and raced ahead. Not many of the
Mau Mau had used guns enough to handle them very well, except at close range on non-moving targets. They were much
more effective with their *pangas* and *simis,* long double-edged
knives.

We started filming, hampered only by the familiar difficulties due to rain, absence of light and the sudden disappearance
of animal life from its usual haunts. These are occupational
hazards in nature photography and, although they drive one
frantic at the time, are accepted as part of the job. But then
three incidents occurred within the first two weeks of my stay
at Hartley's that were far from the expected run of troubles.
First, the head of the police in the district called to advise me
to leave the area.

"It is just too dangerous a situation," he said, "and I don't
like to feel responsible for your lives. Mau Mau bands infest
these hills and swamps. You are living within five hundred yards
of an almost impenetrable swamp where we know scores of
Mau Mau are hiding. They are out for blood, and it won't make
any difference to them if it is your blood or some other white
man's. Please go somewhere else. There are wild animals all
over East Africa which you can photograph. I advise you to go
to one of these places where the danger comes only from the
animals and not from men too."

He was very polite about it, but very serious. And he was
right, of course, about the fact that there were many other areas
in which I could film wild animals. Hartley's captured beasts
and his enclosed arena were not important enough for me to
take any avoidable chances. His son Mike, however, was the
slim thread upon which I had decided to string many of the

events of my film. If I wanted Mike to appear in several good
sequences, I would have to stay in the heart of the Mau Mau
country for at least a month and perhaps longer.

It was a difficult decision to make, and not one to be made
lightly. I had three alternatives—abandon the whole project and
go back home, which I rejected immediately; leave Hartley's
as advised by the authorities and work in a safer region, thus
abandoning my sequences with Mike and hoping that I would
be able to come up with another theme in a hurry; stay at Hartley's and continue with my work in spite of the danger, taking
all sensible precautions at all times.

If at that moment I'd been struck with inspiration and
found another theme for the moving picture, I believe I would
have left Hartley's, but I could not think of a thing. But more
than my own life was involved in staying, so I took the matter
up with the other men. By this time they too realized the situation was in all truth dangerous, but they urged that we stay on.
We had a job to do and such work was always filled with a certain amount of danger. They were willing to face it if I asked
them to. So I decided to stay on and film whatever I could.

We had been working only a short while, however, when
the second incident occurred. The police came and arrested
more than twenty of Hartley's African workers. Several of
the men were known to have taken the Mau Mau oath and
others were strongly suspected, so they were put in jail. They
were most of Hartley's best helpers, too, among them the head
man, called Wilson.

We were all a little shaken to know that we had been working side by side with Mau Mau terrorists who had taken a most
sacred oath to kill white men. Hartley did not seem particularly surprised, since he knew that many farmers had discovered some of their most trusted servants to be Mau Mau
members. But he was exasperated at losing so many workers
when there was a great deal to be done. Their absence definitely
slowed down our filming and resulted in a near tragedy during
the leopard sequence, as I'll explain shortly.

Then came the third incident that helped hamper our work at Hartley's. Gordon Pollman, Carr's half-brother who was himself an admirable handler of wild animals and a great aid in our work, was called up for duty with the armed forces serving to combat the Mau Mau threat. Every able-bodied white citizen of Kenya was subject to such draft and all served willingly, but no one's service could have come at a more inopportune moment for us. But after a good deal of petitioning, the authorities postponed his service for one month in view of the fact that he was helping with our project which was already under way.

These affairs were scarcely out of the way when an African brought Hartley the warning that his house was going to be attacked that evening by a band of Mau Maus from the swamplands that began only five hundred yards away. Our work had ended for the day and my staff had driven home to their fortress. Hartley called everyone left on the farm into his home. There we ate and armed ourselves and waited for the attack to come. We did not listen to the wireless, a common evening entertainment, because its noise might have obscured sounds of approaching attackers. Some of us tried to play cards but had little heart for it. We talked in desultory fashion, listened intently during the long silences, and wondered what might happen. I was amazed to see the quiet calm of the women—Mrs. Hartley and her sisters, Dulcy Wedd and Thelma Randall, and Hartley's secretary, Nancy Drew. They were ready for anything.

The attack never came, however, probably because we were prepared and well armed. The next morning Carr found that some of his cattle had been stolen. The Mau Mau had made a raid, all right, but to get food rather than kill people. We went back to our work.

The incident apparently gave Carr Hartley an idea. He must have been the kind of child who set off firecrackers under old ladies' chairs, and he still had a fondness for practical jokes. The evening after the false alarm, I was sitting in my *rondavel* writing some letters. Darkness had not completely fallen, but one could not see far. The animals had gone to sleep and the

whole place was quiet, as only a remote farm can be. Suddenly
the night air was split by a piercing scream, a scream that came
from Carr Hartley himself, somewhere outside my *rondavel*.

"Mau Mau!" he yelled. "Mau Mau!"

I dropped my pen, snatched my rather unfamiliar gun from
its holster and tore out of the rondavel at top speed, only to
collide with the chunky, barrel-chested figure of Carr Hartley.

The big man burst out laughing—and his laugh boomed
over the plains. Other people rushed from the main house, and
Hartley, still laughing heartily, explained how funny I had
looked racing out of the hut gun in hand when he shouted his
practical joke.

Nobody thought it was very funny, but Hartley persisted in
enjoying his little fun whether anyone else did or not. I put the
incident down as evidence of an unusual—to say the least—sense
of humor, and went back to finish my letters. Hartley went to
his house still chuckling.

The next evening at dinner Hartley left the table a few
minutes before the rest of us. Hartley's secretary spoke to me.

"He's planning another Mau Mau joke on you," she said.
"I don't know just what it is, but I don't think it's very funny.
Come on, let's go outside after him. Pretend that you are not
aware of anything."

We all left the room, following Hartley outside. There he
stood, grimly serious for a change, staring down at the blacker-
than-black patch that we all knew represented the beginning of
the thick and tangled growth of swamp where the Mau Mau
were in hiding. We looked and saw a flash of a light, then another and another. There seemed to be a regular rhythm or pattern to the flashing of the lights. There was no doubt about it
—the Mau Mau were signalling to each other, perhaps to someone up on the farm or to other Mau Maus somewhere. Hartley
pulled out his flashlight and pointed it toward the swamp and
the blinking lights. He flashed it on, then off, then on again, as
if he were sending a signal. There was no code in his flashes, but

he let them know that Carr Hartley had seen their signals and
was ready.

End of joke.

The atmosphere, obviously, was not conducive to concentration on the work at hand, and the reduced staff, plus normal
difficulties, threw many monkey wrenches into our plans. But
we managed to obtain some of the sequences we wanted, among
them one with Chui, the leopard. Hartley had trapped the magnificent creature some time before and kept him in a strong
cage in the compound. He was not tame by any means, but his
wildness seemed to have been tempered somewhat by kind
treatment since his capture. My one worry, in fact, was that he
was too mild a beast to make a good movie sequence. Graceful
and lovely as he was, I was not interested in pictures of a leopard
purring and licking one's hand. He did not quite purr for me
when I first visited his cage, but he let me put my hand through
the bars and scratch his ears. I decided that perhaps he was not
a wild enough wild animal for my needs.

The next afternoon after my affectionate tryst with Chui
(the Swahili word for leopard) I was walking around Hartley's
compound with Dulcy Wedd. As we approached Chui's cage he
snarled, laid back his ears, lashed his tail, and sprang against
the bars. I talked soothingly to no avail. The beast obviously
had just one thought in mind—to get out of that cage and kill
both of us.

Maybe Chui would be all right after all, I decided. But he
had been so friendly with me the first time! Perhaps he didn't
like women, and grew furious at the sight of Mrs. Wedd. So the
next day I tried visiting him alone again. He snarled at me
angrily. I concluded that Chui might indeed act like a real leopard for the film sequence. It was worth a try, at least, because
there was little likelihood of our getting good leopard pictures
anywhere else. They are primarily nocturnal and prefer wooded
areas, so you just don't encounter leopards the way you do lions,
elephants, hippos, rhinos and the multitude of antelopes in Af-

rica. If you do, it is likely to be in circumstances that do not permit you to take pictures—you are running or it is too dark or both.

To tempt the leopard into a little action, we decided to use his great fondness for baboon meat. Hartley had in his private menagerie a mother baboon, with her baby on her back and a slightly larger adopted baboon child at her breast. We didn't use the baboons for bait, but rather their smell.

First we transferred the touchy and temperamental leopard to a portable cage, which was trucked to the big arena about three miles away. Then we took the baboon and its children to another spot about a hundred feet away, and allowed them to sit and play and eat within sight and smell of the leopard. We could see and hear the beast pacing more eagerly back and forth in its cage.

Finally the baboon and her children were removed, two cameramen were stationed at strategic spots for taking pictures, within the arena, and several of Hartley's helpers were ready farther along to divert the leopard and help keep it to a course that would be within camera range. I stood with Hartley close to the path Chui was supposed to take on his way to the spot where the baboon had been. Since we had already taken some shots of the baboon and its children, we hoped to establish the idea that the leopard was after them. The soundest way to accomplish this was obviously to make the leopard actually go after them. He would, we hoped, spring immediately to the spot where he had seen them and could smell them. Then he would follow their trail to the far gate from which we had taken the baboons out of the arena. At that point he would be balked and would get no baboon meat, but Hartley's men would have some other choice food waiting for him.

It was a good plan if it worked. But when men are around, few animals act precisely as they would in their natural environment, so we just hoped for luck. At the last moment, I thought of another kind of luck—involving my life rather than the taking of a picture. I turned to Hartley and asked, "What if the leopard

comes for one of us?" Hartley replied, "Stand still. Don't move
an inch. He'll probably go on past. And anyway, I'll take care of
things."

The leopard was released from his cage and came stalking
swiftly down through the trees and underbrush along the route
we had intended. Chui was an impressive creature. Beautiful
as he had seemed in his cage, he was far more spectacular out
in the open, moving ahead almost like liquid, and I was delighted to see two cameras trained on him from different angles.
Once he slowed down and darted quick and uncomfortable
glances at the humans around, but the smell of baboon meat
overcame his worries, and he went straight ahead to the spot
where the baboon and her babies had sat and eaten for some
time. This brought Chui within about fifteen feet of Hartley
and me, and I held my breath as he passed. But he ignored us,
after that first glance, and went on his way.

He sniffed at the spot, looked up, and started off in the
right direction, more swiftly than before. He didn't want that
baboon to get away. Then quite suddenly he veered to the right,
away from the baboon's trail and almost out of range of our
cameras. Perhaps the wind shifted and fooled him, or our presence threw him off. Hartley signaled to one of his natives up on
a hill to move toward the leopard in an effort to turn Chui back
on his prepared route. The men who had most experience in
working with Hartley knew that wild animals usually turn aside
when men approach them. But Hartley's best men had all been
arrested, and the workers we were using had neither the experience nor the confidence of those now in jail. The fellow
obeyed Hartley's signal readily enough, taking half a dozen
steps toward the leopard's path, at right angles to it. Chui *should*
have angled off to the left, back onto his route within camera
range. But he didn't. He stopped, faced the man, and lashed
his tail in annoyance.

This was too much for the inexperienced African, who was
seized with sudden fear. Hartley and I could sense it a few
hundred feet away, and I'm sure the leopard sensed it, too. Fear

made the man do the worst of all things—run away. If he'd
possessed the courage to hold his ground, as Hartley's more experienced men would have, Chui would almost certainly have
continued on his way. But the fellow panicked and took to his
heels. In that instant the leopard was after him. In two terrific
bounds Chui was on the man's back, knocking him to the
ground, but Hartley was already running fast toward the spot,
with me not far behind. Just as we rushed up, the leopard turned
the native over and sank his fangs in his throat.

It was a tough shot for Hartley to make, with man and
beast so close together, but he did not hesitate. His first bullet
struck the leopard, who leaped off the native and bounded away.
Three more quick shots dropped the animal about ten feet from
us.

The man was horribly mauled and bleeding profusely, but
still alive. Hartley ordered men to carry him at once to a truck
and rush him to a hospital—which was quite a trip but the only
hope for the fellow. The man hovered between life and death
for weeks but he finally recovered.

At the time, Hartley's chief emotional disturbance came
from the loss of his beautiful leopard. He actually wept as he
looked down at the sleek spotted creature lying lifeless on the
ground. I was very upset, of course, at the turn of events—the
near death of the native and the death of a prize leopard. It was
the first serious accident on any of my expeditions.

We did not get the attack on film, unfortunately, because
Chui had wandered out of camera range. But we did take one
final shot of the leopard as it lay on the ground dead. Then I
was faced with a problem. Should I scrap all the good leopard
footage we had taken? Good as it might be, it led nowhere, told
no story at all, and was so incomplete as to be unusable as an
important sequence in the film. To make an acceptable dramatic
sequence we had to fill in the gaps, for which I needed a leopard. Hartley had no other leopard in his compound, and capturing this animal was not something one did on order in a day or
two.

Then Thelma Randall heard through a friend on a nearby farm that a leopard had just been caught in a trap about forty miles to the north. Off we dashed in the trucks, hoping that we had found a substitute for Chui in filming the balance of the leopard sequence. The beast had been put in a temporary cage, but when I saw him I wondered how long he might stay there. The leopard's face was bloody as a result of his lunging with all his strength against the wire mesh of the cage. As I approached him, he sprang at me, crashed against the cage and fell to the floor, picked himself up and catapulted his body once more against the cage walls.

We hauled the animal back to Hartley's farm, hoping that good food and a calm environment would quiet him somewhat. But for three or four days he did not eat a bit of meat, did not even drink water. That beast wanted just one thing in the world —out! Finally, however, he took some water. The next day he ate some fresh meat. At the end of a week he was still a ferocious and vindictive animal, but he did not spend all of his time try-ing to escape. He ate, slept, and paced back and forth in his cage. If anyone came near, he threw himself against the cage with full fury, but the rest of the time he was relatively quiet. We decided that we might use him in some film shots.

Meanwhile, we had gone about other picture chores, of course, but as soon as possible we went back to our leopard sequence, using the understudy. This time, however, our camera-men were stationed in strong cage-like enclosures, with apertures for camera lenses to poke through. In one magnificent shot, the cameraman kept shooting film even as the leopard leaped at his fortress. At any rate, we finally succeeded in getting our leopard sequence for the picture.

It was the only sequence for which we used the arena. This experience proved to us that "staging" an animal scene in an enclosed area was neither very safe nor satisfactory. A wild ani-mal is a wild animal, even inside an arena. It may be more ferocious than usual because it is hemmed in, cornered, unable to run away—which is the first impulse of just about every creature in contact with man. On top of that, it has been captured and caged before being brought to the enclosure, which is sure to infuriate any self-respecting wild beast.

Staging sequences in any way rarely works out well, for most animals just won't behave naturally. If you use somewhat pacified beasts, they act and look like tame animals, and that's not what the public wants. It can see such animals in circuses and zoos. The movie-goer wants action, excitement, and a sense of danger, so producers try to get scenes of animals battling each other or chasing a man—both very difficult. Few wild animals chase a man unless cornered or provoked seriously. As for animal fights, it takes infinite patience plus uncanny luck to get such pictures unless they are caged together—and even then it rarely works. Fortunately, the law has for some years prohibited the staging of man-made battles between natural enemies starved and then put together in a cage or enclosure.

I tried to get some lion shots in Carr Hartley's arena, but the lions would not act as they were supposed to. They were hungry, and meat was placed on the ground for them some distance from the spot at which they were released into the arena. When they headed for the meat they would pass in front of our cameras, and Hartley would try to lasso one of them. But the stage-frightened lions would have none of our act. They ignored the meat and took off for the fence, out of range of our cameras. Hartley's half-brother, Gordon Pollman, was ready for such an emergency and drove in a truck to the spot at which the lions were trying to escape from the enclosure. One of the big beasts climbed up a supporting pole on which the wire fence was fastened and was about to leap over when Pollman courageously tried to shove him back with his bare hands. The lion clung to its pole at the top of the fence and freed one murderous forepaw to brush the man out of the way. Pollman's arm was slashed and he was badly mauled, but he finally pushed the beast back into the enclosure. This may sound foolhardy, but Carr Hartley himself once conquered a wounded lion with a roundhouse right on the nose when his gun-bearer dropped his gun at a crucial moment. Hartley avoids shooting animals whenever he can, not only because he likes them but because they are valuable property, the assets of his business.

We got many sequences in the country around Hartley's farm, most of them involving young Mike. There was one with a hippo caught in a pit trap, which was interesting, but could not find a spot in the film when it was finally cut and edited. There were several showing Mike feeding and caring for the many different animals at the Hartley place. One of the most satisfying was the giraffe hunt and capture. During a rare period of several dry and clear days, we all drove in Hartley's trucks to a region of flat grassy plains about fifty miles away. There we maneuvered around until we located a good herd of giraffe which, at our approach, ambled away in the typical sedate and rhythmical gait of these beasts. The open truck, equipped with long pole and looped rope for lassoing, and containing Pollman and young Mike Hartley in addition to a few workmen, picked up speed, while the photography truck tried to keep pace over the rough terrain. As the first truck came near to the herd, it split in several sections, so the truck was able to cut off from the others a couple of medium-sized giraffe. Selecting one to be captured, the truck pulled up alongside and just a little ahead of the careening animal. Mike and Pollman extended the long pole, then lightly dropped the noose over the giraffe's neck. The other truck was taking pictures of the whole incident, of course.

This is the crucial moment in any giraffe capture, for a giraffe's neck can be broken if he is stopped too abruptly. And even if his neck is not broken, his heart may actually burst at the sudden strain put upon it by an abrupt stop.

The truck slowed down gradually as the rope tightened on the giraffe, restraining the animal gently but firmly. Then when the truck was traveling about fifteen miles an hour, two workers leaped from it, with the rope in their hands, and ran along with the giraffe, pulling it finally to a stop. One immediately grabbed it by the tail.

Once the animal knew it was captured, it abandoned all efforts to get away and apparently accepted its fate philosophically. The giraffe is not a mean animal, and is provoked to kick out with its powerful legs only on rare occasions. Now Mike talked soothingly to it as he approached, and in a short time was patting its flanks affectionately.

Then came the job of getting the big animal in the truck for the trip back to the farm, a forbidding feat. Our cameras took films of the whole affair and, I'm happy to say, one of them kept going even after the giraffe was safely in the truck. For as Pollman climbed up on the truck cab to arrange the ropes securely and had his back turned on the animal, the giraffe stretched out its long neck and gently nibbled Pollman's hat right off his head. It was just the kind of shot that you always want but usually miss because cameras have stopped one minute before.

Getting the giraffe off the truck and into a pen in Hartley's compound was a more troublesome job than loading the animal. Hartley's men dug a big sloping hole in the ground right outside the pen that had been prepared for the giraffe, wide enough to accommodate the truck. The vehicle then backed down the slope into the hole so that its platform was at ground level. A door was opened in the pen, directly behind it, and the giraffe was freed from its bonds so it could walk into the enclosure. The truck ground its way out of the hole, which was then filled in.

Among the Africans working at Hartley's farm were several men from the Turkana tribe which lived far to the north, around Lake Rudolf and near the border of the Sudan. They were tall, long-legged Nilotics, with distinctive lower-lip plugs and white ostrich-feather head-dresses. I became interested in them and made a note to try to work in a visit to their remote territory. Since the Turkana men at Hartley's had appeared in the leopard and other sequences, I knew that any pictures taken later in Turkanaland could easily be tied in with the rest of the film.

A Turkana woman played an important if unusual role in another sequence taken at Hartley's. One day while out in the truck we saw a lioness with several very small cubs. We were downwind from her and well concealed, so she was not aware of our approach. We shot the scene with a telephoto lens and while we were filming, the lioness, who seemed quite restless, wandered away from her cubs—probably to search for food. In a few seconds the father appeared, a big shaggy-maned lion. He was probably supposed to baby-sit while mama was off hunting, but he didn't like the job and soon sauntered away. One of the little cubs was lively and curious, and walked on very shaky legs away from his brothers and sisters. Finally he was far enough away for Mike to get out of the truck and pick him up. The little fellow didn't mind; he was too young to know fear of men.

We drove away quickly, before the lioness might discover her loss, and took the cub back to Hartley's farm. Mike filled a nursing bottle with warm milk and tried to feed the cub as he had often fed many other baby animals. But the cub could not figure out the strange rubber nipple, although he seemed eager for food. Mike tried several times to give the baby lion the bottle but even the next day the little fellow could not manage it. We were all worried. If the cub didn't swallow some food soon, he'd weaken and perhaps die.

While we were debating what to do, I suddenly remembered an experience from one of my trips to the head-hunting Jivaros of the upper Amazon. A hunting dog had been killed by a panther, leaving behind a puppy only a few days old. Dogs are valuable, and the Jivaros did not want to lose the puppy if they could help it. So a Jivaro woman with a new baby nursed the puppy along with her own offspring. I had taken pictures of the scene, which the censors removed from the movie, "Jungle Head Hunters," but a still shot appeared in my book, *Amazon Head Hunters*, which told the story of my three South American expeditions.

I had no idea, of course, if a Turkana woman would nurse a lion cub, but I had learned that primitive people the world over were much alike, especially about down-to-earth matters. Anyway, it was worth a try. Mike and I took the cub to the nearby Turkana village, where Mike was a great favorite. We found a young mother nursing her baby and Mike told his story about how the cub would not drink from a bottle. The woman smiled and nodded understandingly, grasping Mike's request even before he uttered it. With calm self-possession she took the lion cub and put it to her breast. She did not mind my taking pictures of her with a baby at one breast, a lion at the other.

Another out-of-the-ordinary sequence taken at Hartley's was the tea scene. I felt sure that pictures of the relatively tame creatures on the farm would appeal to people everywhere, so we set up a card table outside the house where the light was good. Near by was a cot. We confined the human actors to Dulcy Wedd, Mike Hartley and myself. On the table, in addition to various items of food and drink, was a deck of cards with which Dulcy and I could occupy ourselves, while Mike lay down on the cot for a nap. I put a few pieces of hard candy in the pocket of my jacket, which hung over the back of my chair. My hat was on a stool close by.

With our cameramen set, the scene began. As Dulcy and I played cards, the camera caught a kudu and an eland grazing peacefully in the background, occasionally looking with some interest in our direction. Then Coco the baboon sauntered in, and I pretended not to notice as she sneaked to my chair, reached a paw into my jacket pocket, and stole some candy. She rushed a few feet away with great glee, removed the paper wrapping, and stuffed the candy in her mouth. Next a small zebra wandered up close and nudged Dulcy with its nose. She took a nursing bottle from the table and gave the striped animal a welcome drink of milk.

By the time the zebra was satisfied, the baboon was back again, with her two babies, one on her back and the other clinging to her breast. She took an open bottle of Pepsi Cola and tipped it up to drink, but some of the liquid spilled messily down her front, much to the delight of the baby there who lifted eager lips to catch what it could of the beverage while blinking to keep it out of its eyes.

We shooed Coco and her children away and, as I turned back to our continually interrupted card game, another creature came into the scene silently—an animal with a winning personality. I say this reluctantly, for I know that not many people will believe me. But Eric was—once you got over the first distaste of his appearance—a charming fellow. Eric was a hyena—even if totally different from all other hyenas. They are misshapen, ugly, and generally revolting animals, and I've never heard a good word said for one until coming to Hartley's. Even then, I found him repulsive at first, but it did not take Eric long to win me over with the mischievous light in his eye, his friendliness and his sense of humor. Eric played endlessly and joyfully with Hartley's dogs. And he loved to play tricks. Several times as I sat in my *rondavel* writing, Eric sneaked in and snatched up some article of mine, hoping I would give chase. Once he picked up a shoe, making sure that I saw him at the last minute. I ran after him yelling, for I needed that shoe, and Eric dashed into an almost impenetrable growth of cactus, where I could not follow.

In addition to shoes, Eric had a penchant for felt hats. That's why my hat was sitting on a stool, to tempt him into his mischievous thievery. It was irresistible to him, of course. He grabbed it in his teeth and tore away at top speed. This time I caught him, rolled him over on his back, and took my hat away from his snapping mouth. There was a hole in the hat, but that was small cost for a good scene.

Back at the table again, I put a cigarette in my mouth only to have the eland step up and take it gently from my lips. He chewed it thoughtfully, swallowed it happily and gave me a look of thanks before stepping back. This eland loved cigarettes so much that it had been known to sneak through an open door of the house and steal an open package.

Apparently the cigarette pepped him up, for he proceeded to tip over the cot on which Mike Hartley was supposed to be napping. Mike was furious, and the eland scampered away happily, delighted with his practical joke.

The humans, at this point, decided that they had had enough. We all left the scene, but the cameras kept going, hoping that the kudu would come through with his expected act. He did, entering the scene and eying the plates on the table. He looked around cautiously, then walked to the table and began licking the plates, as though knowing that he was doing something he shouldn't do. He stopped his licking occasionally to cast his eyes up at the cameraman, who might stop him at any moment. This meant, of course, that he looked directly into the camera during his rather guilty but happy cleaning of the plates.

It was only later that I thought of the white owls. We set the two of them on a beam above the door. They often made small growling noises at each other, turning as if in conversation as they did so. Then they looked forward, or down, at anyone who happened to be nearby. Their eyes would ordinarily be mere slits, but at sight of someone they would open wide as if in dismay or surprise. One owl would give this startled look, then turn to his fellow with a tilted head and small disapproving mutters. The friend would also look, turn, and make his own comments.

We set up a camera and waited for enough of these shocked looks and exchanges of comment to be impressed on the film. My plan was to cut these shots into the tea sequence. When Eric snatched my hat, or Coco spilled her drink, or the eland took my cigarette, the scene would cut to the owls with their amazement and disapproval. I reserved the most disapproving look of all for the kudu and his plate-licking, of course.

There was nothing to keep us in the Hartley area any longer. I had to have more wild animals, more herds of wild animals, more wild animals in action, as well as tribes strange and wonderful. Two months had gone by and I had just scratched the surface. Some weeks before, our trucks had arrived in Nairobi, where they were waiting for us. We had enough footage involving Mike and his father to use their experiences with animals as a theme for the picture. We had safely weathered the peak of the Mau Mau terror in the heart of the Mau Mau country. We were all eager to get our trucks and set out for wild country—the wilder the better.

X

Cats and Their Prey— and Scavengers

THE favorite wild animal of most people seems to be the lion. At a zoo the monkeys will attract a big crowd if they are cavorting, the seals if they are diving and barking, the bears if they are dancing or fighting. But let the lion roar just once and everyone will leave these fascinating creatures to rush for the cage of the king of beasts. Men gave this big cat the name of king, indicating their preference, but the lion is not necessarily top dog in Nature. The elephant may be more intelligent, the leopard more cunning, the buffalo more deadly— although you can start a hundred arguments among big game experts by such statements—but the lion is king in men's eyes because he combines dignity, beauty, grace, speed, power, courage and ferocity.

I always admired lions, like everyone else, but I had a feeling that the whole story had not been told in the scores of books, fiction and fact, that I'd read. There were plenty of contradictions in what I read, which didn't bother me too much. Some writers—particularly those who had hunted lions in the old days—pictured the king of beasts as a bloodthirsty killer, with a nasty disposition and a chip on his shoulder, who went out looking for trouble, especially with nice harmless hunters who just wanted to shoot them for trophies. Others described the lion as a courteous gentleman who wouldn't hurt a fly unless the fly made a terrible nuisance of itself—and unless, of course, the lion happened to be hungry; even then the lion would just kill some zebra or antelope too lame or sick or old to run fast. This, they said, was all for the best, a genuine service to zebras or antelopes in general who should thank the lion for weeding out their unfit and thus proving the correctness of Mr. Darwin's theory. These same writers also point out what good family men lions are and what a fine mother a lioness is, playing with and teaching her little cubs which are as cute and appealing as human babies and perhaps more so.

People are always searching for human attributes in animals, and the more likenesses they can find the better the case they can make for the animal. Actually gorillas and chimpanzees are much more like humans than any other animals, which is not surprising in view of the closeness of the blood relationship, but few nature writers emphasize this because people don't find gorillas and chimpanzees admirable. There are some human beings in this world with a surprising number of the attributes of the hyena, some who remind me of nothing so much as a vulture. I even know a few women with the grace and the saucy posteriors of Thomson's gazelles. In general, however, I think it is a little silly and probably futile to try to understand animals in terms of human characteristics.

In spite of this belief, I can see numerous resemblances between lions and men. In the main they both kill other animals for the sake of food and for no other reason. There are exceptions to this rule, such as mother lions killing in order to teach their cubs how to do it and, among men, big-game hunters who kill for the thrill of it. Generally, however, lions and men kill for food; in the last few centuries men have learned how to delegate this task to a few specialists.

There are other similarities. Lions and men are both insatiably curious, and both walk the earth as if they owned it—as if it were created specifically for their enjoyment and stocked with birds, game, shady trees and clear streams solely for their pleasure and sustenance. There's nothing particularly cocky about this feeling, in most cases; it is merely a never-questioned assumption that he, whether lion or man, is the center of things, the reason for things. The zebra has none of this feeling, nor does the topi, the giraffe, the hippo, rhino, buffalo or even the leopard. Perhaps the elephant has something of it, for he goes his own way unafraid of anything except man; but the elephant is more removed from the world, above it all, having little truck with other creatures. Lions and men, on the other hand, have plenty to do with the world and most creatures in it; both demonstrate daily that they are kings. Their calm assumption of superiority is half the battle in making them kings, for all other animals seem to sense the air of confidence that wraps itself around most lions and most men wherever they go.

Kings are interested in other kings, so men have always shown more interest in lions than in other beasts. I shared this interest, but I was just about through with my scheduled trip in 1937 when I realized that I had not even seen a lion. I had been in Simba's land without seeing Simba. I had seen elephants, buffalo, rhinos, hippos, okapi, and even gorilla—which most hunters and explorers rarely see—but not one lion.

I was bemoaning this fact with Cézaire over the dinner table in the old Arab town of Usumbura at the northern end of Lake Tanganyika. He and his old Chevvy had taken me over thousands of miles of Africa and the months we had spent together had provided him, he said, with more adventures than he'd had in his previous ten years in Africa. The following morning he was heading back north for Kampala, while I was going to take a boat down the lake, spend some time in Rhodesia and South Africa, and catch the liner *Duilio* from Capetown.

But there was this business of having seen no lions, plus a natural reluctance to end an association and a trip that had meant so much to me.

"The Serengeti Plains—" I said, half to myself. "That would be the place to see lions for sure, I guess. You couldn't *miss* seeing lions in Kenya or Tanganyika—two places I haven't been. Lots of other wonderful animals there, too. It seems a shame when I'm right here in Africa———"

Cézaire, with a light in his eye, produced a road map. We leaned over it, pointing, figuring distances. Even allowing time for repairs to the car and proper outfitting, we could be in the heart of the greatest game country in the world in ten days!

Rhodesia and South Africa suddenly became unimportant places in my mind. I could shorten my itinerary by several weeks there, and I could fly when necessary to make the *Duilio*, on which I had reserved passage from Capetown. That's how I managed to see a lion—indeed a great many lions—on my first trip. But I never expected that my first sight of the king of beasts would come on a black night on a narrow road that seemed to be miles from anywhere. We had gone back to Kampala for tires and car overhaul and other essentials, then driven over dreadful roads to Nairobi, and were on our way to Arusha, in Tanganyika, from which we planned to take off for the Serengeti Plains. We were rather late because of a delayed start from Nairobi and numerous stops or slow-downs to see animals in such numbers as I had never seen before—great herds of fat-rumped zebra, wildebeest, hartebeest and Thomson's gazelles, not to mention a group of about fifteen baboons that crossed the road in front of us and barked at us as if we were trespassers, which I suppose we were.

It was still light when we reached a rhino-hunting camp on the Namanga River operated by a middle-aged English couple with two very lonesome daughters, nineteen and twenty. The owner told us that the night before a number of lions had ganged up to attack a near-by kraal where some Masai herdsmen kept their cattle, eighteen of which were killed.

"You can't help seeing lions around here," he said. "At this time of day, particularly, you will see lions on the road between here and Arusha."

We left at once, to take advantage of all the daylight that might be left, but within half an hour the sun had set and darkness came down quickly, only to be lightened by a big moon that periodically went behind clouds with the effect of dropping a black cloth over us and our surroundings. When it reappeared, we saw quite well—well enough to make out a good-sized herd of giraffe only a few yards from the road. As we approached, they moved away like sedate rocking horses, in complete silence, but only a short distance. They then turned to look at us curiously, as if they could not understand such creatures roaming around in the night. But they showed no real fear.

We left the giraffes behind, and picked up speed slightly as the moonlight showed the road ahead for a reasonable distance. It ran between thick scrub growth of grass, thorn bushes and low twisted trees. When the moon plunged suddenly behind a cloud again, our view was constricted to the narrow shaft of white made by our headlights and the special searchlight Cézaire had improvised for night driving. At that moment of sudden darkness, an immense form plunged from the bush at the right of the road, flashed across in front of the car—actually clearing the hood by no more than a foot—and disappeared on the other side of the road. Cézaire jammed on the brakes, which squealed and raised a cloud of dust, then threw the car into reverse and backed up slowly as we both peered into the bush at the left.

The strong lights finally picked up the creature, and Cézaire maneuvered the car so that they shone squarely on him—a huge male lion with a dark ruffly mane. He just sat there, seven or eight yards off the road, staring at us and blinking his eyes in the bright light. There was neither animosity nor fear in his expression and attitude, but rather surprise and curiosity—pretty much the same feelings we had. Apparently he had been in the bush alongside the road, had spied our lights as we approached, and finally succumbed to that universal African impulse, shared by animals and Africans alike, to leap in front of the car and cross the road.

The lion looked at us and we looked at the lion for several minutes, disproving all theories about animals hating bright lights. Finally he strolled slowly toward us and sniffed our front bumper. Obviously satisfied with his findings, he turned and ambled off down the road gracefully and nonchalantly, swinging his tail languidly.

"Follow him slowly," I told Cézaire.

We crept along about ten or twelve feet behind the big animal. After we'd gone about fifty yards he turned to stare at us. We stopped, and he walked on again, then turned and sauntered off into the bush where he disappeared from view.

Cézaire and I looked at each other. We shook hands, smiling happily.

We drove on slowly, discussing what might have happened if the lion had struck the car instead of missing it by a few inches. Four hundred pounds of leaping lion might have caused considerable damage and if he had injured himself in the act he would have been very nasty. Suddenly Cézaire broke off in the middle of a sentence and pointed. Two lionesses stood near the edge of the road, as if waiting for us to approach. We drew up about fifteen feet away with our bright lights fixed directly on them. These beasts, too, seemed to bask in the light rather than avoid it. And they too showed no animosity—only amazement and curiosity. One turned to the other as if to make a comment, but the second lioness was apparently bored by us. She gave a prodigious yawn which revealed not only her murderous teeth but her lack of fear.

The window on my side of the car was open, and suddenly I was aware of something moving beside me. The short hair on the back of my neck rose before I knew I was frightened, and by the time my eyes and brain took in the fact that a lion had passed close enough for me to touch him, he had moved on ahead into the shaft of light. The big fellow took the center of the stage at once, turned and stared at us.

For no less than five minutes—and that can seem like an eternity in such situations—the lion family stood and looked at us. I knew that we were safe inside the car, so after the first shock of surprise I could devote my whole attention to studying, at unusually close range, these beautiful and supremely confident animals. I could see them breathe, shift position slightly, lift their noses to sniff the night air, turn to one another as if in whispered conversation. Finally one of the lionesses became thoroughly bored, sauntered up to the front of the car to smell it and thus make sure there was nothing she had missed. Her friend followed her, and then they both walked off into the bush without another backward glance. The lion looked at them, looked at us once more, and leaped lightly over a thornbush to follow them.

That was an excellent and unexpected introduction to lions, of course, with only one drawback. At night I could take no pictures. I missed another camera shot on the Serengeti Plains on that first trip when we came upon a pride of seven lions—two males, four females and a toto about six months old —two hundred feet away. The light was right for once, but the lions proved unexpectedly fearful. Not at first. Cézaire stopped the car, and the whole group came up quietly to investigate us more closely. When they were about twenty-five feet from the car, Cézaire snatched up the Leica camera to get a shot. At the movement, six of the pack bounded back up the hill yipping bloody murder and the seventh took off across the plains in the opposite direction, his tail between his legs, yelping like a scared dog.

When I saw the District Commissioner later, I asked him about the cowardly lions. He laughed. "Yes, that's rather unusual," he said, "but I think I can explain it. A few nights ago a large pack of lions attacked a Masai kraal and killed many head of cattle. I sent out some askaris who shot a number of the gang. Probably your seven had been a part of it. When they saw Cézaire raise his arm with the camera, they associated the movement with guns and gunfire, by which their friends had recently been killed. So they took off in a hurry, forgetting all dignity."

On my later trips to Africa, I learned how rare this sight really was. A lion will do almost anything to keep his dignity, to save face. I'm sure, for instance, that the big lion I mentioned in the first chapter, which was being tantalized by so many succulent gazelles, was annoyed as could be. But he would never lower himself to show that annoyance, particularly when it would get him nowhere.

Ace DuPreez, who convinced me on my 1954-55 trip that he not only knows lions but most animals thoroughly, insists that no one should be afraid of a lion.

"If you come upon a lion unexpectedly," he advises, "remember that the lion wants to avoid trouble as much as you do. Give him a chance to retreat gracefully and with dignity, and he'll probably take it. But don't back him into a corner, or what he thinks is a corner, and don't do anything to make him look silly. He's the king and he must act like a king. Once I came upon a lion in the grass, much to the surprise of both of us. The wind was just right so he had no warning that I was near. We stood stock-still staring at each other, about ten feet apart. Then he haughtily turned to one side, going behind a tall anthill as if that were where he had intended going anyway. I was able to peek over the top of the hill, though, which he didn't realize. Just as soon as he thought he was out of sight, he dropped his dignity in a hurry, and ran like a scared rabbit. But I want to warn you—don't depend on a lion's always acting that way."

Here is the universal refrain of everyone who really knows lions—don't depend on it. A lion's actions are unpredictable, and generalizations are dangerous. Allan Tarlton, noted white hunter and expert on snakes, who has killed more than 150 lions, gives the same warning after telling about the time he was hunting guinea fowl with a twenty-two rifle. Walking through the long grass he almost stepped on a lioness suckling two newborn cubs. Now, everyone knows that any wild animal with young is most dangerous, but this lioness just sat up on her haunches, with one cub still clinging hungrily to her breast. Tarlton saw the blazing ferocity in her eyes, the twitch of her tail, but he could do nothing except stand still. His twenty-two was ineffectual against a lion—particularly a lion only eight feet away—and turning to run would have been the most fatal move. He thought he was a goner, but the lioness did not spring. She

stared, and Tarlton stared. When nothing happened to the
lioness or her cubs, the fire died slowly out of her eyes and she
relaxed slightly. Tarlton slowly moved to one side into the grass
and walked away. The lioness looked after him a moment,
then settled herself in the grass again as her cubs went on with
their interrupted meal.

Despite this pleasant experience, Tarlton gravely advises
that no one should take either the tameness or apparent inof-
fensiveness of any lion for granted. He recalls the fact that three
of the lions he has shot were man-eaters and he was requested by
the government to shoot them—as professional hunters are whenever these psychopaths among lions are discovered. They are discovered, of course, only by virtue of the fact that they have
eaten someone, making it too late so far as the digested man is
concerned but not too late for everyone else in the neighborhood. It seems that once a lion has cultivated a taste for human
flesh he is not really satisfied with anything else. So when a lion
kills one person, strenuous efforts are made to hunt him down
and kill him at once, before he can indulge his new appetite further.

Fortunately, man-eating lions are relatively rare—far less
common than sensational Sunday supplement tales or the exag-
gerations of some travelers would lead us to believe. It obviously
is not normal or customary for lions to eat human beings, any
more than it is normal or customary for human beings to murder
other people. You can walk down the street and be perfectly
certain that almost everyone you meet is not a murderer, and
you can go through Africa with equal certainty that almost every
lion you see is not a man-eater. A man-eating lion is a twisted,
warped, abnormal lion. What makes him that way is perhaps
easier to figure out than what makes a man into a murderer, because a lion's life is less complicated than a man's.

For many years the theory was that man-eating lions were
old or sick or lame animals that were not fast enough to catch
their normal prey such as zebras and different varieties of antelope. In these circumstances, they were often driven out of any

group and forced to hunt alone. They turned to domestic animals such as cows as their hunger overcame their natural reluctance to linger around human habitations. In the course of such raids, they might have to kill a man who was trying to protect his herds. With this first taste of human blood and human flesh, the lion was lost to normal ways. Just what makes human meat so tasty has never been explained. But then no one has quite satisfactorily explained what makes alcohol so irresistible to an alcoholic. Perhaps it helps build up the lion's ego.

In any event, the hypothesis about man-eaters being lions unfit for ordinary lion life no doubt holds good in many cases, but it does not explain the man-eaters that are occasionally shot who turn out to be strong males in the prime of life, obviously capable of catching zebra or topi or wildebeest.

But perhaps there are not many zebra or topi or wildebeest around that season. Lions are not long-distance travelers, like the elephants, and like to stay within a large area that they consider their own. If for some reason—drought, migration, or the conversion of wild land to farm land—the natural food supply of the lion is considerably diminished, some few beasts will turn to whatever animals are at hand for their meals—cattle or humans. In many sections of Kenya and Tanganyika, the last few decades have seen a vast extension of settled agricultural areas. The herds of antelopes and zebras move farther away; many lions move along with them, but others are reluctant to leave their old haunts. Thus civilization tends to make lions into man-eaters.

The most famous man-eaters were very definitely connected with the advent of civilization. The man-eaters of Tsavo held up construction of the railroad from the coast into the interior of East Africa in 1899 because they ate so many of the workers. Colonel J. H. Paterson, who eventually wiped them out, felt that the laborers might have started the whole thing because they did not bother to bury properly a few men who had died on the job of natural causes. Although ordered to take the bodies into the bush and bury them deep, the workers just left them in the tall grass or among the thornbushes. Along came some lions, ate this flesh someone had left out for them and liked it. They wanted more of the same and went looking for it, even to the extent of occasionally dragging a screaming African from tent or hut.

But if civilization has perhaps created man-eating tendencies among lions, so has this custom of refraining from burial of their dead. Many tribes of Africa *do* bury their dead, but the Masai and others in the big-game areas do not. They apparently have no sentimental feeling about the body of a person and find that the most convenient way of disposing of it quickly and efficiently is to leave it outside the village for the vultures, hyenas and jackals to take care of. Occasionally a lion finds the body first, eats, and may go haywire.

It is not known, of course, that all lions who have once tasted human flesh gain an insatiable appetite for more of the same. There may be many lions who try it and don't like it, or others who eat one meal and go back to zebra as if there were no difference between the two meats. But it is best to assume that one taste is enough to change the lion, for it has been proven that a man-eater in a certain area will go on making human kills every few nights until he is shot.

Happily, I never, to my knowledge, encountered a man-eater. On my 1954-55 trip, when we were going to Ifakara, a Wadamba village on the Kilombero River, to film the native harpooning of hippos, we learned that five natives had been killed by man-eating lions shortly before, one of them within a hundred yards of a Church Mission. I was glad that we were not searching for lion pictures there and that the beasts were not likely to appear near the hippo-infested river. I think that we would have abandoned lion filming in any area in which I heard a report about man-eaters. It is one thing to approach on foot within twenty feet of a normal lion who would look upon me as little more that a prying nuisance, and quite another to move up close to a lion that might consider me as a great delicacy.

Actually, the danger of encountering a man-eater never entered my head when I was out in the field looking for lions to photograph. But there was always the chance that a lion might be in pain or a foul temper from any of numerous causes—an ul-cerating tooth, porcupine quills in his footpads, a lost girl-friend or a plain stomach-ache. Certainly lions must be subject to moods like people, though cause and effect may be simpler and more direct. You do run into a nasty-tempered lion on occasion, ready to slash at mate, friend or annoying man with camera. Such beasts are called by the natives *kali*. They are not psychopaths as are the man-eaters, or rogues that seem to have gone completely crazy. No, they are just bad-tempered animals—at least bad-tempered at the moment. And they are not to be trifled with.

Sometimes I could sense when an animal was *kali*, but I did not rely on my own judgment. A look in the eye, a twitch of the tail, a kind of nervous tension would give me warning. Then I'd look at Mafuta, if he had not already cautioned me. Mafuta could always tell. He even scowled and looked bad-tempered himself, as if sharing the animal's emotions. With a shake of the head and a muttered *"Kali,"* he would warn me off, and I would decide not to get out of the truck to get a close-up of this particular beast.

Does all this mean that if a lion is not a man-eater, not wounded and not *kali*, he is safe? No, unfortunately. It may mean precisely that nine times out of ten, or even twenty-four times out of twenty-five—but not always. That one other time a lion will act contrary to expectations despite the lack of any reason discernible to man. Of course, the lion itself has a reason for charging, ignoring or retreating—a reason that makes sense to him. The fact that we cannot foresee or understand it is of no concern to the lion.

Personally, I have an idea that sometimes when a lion charges without apparent reason he is just plain sick of being pestered. Human beings creeping up close when he wants to sleep or make love or eat or just lie there enjoying the scenery must often seem annoying as the devil. I can understand why an otherwise peaceful and contented lion would suddenly lash out.

In general, however, lions are singularly tolerant and even

amiable creatures. They are intelligent and adaptable. Their adaptability accounts for some of the apparent contradictions in the stories one hears and reads about them. The lions that appear friendliest, tamest and consequently easiest to photograph are those which have seen almost nothing of man or a great deal of man. In the latter category are those Cézaire and I saw that night on the way to Arusha and those I encountered for my best pictures from the first trip, some time later. I had said goodbye to Cézaire in Arusha and hired a Ford with a Kikuyu driver to take me to Dodoma, where I could catch the plane south for Northern Rhodesia. So far as I was concerned, my experiences and filming in the big-game regions had ended. We were going along the road at a good clip when I saw a lion lying under a tree up ahead, a splendid specimen with a rare black mane. He was finishing a zebra dinner all alone, and looked inquiringly up at us as we stopped the car about thirty yards from him. The sky was overcast, and there was not enough light for me to get good pictures at that distance, especially since he was in the shade of the tree, but we didn't dare move closer. The driver was too frightened, even though he should have known he was safe in the car, and I was afraid that I would drive the lion away. Perhaps if we waited he would eventually come to us out of curiosity.

When the lion saw that we were standing still and making no noise, he went back to his munching, looking up at us occasionally to make sure we were still behaving ourselves. We had shut the motor off and could hear the crunch of bones as he worked on the short ribs. It was obvious that he was no longer ravenous, but he didn't want to leave too much for the vultures which were circling closer and closer, occasionally landing ten or fifteen feet away and casting nervous eyes first at the lion and then at us.

For half an hour we sat there as the great beast finished his meal in leisurely fashion. Finally our patience was rewarded, for he rose slowly to his feet, took one last lick at the zebra, and feinted toward two vultures to scare them away. Then he walked diagonally across toward us, his belly so full that he had to move slowly. I could see the mouth and paws that dripped with blood and at that moment he was not so beautiful. But I leaned out of the window, trained the camera on him, and pressed the button. He turned into the road and padded along, away from us, very sedately. I told the driver to follow along behind, which he reluctantly did. The lion did not even turn around as the car started up but kept on his way. The light was just right and I felt sure I was getting exactly what I wanted. Suddenly he wheeled about, opened his jaws wide, and let out a combined yawn and roar.

My driver, scared almost white, threw the car into reverse so violently that it almost leaped backwards and spoiled my shooting of the last half of the long yawn-roar. I know the lion was not angry. For one thing, lions seldom are after they have eaten their fill. This one was merely expressing his satisfaction with the good dinner he'd enjoyed, as some humans do quite noisily. In a moment he continued on his way, although a bit off the road, and for a time we traveled parallel, only a few yards apart. I kept the camera going a good deal of the time, and finally he vanished into the bush.

I felt quite elated with this extra dividend, and then about an hour later the car rounded a turn and almost bumped into a pride of lions basking in the sun—one male, three females and a half-grown cub. They lifted their heads to gaze at us, but did not stir.

"Go ahead, slowly," I told the boy.

"Oh no, *Bwana*, no!" he protested.

"Yes," I insisted.

He put the car into low gear and inched forward. The lions were aware of our gradual approach, but did not seem perturbed. I started photographing through the windshield, but the boy stopped about fifty feet from the lions. "Go ahead," I ordered, and we moved to twenty-five feet. "Farther!" I muttered, though the driver was sweating and mumbling protests or prayers to himself. At about fifteen feet we stopped. The

lions were still lying down, still contemplating us indifferently
—all except the toto that was snarling furiously at us. The rest
of them were not even very interested. After we had remained
still for a few minutes they turned their heads away, and one
lioness, lazy and contented, closed her eyes and dozed off.

Another lioness, farther away and thus unable to see us
very well, rose and started walking toward us, although not
bothering to look directly at us. I still felt relatively safe as she
approached the car, but took the precaution of jerking in the
camera and rolling up the window. She walked right past without paying the slightest attention and disappeared in the bush.

Encouraged by this, I told the driver to edge up even closer,
very slowly. Against his better judgment, he did so, until we
were no more than four feet from the nearest female. I opened
the window and stuck out the camera, training it directly on her.
At the whirr of its starting, she looked up at me and screwed up
her eyes slightly as if wondering what this was all about. There
was a calm and friendly, though aloof, expression in her eyes,
and I could almost have said that she smiled slightly.

After taking all the movie footage I could possibly use, I
picked up the Leica and made some stills. Finally the male
stood up slowly and started off in the bush, the others following
him. They were thoroughly unconcerned and disdainful.

As time goes on, more and more people are enjoying such
experiences in Africa in the great reserves and parks that have
been created. The lions in Kruger Park have long been known
to act pretty much like the bears in Yellowstone Park, and
those near Nairobi are fast becoming as indifferent to the presence of men in automobiles. The Serengeti Plains, where so
many big-game hunters have bagged their beautiful lion trophies, are now a restricted area, with lions protected. And it
doesn't take lions—or any other animals—very long to realize
they are in a safe place. Occasionally, of course, some foolish
person is beguiled by the placid lions into thinking they are completely tame. He gets out of his car, contrary to regulations, and
goes up too close. Even then, the lion is most likely to move away

but he may become annoyed and maul the human pest. It doesn't take much mauling by a lion for a person to wind up with broken neck and a stomach slashed to ribbons.

A man outside a car is not at all the same thing to a lion as a man inside one. It actually seems, in fact, as if the lion looks upon the automobile as one creature with which, in certain areas, it has become familiar.

I said that the least dangerous lions are those either most accustomed to man or least familiar with him. I meant in the first connection those accustomed to men not trying to kill lions, of course—in other words, the lions in parks and reserves and restricted areas where they are protected. But what about the lions that have had almost no contact with man, good or bad? One might think that they would be particularly savage, attacking this strange new creature immediately when he first stepped into Simba's land. That assumes an innate ferocity in the lion, which just does not exist. Except for the very rare rogues and the occasional big cats with toothaches or such, lions apparently haven't got anything against anybody. They haven't even got anything against the zebra they stalk; that animal represents necessary food just as a steer means steak and roast beef to us. Maybe the steer thinks men are fierce and mean, but we don't have any such feelings toward the animal, of course. We're just hungry.

When a lion is not hungry, he is a thoroughly inoffensive animal. The most conclusive proof of this comes from the actions of zebras, wildebeest, and other favorite dishes of the king of beasts. I've mentioned the lion being teased by various species of antelopes. I have also seen, on many occasions, herds of topi, wildebeest, hartebeest, zebra, and "Tommies" grazing placidly within seventy-five feet of a pride of lions. They did not even bother to keep their eyes on their most bitter enemies. The lions were full of food and the prey knew it. When the lions moved around, I could see their bulging bellies that made them walk slowly. They could not run fast if they tried but— more important—they had no desire to run after a zebra and bring it down. What would they do with it? A lion does not kill for the fun of it, as many leopards obviously do. He isn't interested in killing, only in getting a meal when he needs it.

I believe that antelopes and other lion prey know through a sense of smell when a lion is satisfied, when he is hungry. The glandular activity of a lion digesting a big meal is certainly different from that of a hungry lion getting ready for a quiet stalk and a flying charge. In any event, the lion's prey knows when he is dangerous and when he isn't.

As for the animals which are not considered edible by the lion, they show no fear of the king of beasts. A hyena will keep out of a lion's way because lions obviously don't like hyenas. But they never kill hyenas and would not dream of eating their flesh. When these scavengers come too close before a lion has finished eating, the big cat will take a swipe at the hyena or make a short charge to drive him away, but that's only because the hyena is a pest. On the other hand, lions seem to like jackals and have been reported sometimes to toss them bits of meat while they are still eating. Lions have fun chasing vultures away from the remains, but they never try to kill the birds.

Lions do not make a habit of picking fights with other animals—and rarely fight bitterly with each other. Even in competition for a beautiful lioness at mating time, male lions almost never do battle for her favors. Instead, they seem to follow the sensible procedure of leaving the matter up to her and the one not chosen goes off to look for another young lady. Or he may just hang around and wait his turn, for lions are polygamous, and a lioness is generally willing to mate with several males in succession. And a male lion may have a harem—or share one with another male. That's why you will find prides of one male and three females, or two males and four females, or in almost any combination.

Two male lions of about the same age often form very close friendships, too, hunting and palling around together for a long period. There are, of course, similar evidences of deep devotion between male and female over quite a time, but these should not lead people to believe that all lions have family lives comparable to those of human beings.

Although the photographing of wild animals has begun to supplant the killing of them only in recent years, a few men were primarily interested in pictures as far back as the turn of the century. If they traveled far enough to get away from European towns and the villages of lion-hunting natives, and if they stayed long enough for the lions to become accustomed to them, they enjoyed remarkable experiences. An example is Paul L. Hoefler, who in the twenties found himself in some good lion country that had not been extensively hunted. He and his companions came upon a group of lions near a water hole and a clump of shady trees. They were busy eating and did not seem too disturbed at the approach of men, so Hoefler contented himself with photographing them from a distance, with a telephoto lens.

The next day the men returned and came a little closer, still being careful not to annoy or disturb the lions in any way. They killed a zebra and left it for the lions, came a little closer the following day, still taking pictures. For several weeks Hoefler spent almost every day with the lions, and it was soon obvious that the lions had accepted the men as completely harmless features of the landscape. There were six females—one with cubs— and two males in the group, each with distinctive personality. The leader of the group, at least in courage and initiative, was a lioness—and this seems generally to be the case. I've always found that a lioness will come up closest, will make the first move, will display the greatest curiosity and confidence. She is usually the one to make a kill, too, with her mate tagging along behind.

The lions performed regularly for Hoefler's camera, playing among the rocks, teaching the cubs, making love and obviously living exactly the kind of life that lions live with no men and cameras around. By the clever placing of the meat he brought for them, he was able to get them to perform pretty much as he wished, even to the point of having them climb trees—which lions were always supposed not to be able to do.

Some of his photographing was done from a blind, or *boma*, made of thorn bushes, with a couple of peepholes for cameras. He filmed lions fighting over a carcass when they were quite hungry—and licking each other in friendly fashion after the meal as if to say that they had not really meant anything unpleasant by fighting. The boldest lioness used to approach the boma and stand on tiptoe to look through one of the apertures, just to make sure Hoefler was there. And always, after they left and were driving away in their truck, the men saw all the lions go up for a look inside.

They were always aware of the men's presence but were neither afraid nor angry after the first few days. Hoefler had conclusive proof that the lions were selective and intelligent in this behavior, however, and did not extend their acceptance to all men. One day while photographing the lions near the water hole, the man saw them stop their actions, lift their noses and quickly but quietly hide in the nearby grass—and a lion can hide effectively in a spot which, as Hoefler puts it, "a rabbit would scorn."

In a few minutes Hoefler saw the reason for the lions' retreat—three lion-hunting, spear-carrying Masai warriors came over the hill. When these men had passed by and were out of sight, the lions came out of the grass and went about their business.

In spite of these amiable relations with lions, Hoefler never felt that he could predict their behavior so that he felt absolutely safe. Once when he was filming the group from only about fifteen feet—the lions were eating—a female looked up, lashed her tail, snarled, and made a rush at him. He was frozen with fear, but the lioness suddenly stopped about six feet in front of him—he could feel her hot breath—turned around and went back to her meal. He could not explain what had made her rush at him in the first place or what had made her stop. And he repeats that the only thing certain about a lion is its uncertainty.

Most of the early lion hunters had no such concept of the lion as Hoefler presented. They looked upon the lion as a vicious, bloody, vindictive killer that went out looking for trouble and usually found it. They went to kill lions, not to study or understand them. Before the turn of the century, rifles were often not as accurate nor bullets as powerful as those of today, so many lions were just wounded at the first shot. Now everyone agrees that there is nothing much more angry and devastating than a wounded lion. The pain infuriates him, his pride is wounded as deeply as his body. His bloodstream is filled with a sudden great outpouring from his adrenal glands so that his muscles are activated to overpowering strength. He can leap twenty or twenty-five feet at one bound, and his speed over a short distance is almost incredible.

Most of the early hunters had such a creature coming for them at one time or another, and they very naturally concluded that the lion was the most deadly and bloodthirsty beast ever created. They did not understand the lion's insatiable curiosity, either. When they camped out in lion country they built up thick thorn walls around their camps at night, and kept fires burning. The lions, wandering out at dusk, wondered about this new feature on the landscape and went to investigate. Finding a thorn wall in their way served only to intensify their curiosity, just as it would with human beings. The lions found a way under or over or through the thorns and started sniffing around. A sleepy guard screamed, somebody grabbed a gun and shot it, and both lions and men went into a panic in which somebody got hurt. So the hunters concluded that lions were so vicious they would do anything to get at men and kill them.

Nowadays nobody builds a wall around his camp or keeps fires going. I have heard lions padding around my tent at night, sniffing and looking carefully until their curiosity was satisfied, then going quietly away. I will admit that I felt a little uneasy, but I don't think the more experienced professional hunters in the party did.

Most of the lions I have encountered and photographed fall in the category of those which have had enough unpleasant experience with men to be afraid and not too friendly.

There is always danger in such circumstances, of course, but no one gets authentic wild animal pictures without taking risks. I took chances but was never really foolhardy, and for lion filming I was usually covered by professional hunters. They were remarkable men—expert marksmen and canny about the ways of wild animals. On my 1946 trip I enjoyed the protection and companionship of several well-known white hunters, among them Lionel Hartley, younger brother of Carr Hartley, who later died in a small plane crash.

Although most of my time with Lionel Hartley was spent in trying to get moving pictures of a rhino chasing me up a tree, we saw many other animals in the rugged country around the Tsavo district. When I arrived in Mtito Andei, for example, I found a note from Diane Hartley telling me that she and her husband had suddenly been called away to clear a road where elephants had been knocking trees down to get at the leaves. There had been a drought in the area and the only green leaves left were high—but not too high for the elephants, who just uproot trees to get at branches out of their reach. They don't care if they leave the trunks scattered across a road.

Diane Hartley often went hunting with her husband. Once they were called out to shoot a man-eating lion which had killed several tribesmen. They tracked the lion down and Lionel shot him, but the bullet lodged in the big lion's chest and he just tore off into the bush. A lion can carry an astounding amount of lead in him before he falls, but it makes him furious. The inviolable rule of all white hunters, however, is to find and kill any animal that has been wounded. This is the moment of greatest danger for a hunter, for wounded animals hide in good cover, lying in wait for their attacker. This man-eater did precisely that, and sprang at Lionel from a short distance. The hunter had no time to shoot, and would have been dead in a moment but for the fact that the lion's wound somehow disturbed the accuracy of its charge. Its body grazed a tree in mid-air, which made him miss Hartley by inches. Before he could turn to renew his attack, Mrs.

Hartley, who was bringing up the rear, shot the beast in the neck for the kill.

But that was not the end of their close shave. They had their native boys take the big lion back to their camp, where they skinned it and hung the hide on a tree to dry. When darkness fell, the Hartleys went to sleep. They had no tent, but slept under a mosquito netting. The man-eater's mate, which had probably never been far away from the goings-on, came close to the camp, sniffed around the skin of her loved one and began to growl in anger. This didn't wake the Hartleys, but their two dogs then started barking and rushing at the lioness to drive her off. The Hartleys jumped up, grabbed their guns, and saw the angry lioness about to charge in spite of the harassing dogs. At sight of the humans with guns, however, she dashed off before the Hartleys could get in a shot. They were both certain that but for the dogs the lioness would have charged them in their sleep and they would have been killed before they could think of defending themselves. The mate of a man-eater is very likely to be a man-eater too.

For the lion pictures on the 1946 trip I spent some time in the wild country west of Narok, in Kenya, not far from the Tanganyika border. The white hunter assigned to me was David Sheldrick, who was to succeed Lionel Hartley as Game Warden at Tsavo when the latter was killed. Sheldrick and his friend Mark Williams had been ready to set out on a busman's holiday hunting trip of their own when Sheldrick got the assignment. Williams, left with nothing to do, asked if he could come along. So I had the help of two professional hunters, not to mention the famous gun-bearer Mafuta.

We traveled in a truck and a safari wagon, with open sides and a hatch in the top to facilitate filming. The first night we camped out, two lions wandered in and padded around our tents but caused no trouble. Our first difficulty with an animal came the next day, but with a buffalo rather than a lion. We were looking for a place to make camp, and saw a grove of acacia and candelabra euphorbia trees. Sheldrick, Mafuta, and I were in the open-sided safari car and Sheldrick drove right into the grove between the trees, looking for a good spot. About twenty feet in, the growth closed ahead of us and we could go no further. As we looked back to turn around, we saw a huge buffalo, about fifteen feet to one side, glaring at us angrily.

"If he charges, he could cause trouble hitting us broadside," Sheldrick said. "He is a very big one." Mafuta agreed that this was an unusually large buffalo, probably an old fellow that had been thrown out of his herd because of age or cantankerousness. Buffaloes are almost never seen alone in other circumstances.

The buffalo lowered his head, pawed slightly at the ground, but David quickly threw the truck into reverse and backed it around toward the buffalo, confronting the animal with our solid rear end rather than our open side. The idea of attack was psychologically sound, too, for the old buffalo was obviously startled. Startled enough, at any rate, to turn and trot away.

We made camp and ate our evening meal. When the sun set it became very cold, as it often does in spite of hot days on the veldt near the equator, and we needed a fire and sweaters. The next morning we were out early looking for lions and found three within twenty minutes—a male and two females lying under an acacia tree. Sheldrick suggested that we should get some bait to entice them into the open and into some action for filming, so we went off looking for animals. This was an easy task, for in this country there were herds of zebra, topi, wildebeest, hartebeest, giraffe, Thomson's gazelles, eland and other animals almost everywhere one looked. We found a herd of topi and Mark Williams shot one. Strange as it may seem, it was the first animal I had seen shot in all my travels, and it gave me a sickening feeling.

The topi is not the most beautiful or appealing of the many species of antelope, for its sloping haunches give a humorous impression. But it is a graceful and inoffensive animal, with the usual big eyes of the antelope tribe. Mark's first shot didn't finish it off, and it tried to get up, while the other topi in the herd raced off some distance. I noticed one of them which did not run as far as the others but stood and watched its friend, or possibly its mate, struggling to its feet. Mark shot a second time and the animal went down, and Mafuta ran up to put the animal out of its misery with his knife. He then expertly cut off one leg for food—topi steaks are quite good—and we tied a chain from the truck around the remains of the carcass to haul it off toward the lions. During the whole procedure, the other topi looked on dolefully. This added to my unhappiness, and my stomach was uneasy for a time, but I realized this was part of the business and said nothing.

By the time we started to drag the topi across the plain the vultures were circling above and following us. We drove the truck as close to the tree sheltering the lions as we could without chasing them away, then hitched the chain to a small tree in the open, where the lions could both see and smell the meat. We retired a short distance, waiting for them to come out and eat. But they would not come.

"They must have eaten recently," Sheldrick said. "They aren't hungry."

The vultures circled lower and finally skidded to an awkward landing about ten feet away from the carcass. They knew the lions were watching, and kept their eyes on the beasts. We all hoped that the sight of the vultures at the carcass would bring the lions out, but they just lay under their tree as if enjoying the sight. In disgust, we headed back for camp to have lunch, and by the time we returned the vultures had finished off the topi. The lions were asleep and merely lifted their heads when they heard us approach. I was not interested in taking pictures of lions resting in the shade of a tree.

There are at least a dozen such attempts for every shot one actually takes of lions—and then only a few of the shots are worth putting in a feature film. In spite of the fact that we were in a rather isolated area and that the years of the war had considerably curtailed all big-game hunting, we had a difficult time finding lions for a time. While out looking for them, however, we had many spectacular sights to enjoy and some to film. Once we came upon a herd of about three hundred zebra which stampeded at our approach. Thundering across the plains and raising a cloud of dust, they were a breath-taking sight and I thought we had some good pictures. But these films were later lost. I did manage to get a fine shot of a herd of giraffe moving swiftly but sedately across the flat land. The light was just right, and the giraffe, though some distance away, were clearly seen against the bright blue sky and white cumulus clouds. You'd think that a running giraffe might be the most awkward thing in the world, but actually he is graceful in a dignified way, rocking along in a slow rhythm that deceives one as to speed. These shots turned out well and were included in "Savage Splendor." Later I filmed more excellent giraffe shots, as a large group stampeded in single file against a lovely mountain background. It was a real joy to take such photographs and made up for the repeated frustrations in connection with lions.

One day we chased a warthog in the truck, trying to get close enough to film it well, when it suddenly turned and charged at us. Since a warthog is not a very pugnacious animal, and certainly not very destructive, we were all caught completely by surprise. The warthog's move was just a feint, but it served its purpose. We jammed on the brakes, and the animal veered off into the bush, escaping. I was reminded of a story Carl Akeley told about a half-grown warthog that managed to escape from a lioness. This seems incredible, but the lioness was old and heavy and rather slow. Still, she should have been able to get the little pig easily. He eluded her by veering to one side every time she was set to spring, and finally winded her so much —the lion is never fast on the long haul—that he got completely away.

Another time we raced a cheetah in the truck. Since this member of the cat family is probably the fastest creature in the world for a short distance, we didn't have much chance. The cheetah is not really dangerous because it has rather blunt claws like a dog's rather than the usual sharp sabres of the lion and leopard. I've seen young Mike Hartley grab one by its tail when it was climbing up a tree.

Holding a wild animal by its tail looks silly, but almost all men who really know animals grab for any beast's tail in an emergency. They claim that if they keep tugging on the tail for all they're worth the animal cannot get set to spring, cannot keep its proper balance for any sort of attack, cannot kick or claw with top effectiveness. It seemed to work whenever we witnessed the efforts of a group of men trying to get an obstreperous wild animal into a cage or truck at Carr Hartley's place.

After many days spent looking for lions or trying to entice them into action in a good light, we were rewarded by finding a pride of five lions, including two males with beautiful manes, among a small cluster of trees. We found a herd of wildebeest near by, shot one, and brought it back near the lions. There was no tree to tie it to, but we left it in the open not far from the lions and retired in the truck. Several lions came out almost immediately, chased away the approaching vultures, and started to feed. We edged up in the truck with both cameras going. We got a good shot of a female, annoyed at the vultures which had returned, chasing them away.

As we came closer and closer, the lions kept looking up nervously, and we decided that if we went further they might bolt. After all this time we didn't want to lose out, but I was disappointed at our distance from the big cats. I decided to go closer on foot, and told David Sheldrick and Mafuta to cover me.

The lions didn't pay much attention when I stepped from the truck, but they began to glance up as I moved slowly toward them, stopping to film them occasionally. I was happy to hear the whirr of the camera in the truck behind me, for I knew the cameraman was getting both me and the lions on his film. When I was about twenty feet away, all the lions looked up at once from their carcass, blood dripping from their jowls. Obviously the lions did not like my close approach. I don't know if they thought I wanted to take their meat away from them or kill them, but they were obviously seriously annoyed. At such moments you have no way of knowing if the lions are going to go on eating, retreat, or charge. If the decision is the last, it happens in about one second.

There was nothing I could do about it but freeze absolutely still. My blood was so chilled that I don't think I could have done anything else anyway, which is fortunate.

I knew that David and Mafuta both had their big guns trained on the lions, ready to shoot the instant one of them made a move toward me. But could they handle five lions? Luckily, five lions rarely charge at once. One of them, probably a female, would have been the first. Perhaps even two would have come for me at once while the others stood by waiting. Thus the hunters, both with double-barreled rifles, might have been able to take care of four lions before they could get to me, provided each one shot at a different lion each time instead of ganging up on one or two.

But there was no need to test their ability to get four or all of the lions. A second or two after the whirring of the camera stopped, one lioness lowered her head and sank her fangs in the wildebeest's haunch. The other lions looked down at her and decided not to let her have all of it. They went back to their meal, apparently forgetting all about me.

I breathed normally again, then slowly backed up until I was far enough away to turn and get into the truck. In about five minutes I began to feel the thrill of the adventure course through my veins instead of the cold sludge that had been there a short while before.

After that our luck turned and we got more lion pictures. One day vultures in the sky led us to a spot where a pride of eight lions were feasting on a zebra they had killed. Another time we came upon a fine lioness with a cub about six months old. They retreated into the edge of the bush at our approach, and we saw other lions there without being able to count how many. I came up quite close to the lioness and her cub, filming them within eighteen or twenty feet.

Hoping to get the rest of the cats into the open we went for bait and put it nearby. This time we brought two carcasses and placed them about twenty feet apart. We hoped that lions would go to one, vultures to the other, and that some of the lions might run back and forth chasing the vultures away. This would make a good sequence if we could manage it.

Only the lioness came out to the bait, however, while the rest remained in the cover. When vultures attacked the other carcass, the lioness didn't bother to chase them. If she was so tolerant of vultures, I decided she would tolerate a cameraman, so went on foot to within about fifteen feet without seeming to disturb her. Apparently I was downwind and she was so busy eating that she wasn't even aware of me, for when she suddenly looked up and saw me, she was obviously astonished.

Astonishment was quickly replaced by anger, and I saw what Tarlton had meant when he spoke of the fire in an angry lion's eyes. There were burning flames in those two steady orbs fixed upon me. She raised her tail in the air and twitched it angrily twice. This really made me freeze, for I had always been told that three twitches of the tail was the prelude to a charge. Maybe so, but she gave only two twitches. We stared at each other for fifteen seconds that seemed like minutes. Then the angry young lady decided to go back in the bush with her cub. As soon as she was there I retreated hastily to the truck. When I could talk again I turned to my cameraman and said, "That must have been just about the best shot yet of man and lion together."

"Oh—I didn't get it," he said. "I was too scared."

Gazelles and other prey of lions are much easier to film than lions themselves, but no matter how beautiful they are, they are not dramatic enough to take over major roles in a feature film. They are, however, among the most satisfying and thrilling sights in all Africa, for most of them live and travel in herds. I have been reading for years about how the vast herds of animals in Africa are disappearing. A book published in 1900 states that the antelope herds are not what they used to be. An-

other book published in 1910 deplores the fact that the big
herds are no more. Ten years later we read the same thing
about 1910, and so on to the present day.

I have no doubt that these animals have been thinned out
considerably, but I think they have retreated rather than disappeared. You have to travel farther from towns to see many big
herds. Perhaps many herds are smaller, too, though I think that
few people ever saw a bigger one than the three hundred zebra
that stampeded before my eyes in 1946.

The greatest thrill of African animals is their variety. Just
think of the kinds of antelope I have seen in my travels there—
without specially searching for them. The reddish-coated hartebeest with curved and pointed horns; the big and ungainly
wildebeest (the gnu of crossword puzzles) with horns that curve
down and out, and with long hair on the throat that makes him
look bearded; the shiny-coated, slope-haunched topi; the little
solitary duiker, which really means diver, so called from its
sudden graceful dives into thick brush; the agile rock-climbing
klipspringer, only about two or two and a half feet tall; the
tawny oribi with straight horns; the rabbit-sized dik-dik, so
swift that you can scarcely see him when he puts on steam; the
large waterbuck that likes to live along the banks of streams
and is a good swimmer; its relative, the bushbuck, smaller and
swifter; another small relative found primarily in Uganda and
called the kob; the good-sized oryx with long straight horns sloping back over the forehead; the long-necked gerenuk with
thick horns; the medium-sized impala, prodigious jumper with
particularly graceful curved horns; the big eland, sometimes
running as much as fifteen hundred pounds; the situtunga which
spends most of its time in the water with only head and horns
above the surface and whose hooves are specially elongated to
enable it to walk in soft mud; the steinbuck or stembok; the
kudu, of which I have seen only that called the lesser and not
the greater; the bongo, probably biggest of all East African antelopes; and finally those loveliest of all antelopes, Grant's and
Thomson's gazelles.

All these are meat for lions, although he has his preferences among them. The waterbuck is not very palatable, the dik-dik is not a mouthful, and even the "Tommies" offer so little meat as to be scarcely worth a chase unless there is nothing else around. Aside from the larger antelopes, lions love ostriches and zebras.

Lions are not the only enemies the various antelopes have, of course. The smaller gazelles are favorite dishes for cheetah, hyenas and wild dogs. And leopards will eat almost anything— even the meat of the hyena.

Leopards love dog meat, too, as well as other domesticated animals. So they often hang around close to villages, which they raid with regularity. Leopards are not particularly impressed by men, or afraid of them, although they will usually avoid contact if they can. Many leopards, however, will attack a nearby human without any apparent provocation, and leopards like to kill for the pleasure of it. A lion always eats what he kills, even if he doesn't finish it, but a leopard will kill and just leave the victim lying there. His favorite food is baboon meat, which brings up a problem in the economy of many areas. Baboons are a nuisance and a destructive menace. So are leopards. If you kill off the leopards, baboons multiply by the hundreds and drive everyone crazy. If you let the leopards live to keep down the baboons, they will steal your dogs, your cattle and maybe your children.

In spite of the fact that leopards are among the most beautiful of all four-footed animals, I don't like or admire them, as I do lions. They are vindictive, bloodthirsty, swift and cunning —a real challenge to hunters with either cameras or guns. Vivid testimony to this effect was given me on my last trip by Edgar de Bono, a white hunter. For a time he was interested in night hunting—for what reason I cannot imagine except that it is more difficult and dangerous and thus gives a greater thrill. He decided once, while in good leopard country in Eritrea, to hunt leopards at night. He fixed a flashlight securely to his rifle so that its beams covered the front sight on the barrel and the game at which the gun was aimed. The gun-bearer had a similarly equipped gun for the second weapon.

De Bono was in thick bush country when he sighted a leopard, which he was able to approach within twenty-five feet. He aimed and fired—and was enveloped in complete darkness as he heard a screech of pain from the leopard. The recoil of the gun had knocked the flashlight out of commission, and there de Bono stood, listening to the howling and thrashing leopard—which could see quite well in the dark—a few feet in front of him. He started to retreat toward his gun-bearer, who suddenly cried, "He's coming!" De Bono fired the second barrel of his rifle blindly in the dark, felt a huge form crash down on top of him. Pinned to the ground by the leopard he expected claws to slash him to ribbons. But no claws slashed. There was no movement of the leopard.

De Bono wriggled out from under the beast, and by that time the gun-bearer was there with his flashlight. The last shot, fired in the dark, had gone through the leopard's brain, killing him instantly in mid-air.

Edgar de Bono did no more night hunting after that.

XI

Tough Customers with Thick Hides

I WENT to Africa in time to see Lutembe. The grand old girl was dead when I returned in 1946, or at least she was presumed to be dead since she no longer came when called. For at least three generations this famous crocodile had never failed to answer to her name.

You think of wild animals in African game reserves as being somewhat tame, but I doubt that anyone will find there a friendly crocodile. All animals and humans seem to dislike the creatures, and white men have carried on a war of extermination for several decades—a war that has apparently exterminated very few crocodiles.

Lutembe, however, was different. I heard about her in 1937 at Kampala, Uganda, and made a detour to the little fishing village of Dewe, on the shores of Lake Victoria, primarily to confirm my skepticism about this fabulous pet. I half expected to find a stuffed crocodile skin or at best a toothless old beast in an enclosure. But there was no phony crocodile on hand, when I found its native master. He said he'd have to call Lutembe, which he would be happy to do for a modest tip.

Gathering up an armful of dried fish, the native led the way to the shore, where he looked out over the broad waters of the lake and saw precisely what I saw—not a sign of a crocodile. But this did not seem to daunt him. He merely cupped his hands to his mouth and shouted loud and long, "Lutembe!"

The name echoed over the choppy waves. I felt silly,

waiting for someone to bring forth a crocodile from the lake,
just by calling its name. But I would see the farce through, I
said to myself.

The young man called again, louder this time. Still nothing could be seen. He shouted louder, "Lutembe! Lu — tem —
be!"

This went on for five minutes, and I finally shifted uneasily.
The man turned to me and with a gesture and a slight frown told
me plainly that I must have a little patience. I summoned some
patience and squelched my mounting doubts. For ten minutes,
the call to Lutembe rang out over the lake. Finally the young
man pointed triumphantly to a spot far out on the water, and
turned to me with a smile. At first I could see nothing but then
I noticed a commotion in the water, as if someone were swimming vigorously. In a few more minutes I definitely saw the
snout that ploughed through the waves directly toward us. As
it approached the shore I saw the moving tail, the big jaws and
the serrated hide of a crocodile. The beast heaved itself out of
the water and lumbered toward the man. I stood a few feet
away, behind the pile of fish, filming the incredible perform-
ance.

The crocodile looked huge and hideous to me—it was about
fourteen feet long, I believe—especially when it opened its
cavernous mouth and I saw its sharp teeth. I thought it was
glancing hungrily in my direction, but I soon realized its interest lay in the fish behind which I stood. The young fellow
reached for a fish, thrust it in the croc's gaping jaws, his hand
coming within inches of the teeth that chomped down on the
morsel. Fish after fish went into the bottomless pit. Finally the
creature's master took hold of the crocodile's tail affectionately
and sat down on it. One swish, I thought, and he would have
been tossed far into the lake.

"How old is he?" I asked.

"She, *Bwana*," the boy replied.

"Well, I don't see how you know, but *she*, then. How old
is she?"

"Five kings, *Bwana*—Kamanya, Suna, Mutesa, Mwango, and Daudi Chwa."

I had no idea how long Buganda kings normally lived, but I found out later that this span would be about a century and a quarter. While this seemed an exaggeration to me, it was partially confirmed by the fact that the young fellow's grandfather had apparently been the first to make a pet of Lutembe by tossing fish to the ordinarily irascible croc. The creature became accustomed to her daily handout and visited that one spot on the shore regularly. In time, it even learned to know the name "Lutembe," and to come when called. When the original crocodile tamer died, his son inherited Lutembe, or Lutembe inherited him. And he made a pretty good thing out of Lutembe, who was fast becoming a regular tourist attraction. Too bad the old girl could not have lived for the tourist influx after World War II.

There were still a few fish left, and Lutembe was looking hungrily at them.

"What would happen if I fed Lutembe?" I asked.

"She would eat, *Bwana*," the boy said, getting off his pet.

She would eat, yes—perhaps my arm. But I decided to try it. First I asked the boy if he had ever handled a camera. No, never. I showed him how to point it, how to push the right button down. Gingerly, he aimed the camera at Lutembe and me, and even more gingerly I picked up a fish by its tail and held it out toward the crocodile. Lutembe looked at the fish, or at me, with a gleam in her eyes and moved toward me at a speed that made me recoil. I later learned that all crocodiles are considerably faster on land than their appearance would lead one to believe.

I flipped the fish into the open mouth before Lutembe reached me and backed away a few steps. The croc was either disappointed in the small morsel or disturbed at my mistrust. In any event, she slithered off into the water and began circling around, as if still hoping for more to eat. Wondering if she would snatch at something thrown in the water or perhaps even retrieve it like a pet dog, I picked up a small stick about a foot long and tossed it playfully in her direction. But instead of landing in the water in front of her, it hit her on the back and bounced off. Instantly, as if in a huff, she turned about and headed full speed toward the middle of the lake.

"*Bwana*, you should not have done that," the young master said, handing me my camera. "You hurt her feelings." He turned toward the fleeing crocodile and called out pleadingly, "Lutembe! Lutembe!"

Although my stick made as much impression on the croc's tough hide as a toothpick on an elephant, I felt like a bad boy when Lutembe refused to return. But the young fellow persevered, calling lovingly to Lutembe, who finally decided that her temperamental conduct might be depriving her of dessert. She buried her pride and circled back to shore, forgiving and forgetting. This time her master stuffed her until she could have no complaints. Then she lay contentedly in the sun, opening wide her enormous jaws before falling asleep so that the rays of the setting sun shone directly down her throat—a most unusual form of sun-bathing.

And that's the way I left her. Just what caused this particular crocodile to become friendly with men, when all others obviously fear or hate humans, is not clear. But I believe that this is probably the only crocodile that ever had human beings act nice and friendly instead of trying to kill. Certainly, her story lends weight to the theory that wild animals are all nonbelligerent toward men if they are not annoyed, provoked, or hunted. It just never occurred to anyone else in all Africa, except that first native fisherman, to be nice to a crocodile.

Why it occurred to him is incomprehensible, for crocs are ugly-looking and generally ugly-acting, and they cause a great deal of trouble and destruction. There's no doubt that more tribesmen are killed by crocodiles than by any other wild animal in Africa, because they go into so many streams and lakes, fishing, bathing or fording. Snakes are probably the second most common killers since bare legs and bare feet offer ready targets.

I've seen and photographed hundreds of crocodiles since my experience with Lutembe, but I never let her apparent tameness lessen my caution in dealing with them. Another incident from my 1937 trip showed the foolishness of taking chances with them. Cézaire and I had arrived at Pat Putnam's camp on the Epulu River in the Congo. Although this unusual American who had lived so many years in the tropical forest was away in the states, two servants were in charge and made us at home.

It was sweltering, so Cézaire suggested a swim in the river but I wanted to take a few pictures of Putnam's two rare okapi, kept in a stockade, while the light was still good. Although a few of these rare animals have finally reached the zoos of the world in recent years, they had at that time been seen by few people. A leftover from some ancient age, the okapi is probably related to the giraffe, but is about the size of many antelope, which it also resembles. It is a very shy creature with perfect protective coloration for the Congo forests in which it lives. It feeds only at dusk or in bright moonlight, traveling alone rather than in herds, slipping through the forest tangle so quietly, and so alert to danger, that not even the Pygmies can creep up on it. They usually catch the animals in pit traps.

The okapi is one of the neatest and most fastidious animals in the world and spends much of its time grooming itself. In captivity, however, it has a tendency to become infected with worms from its own droppings. At Putnam's camp there was an attendant always on hand to keep the corral clean. He said it was perfectly safe for me to enter provided I kept out of reach of the okapi's legs, for it has a kick like a catapult.

The color of the okapi is a kind of purplish brown but its legs are striped black and white like a zebra's, ending in white stockings on the rear legs. Contrary to the usual order of things in nature, the male is smaller than the female and carries a pair of diminutive, skin-covered horns. With its sixteen-inch tongue it can perform amazing feats, such as licking the back of its own red-fringed black ears. On both sides of its mouth are pockets in which it can store food. And it has the most plaintive eyes I have ever looked into.

I took the pictures I wanted and, as I was leaving the corral, I heard Cézaire shouting. There was such despair in his voice that I dropped my camera and tripod and raced full speed for the river bank. I saw Cézaire about thirty-five feet from shore, treading the coffee-colored water and splashing furiously with his hands. Two Pygmies were jumping up and down on the bank, adding their shrill cries to his. Suddenly I saw the cause of all the commotion—a huge crocodile scarcely ten yards downstream from Cézaire and swimming steadily toward him, against the current. If Cézaire made a dash for shore, the crocodile could put on a little speed and snatch him in his jaws easily. Our only hope of saving him was to frighten the big monster off.

I picked up a rock and let fly, but my aim was bad. Still, the croc slowed down a little at the big splash in the water. The Pygmies, following my example, picked up stones and started flinging them at Charlie Croc. At the same time we all kept up a terrific din. The beast slowed down, stopped, and at that moment a stone caught him fairly on the snout. That was enough for him, for he turned and retreated.

"Come on, Cézaire, come on!" I shouted frantically. "Now's your chance!"

While we kept up the rock barrage against the crocodile, Cézaire started flailing at the water arm over arm, his feet beating like a paddle wheel. I helped pull him from the water, and he stood there trembling, unable to speak. Later he explained that he had been enjoying his swim so much that he paid no attention to the first warning cries of the Pygmies—and then it was too late to swim for shore. He had yelled and thrashed the water mainly to frighten the croc, but he was grateful that I had heard and started the rock-throwing which finally drove the animal away.

It may seem foolhardy to go swimming in waters known to harbor crocodiles. But since almost all rivers and lakes contain

them—except for Lake Kivu and a few other favored spots—
people swim and fish in spite of danger.

Natives use the same technique we did in driving crocs
away—as much noise and turmoil as possible. Crocodiles are
afraid of men and keep out of their way if they can, but it is
hard for them to resist a tasty morsel all alone and not making
much noise. Many tribes fish regularly in croc-infested waters
but some take their medicine men along to help out. A large
group plunges into the water making as much noise as they
can, splashing the water, throwing rocks and sticks. Most of the
crocs get out of the way, but some may find themselves trapped.
In this case, they lie on the bottom, try to hide in a shallow
cove or even burrow themselves into the mud—and they play
dead. Nothing on earth can play dead as effectively as a crocodile.
You can beat it, poke it, hit it with stones and there won't be a
movement from the animal.

When the fishermen encounter one of these they call on the
medicine men to take care of the menace. These gentlemen dive
into the water and spear the croc. Although the others think the
medicine men have special powers and immunity, the truth is
that in such circumstances all crocs play dead and can be speared
easily. The medicine men merely make a good thing of something they have learned about the nature of crocodiles—a procedure which accounts for most of the powers of medicine men
everywhere.

The Semliki River, and especially its delta where it flows
into Lake Edward, is famous for its concentrated crocodile population. On the 1937 trip, Cézaire and I went out in a metal-
bottom boat to see and photograph them. But at that time the
water was so high that it had captured the sunny banks on
which the crocs usually basked during the day; but there were
plenty in the water. Our boat suddenly came upon a concentrated group which thrashed until the water boiled in their efforts to get away. It made a good picture.

In 1946 I came back to the same spot, crossed part of Lake
Edward in a forty-foot steel boat powered by an old Chevrolet

motor, and entered the Semliki River. Near the delta we saw
crowds of white, yellow-billed pelicans and marabou storks. We
had a supply of fish along and tossed some to the storks, who
were the most voracious creatures I've ever encountered.

The water in the river was very low at this time and innumerable crocodiles slept along the banks. But they were hard to
spot, since they look so much like old logs or lumps of mud, until
they slithered into the water at our approach. The water was
so low that on several occasions the boat got stuck on sand bars,
and some of the boys had to jump out and push. It was dangerous, of course, in the croc-infested stream, but they face
such dangers daily and think nothing of it.

Men hunt crocodiles, but not for sport. In places where they
abound, the animals are sitting ducks for a rifle, as they sleep
on the bank with little birds cleaning their teeth and jaws for
them. Hunters are interested in the valuable skins, from which
pocketbooks, shoes, and other articles are made. Some game
wardens have the task of searching out croc nests at the right
times of the year, so they can destroy the eggs. A crocodile
scoops out a depression in the sand, lays sixty or seventy eggs in
it, and covers it up again. There are small lizards which love these
eggs, but some crocs usually manage to grow out of one clutch of
eggs. In spite of the fact that other animals and all mankind
try to wipe out the crocodiles, they keep on reproducing plenti-
fully.

Crocs are well adapted to their environment and are formidable beasts. They eat fish, men, women, children, dik-diks,
baby hippos and almost anything they can get their jaws
on. A crocodile can kill a rhino ten times its own weight—if
the situation is just right and the rhino reacts the way rhinos
usually do. The croc lies in shallow water, hidden, at a favorite drinking spot. The rhino comes along, steps into the water
a few feet, and begins to drink. The croc grabs him by one
leg, the rhino is angry and charges. This is where he makes his
big mistake. If he pulled back he could get away, but a rhino's
mentality is such that attack is his first thought. He charges, and

the croc merely hauls him in a little deeper until his snout is below water and he drowns. Then the croc has a big feast.

A crocodile can kill a small elephant the same way, but a full-sized elephant can lift a croc from the water with his trunk, smash him to the ground and then trample on him. A hippo can cut a crocodile in two with one bite, but hippo calves are favorite dishes of Charlie Croc. When hippos are about to have babies they usually clear out that whole section of the river so no crocodiles are around. And mother hippos take the precaution of carrying their little ones on their backs when they are traveling around. Most of the time hippos and crocs may be found in the same areas, but the crocodiles keep clear of the "river horses" unless they think they can sneak in a quick kidnaping of a hippo calf. They won't risk a fair battle with an adult hippo.

It is amusing to watch a big group of hippos together, in clusters of fifty to a hundred, provided you can sit in some safe spot, off the regular deeply cut tracks from water back to feeding places. Even if the hippos have noticed you at first, and submerged, they soon get used to you and go about their business. In the Rutshuru River, which I visited on my first two trips, and in the Kazinga Channel between Lakes George and Edward, along which we saw and photographed dozens of different animals in 1954, hippos are protected and thrive in great numbers. You can watch them for hours without getting bored, chiefly because they have such a good time. You find yourself smiling at their antics, trying to figure out how long one can stay under water, and marveling at the ease with which they handle themselves. A cow hippo plays happily with her little calf, making him slide off her back into the water, then helping him climb up again for another go at it.

If all the hippos in sight from your vantage point go to sleep, you can usually walk or move along the water's edge, or move by boat, a few hundred yards and you will find another group of a hundred or so hippos, and they will put on a show for you. Even in such hippo housing centers as the Rutshuru and Kazinga Channel, there are distinct herds that keep a little apart from each other. If a bull from one herd should approach the watery territory of another herd, he would quickly be driven off.

Now, it's one thing to watch these fellows from shore, or from a boat traveling thirty or forty feet away from them. But it's quite another thing to stand in a tiny shell of a dinghy right in the midst of such a herd. That is just what my friend Ace DuPreez did, all for the sake of my moving pictures. Some of his acts seemed foolhardy at first glance, and would have been foolhardy if I (or most people) had undertaken them. But Ace was not foolish. He knew animals better than most men, that's all, and could thus do more with them, just as an expert sailor can handle a squall which others could not come through safely.

"Safely" is perhaps not the word to be applied to Ace's voyage to the middle of a herd of hippopotami, but he felt confident throughout. He took it quite slowly, allowing his fragile dinghy to drift toward the cavorting herd while he sat quietly. From a little distance, we photographed the scene from another boat. As Ace's dinghy came within a few yards of the first hippos in the group, they saw him, submerged quickly and noiselessly, then came up again, showing only eyes and nostrils. The boat still moved only at the gentle speed of the water itself, and Ace made no sudden gestures. Some of the hippos stayed under water, but some let the rest of their heads appear, staring at the invader curiously but not belligerently. So long as it was not a crocodile after their youngsters or a hippo from another herd they apparently had nothing to fear. The hippos did not consider men a serious menace, as they lived in a protected area and had not been hunted for years.

Ace drifted into the center of the hippo herd, but by the time he was there, it no longer looked as large as it had been. Where there had been eighty to a hundred of the river horses, we could now see only twenty or thirty around the little boat. The rest had submerged and were staying under water. Ace did not seem worried as he stood up in the boat to take closeups of the hippos nearest him. But until he had gone past the herd, I was afraid that he would be tipped over by some well-intentioned hippo just coming up for a look. And that would be the end of Ace, I thought.

I mentioned this fear to Ace when he joined us again.

"Oh, I don't think they would hurt me even then," he said. "By the way, that should make a wonderful picture—of the boat tipping over and throwing me into the water in the midst of the hippos. Would you like to get that?"

I didn't take him seriously at first. Of course, I said, it would make an exciting picture, but I didn't expect anyone to be foolish enough to try it intentionally, and when it happened accidentally you were never right there with your camera, or the light was wrong, or something.

"Tomorrow we'll do it," Ace said happily. "You will have your cameras all ready, and the light will be just right. If a hippo won't tip the boat over, I'll help, but I can make it look right."

I protested. I wouldn't allow it. But Ace would think of nothing but the fine picture it would make. He insisted that if he took his time, let the hippos get accustomed to him, they would not hurt him, even when he fell in the water.

"They'll just get out of the way," he said.

So the next day, against my wishes and better judgment, Ace boarded his dinghy again while we got in the other boat with our cameras trained on him. Once more he drifted slowly to the middle of the herd of hippos—the same ones he had visited the day before—but maneuvered so that he was somewhat closer to shore. The scene would be exciting enough without making him swim too far to reach safety.

I knew when the time was ripe because Ace signaled with his hand and stood up in the little boat. We were filming with our cameras, and the light was good. Suddenly the boat tipped, Ace lurched as if trying to keep his balance, and then tumbled over into the water with a splash. It looked so real that I could not believe that a hippo had not actually done the job without any help from Ace. Later, he told me that he didn't need to help much, for the boat had been nudged vigorously several times by the hippos and at that particular moment one almost tipped it over.

And there he was in the water, surrounded by hippos, swimming for the shore, about two hundred feet away. I held my breath, expecting to see a thrashing in the water, a huge gaping mouth, and then no more Ace. But he had been right all along, as I should have known. The hippos nearest him quickly submerged and obviously swam away from this sudden disturbance in their water. By the time they came up again, Ace had almost made it to shore, and they just looked after him inquiringly. A few snorted loudly, and one even swam after him—but lazily and curiously, not with speed and anger.

Ace pulled himself up on the shore, dripping and muddy, then turned with a big smile to wave at us in the other boat. I was sweating and a little limp, but waved back. Then we circled around to pick him up, for he stood on a shore along which we had seen elephants, buffalos and rhinos the day before.

A few days later Ace and I and a cameraman were out on the plains looking for a herd of buffalo to photograph when we came upon a muddy pool overflowing with hippos. We stopped the truck, and Ace and I approached cautiously on foot. We saw a herd of at least fifty hippos, all so thickly covered with mud that we could hardly identify their shapes or tell where one hippo left off and the next began. Some were on top of each other, a few were squirming around for even muddier spots, but most of them were just dozing there in utter bliss.

I wasn't sure how good a picture the scene would make, but it was worth a little time and a few feet of film. Ace and I walked toward the pool while the cameraman stayed behind with the truck, shooting our approach and my own filming of closeups. As we drew near there came a sudden restless and annoyed heaving of that entire mass of muddy hippos, almost as if some subterranean rumbling had shaken the mud beneath them. Those nearest to us turned their heads and stared. We stopped, and the heaving subsided. We walked closer, and once more the muddy mass of animals stirred, and some of the hippos bellowed like sick cows. One gigantic bull hippo at the edge of the pool lifted his head and glared at us. He was obviously not pleased with our presence.

In my view-finder, I could see that the pictures I was taking would probably look like nothing but a waving mass of mud. I wished that we could get a little action, and Ace decided to fulfill my wish. He took a couple of steps at the suspicious hippo and yelled at him. At that, the big beast decided that we had interfered enough. I cannot understand how such a bulky animal mired in mud could move so quickly, but before we could think he was coming toward us, head lowered, eyes blazing— and he was coming fast. We turned and raced for the truck, and the driver saw our predicament at once. He shoved it into gear and angled swiftly toward us so that we could leap on the moving vehicle just a few yards ahead of the angry hippo. Luckily, the cameraman had recorded the entire scene, which gave us more action than we had bargained for.

Hippos continued to give us plenty of action on the 1954-55 expedition, including two long and arduous trips to remote regions. The first was to Lake Rukwa, in Southern Tanganyika, where a severe drought had been bringing slow death to hundreds of hippos. Conservation authorities told August Kuenzler, brilliant collector of wild animals for zoos the world over, that since the hippos were sure to die, he might capture any animals which he thought strong enough to survive. I had fortunately met Kuenzler in Arusha, near which is located his fabulous wild animal farm, through Mrs. Margot Rydon, who knew how helpful he might be to me. August Kuenzler was a Swiss who came to Tanganyika in 1929 and eventually developed his business of capturing, and training for zoo life, many kinds of wild animals. He is a dedicated man, devoted to the idea of preserving animals, of treating them with kindness, of sending good specimens to good homes around the world so that people can learn about them. He was one of the first to capture baby rhinos, elephants and other animals without killing the mothers—a method now enforced by law in Tanganyika—and has trained his remarkable associate, Pellegrini, in this technique.

We obtained some of our best sequences on catching expeditions with Pellegrini, but the Lake Rukwa hippo safari was the first and toughest. Dave Mason, one of my most conscientious and competent staff members, was the only cameraman on this particular project and he took some dramatic footage. But it meant a bruising, battering trip of thirty-six days over some of the worst country imaginable, with roads so rocky that two trucks broke down and we had long waits for repairs. It meant sickness and fever of several days for Dave Mason, and work in the sun under a blistering heat of 102 degrees in the shade. All this for about four minutes in the final picture!

Lake Rukwa lies more than eight hundred miles south of Arusha, and has on several occasions suffered such drought that many hippos died for lack of water. In such a drought, the vegetation for many miles around shrivels, dries and dies so the big herds of hippos have nothing to eat. The burning sun kills them if starvation doesn't, for a hippo must spend many hours a day in water or mud to withstand the strong rays of the sun. Without regular submersion, the heat literally cooks the thick layers of fat beneath its skin. As the lake shrinks, more and more hippos crowd into a smaller and smaller area. Then there is a sea of mud, growing daily thicker and harder. Many hippos become trapped in the gluey mire and die there. Others are so weak that they cannot pull themselves toward the receding water and mud.

This is the scene we wanted to photograph but, after the long trip, circumstances at Lake Rukwa were not suitable for a combination of filming and catching. The hippos were scattered over a wide area; they could not be approached by trucks or cameramen because of the dried earth which had developed impassable cracks and crevasses. But Pellegrini had gone out after hippos and he meant to return with hippos. Since the drought covered a wide area, he determined to find another place. Back we went, retracing our steps to the Rungwa River, which contained nothing but mud and hundreds of hippos. On one side the terrain made filming impossible, and on the other side photography had to wait until afternoon because of the sun, but these were common hazards. Mason just stuck to one side and took pictures in the afternoon.

The trucks could come within a reasonable distance of the hippos—a necessity because of the difficulty of transporting a captured hippo any great distance on foot. On the evening of our arrival, in fact, the trucks stopped so close to about two hundred hippos that no tents could be pitched. Everyone slept in the trucks because the huge beasts were wandering around too near for comfort. And they were not happy animals.

A drying and muddy river bed in southern Tanganyika has a foul stench arising from it because of rotting vegetation, dead fish and such. On top of this odor there was the pungent and sickening smell of the rotting flesh of many dead hippos. The vultures were busy taking care of this carrion but they could not keep up with their work fast enough for good sanitary conditions.

Over a priod of several days, Mason managed to get many good shots of hippos stuck in the mud, of hippos collapsing. Pellegrini's job was not easy, for he had to find a hippo strong enough to withstand the trip back to Arusha, where he could have plenty of food and water, and at the same time small enough to fit into a truck. Thus he had to find a hippo about half-grown and in fair condition—not easy since most of the smaller hippos were shoved out of the best places by the big cows and bulls.

Pellegrini reconnoitred, searched, hunted for the right hippos—with Mason alongside at all times. He finally caught one hippo, then another—and this time Mason got some good pictures. Pellegrini found the second one at some distance from the truck, which could not be brought any closer. He and Mason were in the midst of hippos, dozens of them, some dead, some dying, some lethargic but with strength left for an emergency.

These resented the men walking among them, but not enough
to charge in their weakened condition. It might be another matter, however, when Pellegrini had caught one hippo and was
trying to get it to the truck. By this act, the men would at once
become more than mere nuisances to the hippos; they would
constitute serious threats to be challenged and charged. And it
would take only one aroused hippo to bring the whole project
to a nasty end. Pellegrini was counting on the weakness and
despair of all the living hippos to prevent their aiding the captured young one, who could be counted on to put up a big fight.

Pellegrini threw his lasso, caught the young hippo securely,
and pulled his rope tight. The beast was not full-sized nor up
to his normal strength, but he weighed between two and three
tons and was in better condition than most of his fellow hippos.
He tugged, pulled, twisted, charged, but Pellegrini ran back
through the other hippos toward the truck, holding his rope
tight but paying it out at the same time. Some of his helpers
were ready with another length of rope, which they quickly
tied to the end of the lasso rope in order to gain sufficient length
to get them clear of the cluster of hippos, some of whom had
stirred and looked angry about the whole proceeding.

Finally everyone hauled on the end of the long rope, tugging the reluctant hippo toward the cage truck. Foot by foot
he came, his strength finally ebbing so that the job became a
little less back-breaking for the men. But then as he was hauled
past a dead cow hippo all his fight and strength seemed to be re-
newed. He was determined *not* to leave the side of this particular beast, bloated and rotting as she was, her hide split so that
the fat beneath could be seen as yellow lard that had literally
boiled in the intense heat.

"That must have been the young hippo's mother," Pellegrini said, when they had finally pulled the prisoner past the
carcass and brought it beside the cage truck. Then they performed the supreme act of kindness for that young hippo—
they poured a few buckets of water over his parched hide, precious water that they had hauled many miles by truck. Pellegrini

wanted to soothe the beast, strengthen it, and teach it that captivity might mean pleasure and comfort. And both men and animals still had a long, tough trip ahead of them.

On the way back to Arusha, one truck broke a spring, another lost a shock absorber, another's gasoline line became blocked, and one of them broke a radiator hose. But Pellegrini had his hippos, and we had an interesting sequence.

A second detour for hippo shots was made to the Kilombero River, a tributary of the Rufiji in the south central part of Tanganyika. Here hippos are looked upon as vermin to be exterminated because of the great damage they do to crops and fishing traps—so much that at times the Wadamba tribe, which lives there, doesn't get enough to eat.

It is always confusing to find that wild animals which are protected in some regions are exterminated, if possible, in others. On the Kilombero the government helps the natives kill hippos, but our primary interest was the Wadamba method of killing these evil spirits of the river. The Wadamba are still quite primitive, deeply superstitious and under the influence of their witch doctors. They are poor, not colorful except in their hippo hunting, and are certainly not a tribe I would photograph for the sake of the people alone. Their lives are lived against great odds, for they had been plagued just before our arrival by some man-eating lions, on top of their customary curse, hippos. Malaria, endemic sleeping sickness, and relapsing fever are rife in the area, too. This pitiful situation will not last long, however, as government authorities have drafted plans to clean up the entire area so it will become a rich agricultural land— which it can readily become since conditions are very favorable for the planting of rice and sugar cane. But first the hippos must go, and the swamps, the low bush, the mosquitoes. It is a big job, and it ought to be done—but there is one more primitive region that will disappear.

I wanted to put on film the Wadamba hippo killings before civilization caught up with the Kilombero River. There was no difficulty in persuading a group of men to go hunting for hippo in front of our cameras, so we got many good scenes over a period of several days.

The natives entered canoes some distance upstream from the spot where a herd of hippos was swimming, sleeping, playing and making love. Men with harpoons sat in the bow of each boat, spearsmen along both sides, and a paddler or two in the rear. But there was not much paddling. The canoes drifted down toward the hippos silently and smoothly, carried by the current. When a hippo near the edge of his group was spotted, the paddler of the first canoe guided the craft toward him. But it is almost impossible to approach a hippo within striking distance without his seeing what is coming. He submerges in the muddy water, leaving scarcely a ripple on the surface.

When a hippo submerges he may then do one of many things. He may just go down and lie quietly on the bottom, waiting for the intruders to pass on or go away. He may swim *away* from the menace, retreating to the middle of the herd just below him. He may advance toward the approaching craft with the intention of attacking it. Or he may turn to one side and hide temporarily in a muddy nook below the surface.

The natives assumed, first of all, that he might be just below the surface where he submerged. So they drifted over that spot and the harpooners thrust their sharp weapons blindly down into the water, hoping to draw blood. When their weapons struck only water, the paddler came to life and sent the canoe zigzagging back and forth across the river, hoping to catch the hippo as he surfaced again. But the first hunters had no luck with any of the hippos on their downward drift. When they were below the herd, they headed for the shallow waters along shore and poled their way upstream again, to repeat the whole maneuver.

Meanwhile four other canoes followed the first, but not a single hippo was harpooned that day—or the next two days. Finally, however, the infinite patience of the natives—and our cameraman—was rewarded. A harpoon struck home and blood boiled up through the muddy waters. There was a violent thrashing in the water as the wounded hippo turned to attack, and the canoe rocked until we thought it would turn over. But in that brief encounter two more harpoons and several long spears were plunged into the big hippo, reaching vital spots that knocked the fight and life out of him in a hurry.

The job was not over, by any means, for the men then had to haul the animal to shore. But they had enough ropes attached to make it, and he was finally rolled up on the bank, to the joyous shouts of the Wadamba, who had not only rid the river of one more enemy but had found much needed food aplenty.

While hippos were often interesting and sometimes dangerous, they could not hold a candle to rhinos in either department. A rhino will eagerly attack a two-ton truck—and sometimes he'll win even that battle. The theory that all wild animals will let man alone if not annoyed or hunted is put to a severe test by the rhino, who seems to go around permanently angry. On the other hand, there are Carr Hartley's two tame white rhinos, who allow people to ride them piggy-back. They prove that *faru* is susceptible to kindness. And when I recall the number of times I *wanted* a rhino to charge for the sake of good movies, and the beast retreated or just paid no attention, I know that some rhinos occasionally remove the chips from their shoulders.

There's no way of knowing what a rhino will do, and that is what makes him so dangerous. You can only be sure that half the time he will charge a man anywhere near him, whether there has been provocation or not. And when a rhino charges he means business. He's fast and agile and determined.

To prove that stories of the ferocity and unpredictable behavior of the rhino are not exaggerated, I want to quote briefly from two news items in the *East African Standard* which I read during my 1954 trip. They served to increase my caution in dealing with these animals.

> Col. Charles Haynes of Nyeri was killed by a rhinoceros
> which charged him and his wife as they were walking near
> their home at Nyeri airstrip. Col. Haynes saved his wife by
> thrusting her into bushes when he saw the rhino was going
> to charge. He was badly gored in the groin and died later
> in Mt. Kenya Hospital. The first indication of the animal's
> presence came when Col. Haynes's dog ran out from the
> bushes, frightened. The rhino followed . . . Nyeri resi-
> dents have been increasingly worried by the animals which
> now appear regularly near houses and the airstrip.

Obviously the rhino, in this instance, considered the dog a
sufficient provocation, became angry and charged, when most
other wild animals would have stayed hidden in the bush or retreated, with or without dignity. The second item was more
dramatic.

> A bull rhino, disturbed by an operation in the forest around
> Treetops, charged into the Ol 'Gatai Sisal Estate, killed two
> cows and then attacked cars on the Mweiga-Nyeri Road.
> The animal went for a car driven by Mrs. Ruby Beyts, wife
> of Brig. G. H. Beyts, District Officer, Mweiga. She swerved
> past it and on arrival home told her husband who phoned
> the police.
> Meanwhile the rhino charged a truck owned by Col. G. Jar-
> man, a Treetops White Hunter, who stopped the vehicle
> to let an Asian passenger alight. The Asian's shirt was ripped
> up the back—but he was unhurt. The animal charged the
> truck five times and later went up the drive to Brig.
> Beyts' house. A truck with four African policemen, in-
> cluding a sergeant with a Bren gun, came to the scene. The
> rhino made for the truck, threw everyone out, dug his horn
> into the floorboards of the vehicle and lifted it bodily. The
> sergeant opened fire and killed the animal.

Why is a rhino so belligerent? The most likely theory is
that he is not very bright and his eyesight is poor. He cannot actually see anything clearly until it is about ten yards in front
of him. But the beast makes up in courage what it lacks in

brains, and a keen sense of smell compensates for its poor eyesight. If you approach a rhino downwind, as any sensible person does, the animal is not aware of you until you are very close. He dimly makes out the menace in front of him; if there's danger where he's looking, he figures there is probably also danger behind him and to right and left. At least, he's assuming the worst and taking no chances. So he charges to break out of the supposed encirclement—and he goes in a straight line. The thickest brush growth is no barrier to him, as he can crash right through it. Don't think that because he looks so bulky and clumsy that you can dodge out of his way and his speed will carry him past you. He can wheel and turn in his own length, no matter how fast he is going, and would put to shame a polo pony in this department.

All other animals make way for a rhino. If *faru* and *tembo* meet on a narrow forest path, the elephant is the one that will detour. I doubt that a rhino could do much damage to an elephant, but the elephant will still decline an engagement. All natives feel the same way about the rhino. The Masai, bravest of the brave who kill charging lions with their thin spears, fear only one animal—the rhino. Incidentally, rhino horn—which is not genuine horn but compacted hair tissue—is more valuable than ivory. Throughout the Orient, many people consider powdered rhino horn a powerful aphrodisiac.

Perhaps it was foolish of me to set out to provoke a rhino to charge me. But a moving picture of a rhino is nothing unless he is charging. He's an ugly brute, and nobody enjoys looking at him in repose, as you can enjoy a reclining lion, an elephant quietly drinking water, a giraffe nibbling at leaves on a tall tree. With their thick hides that fit so badly that they seem to be made for some other creature, and their long, forward-sloping horns placed in the most unlikely position near the end of the nose, rhinos would look like amusing caricatures if they were not obviously so cantankerous.

My first intimate knowledge of rhinos came from the late

Lionel Hartley, who helped me in 1946 in the country around Mtito Andei. It was a rugged area, dry and covered thickly with thorny bush, including many of the aptly named "Wait-a-bits" whose thorns snatch at one's clothes and hold on. It was good rhino country.

After all the talk about the bull-headed belligerence of the rhino, you would think that it might have been simple to get one to charge me. But there were so many essential elements in my planned scene that we never managed to get them all together at once. There had to be, first of all, the rhino. Then there had to be a good tree for me to climb when *faru* charged me, plus a safe spot for my cameraman, preferably another tree, from which he could photograph rhino, me and the tree I escaped to. And the light had to be right. Hartley, of course, planned to cover the whole thing with his big .475 gun—it took a mighty jolt to stop a charging rhino, and there wouldn't be any time for second shots. Another essential was Hartley's ability to save me in an emergency, and he always inspired so much confidence that I was never really worried on this score.

We went out in a truck and saw our first rhino right away, but he heard the motor and didn't like it so ambled away out of sight. A few hours later, during which time we saw a fine pride of lions, we sighted a big bull rhino about two hundred yards away. When we stopped the truck, he retreated.

As we jolted our way over the countryside for several more hours I began to express doubts about the ferocity and even the presence of rhinos. The words were hardly out of my mouth when a big rhino suddenly lunged at the truck from behind a bush about seven feet away. But the truck was going fairly fast, and Hartley stepped on the accelerator, so the rhino missed. He took up the chase, however, and came so close to the rear of the truck that one of the Africans sitting there was petrified with fright and rolled over to get as near the truck cab as possible. Hartley speeded up and we finally pulled away from the angry beast, who might have toppled us with a charge against the side but couldn't do too much damage with a collision on the rear of the vehicle. While this was all very exciting, I didn't get a picture. The rhino had not given me any time to get set.

During the next few days, this same sort of thing happened many times—a rhino suddenly charging from the bush—but these meetings were totally unproductive photographically. Hartley explained that we had to find a rhino quietly feeding, approach him downwind, find the necessary trees, then let the rhino know we were there, whereupon he would charge. After several days, we came upon a feeding rhino who did not hear or see us. We watched the little tick birds that walked up and down his back, picking lice from the folds of his skin, and hoped we would not disturb them. They are very alert, and often serve as the rhino's eyes. If they became alarmed at our presence, they would fly up with little cries and head in our direction to tell the rhino where to look for trouble.

We inched the truck to within a hundred yards of the animal without disturbing anyone. From here the cameraman could photograph the scene with relative safety, since the rhino would presumably be charging me rather than the truck. We found a tree off to the left that I might climb, but Lionel decided it was too fragile; the rhino might knock it over. Farther away we found a tree that was good, but it was out of position for the cameraman. So we switched around, put the cameraman in the good tree, and decided that I would run for the truck. All set at last, I walked slowly toward the feeding rhino, taking pictures with my own camera. I wanted to catch that moment when he looked up, saw me, and started his charge directly for me. Then I'd fly and hope to make the truck in time.

He finally looked up, all right, but instead of charging he just turned and trotted away into the bush. And we had lost a couple of hours!

Patience, patience—how much of it is needed! And how thin it was running by that time. That is when camera hunting becomes dangerous. After days of frustration—from uncooperative animals, rain, poor light or any of a dozen causes—the photographing explorer is too eager. When he finally encounters an animal in favorable circumstances, he is likely to take foolish risks.

I know that I finally took chances I shouldn't have when we finally came upon a big bull feeding. Although he looked peaceful to me, Hartley said this particular animal was *kali* and ought to be "full of fun." I have no idea how Hartley could tell. Perhaps it was the rutting season, when rhino bulls are all nervous and irritable. They have a right to be, for among rhinos, the female is the aggressor in love-making and will chase an attractive bull for miles, then butt him furiously until he agrees to give her what she wants.

We found a tree for the cameraman, a sound tree for me about forty-five feet from the rhino. The light was right, and Hartley stationed himself with his gun to cover me. I approached the rhino, but the wind was wrong and he had no idea I was there. I picked up a branch and threw it at him. It fell short, but *faru* heard the noise and looked up, eying me suspiciously; but he did not charge. I threw a rock, which came a little closer and angered him. As he lowered his head, I was sure he was going to charge, so took off for my tree at full speed. I grabbed the lowest branch, swung my right leg up over it, managing to strain a muscle badly as I did so. Breathless but safe on the branch, I turned and looked back. The rhino was in the same spot, looking at me wonderingly. He had not charged!

Hartley said later that he felt sure the rhino would charge when I took off. But I ran about a second too soon. If the charge had once begun, the rhino would not have stopped, but just before he moved I ran, and this confused him.

But we didn't give up. I approached the rhino again, though he didn't seem very interested. Hartley sent a boy to circle around in back of the rhino, hoping the animal would get the boy's scent, feel surrounded, and charge me. The boy climbed a tree to reconnoiter, and then saw a sleeping cow rhino, the mate of my friend, near the foot of it. Hartley and I did not know this at the time, of course, and Lionel could not make out the boy's signals from the tree. The boy was afraid to descend for fear he would waken the sleeping rhino, which would charge him. And if that cow rhino had awakened, she might have charged me suddenly from the side and cut off my retreat toward the tree.

But I could not get a rise out of the feeding rhino. *He* knew that he was not surrounded, for he had left his mate asleep back in the bush a little way. The light was growing dim and finally the big rhino, his belly full, turned and went back into the bush where he awakened his mate. They went off together.

Conclusion—I obtained no good rhino pictures in 1946, but I learned a good deal and had some exciting times trying. During my 1954-55 trip, I more than made up for the deficiencies of 1946, although my first encounters with rhinos almost got me into a peck of trouble.

I planned to go into the same general region, which by this time had become a protected area, the Amboseli National Park. Just before leaving for Amboseli, however, I heard from two good friends of mine from San Francisco, Marsden Blois and Earl Douglass, two fine sportsmen who were on a trip around the world. They asked if they could join my expedition for a short time, and I was very happy to have them come along. My one hope was that we would not strike one of those deadly stretches when nothing happens, when skies cloud over and no wild animals can be found.

I met them in Nairobi, and we set out almost immediately for Amboseli in the Volkswagen bus and one truck, along with cameramen Johnny Coquillon and Dave Mason and an excellent African guide. Shortly after entering the sanctuary, we saw another truck and, of course, stopped for a chat. It contained two Americans, a missionary named F. G. Reid, and Dr. George W. Allen, who had been a medical missionary in Nigeria for years and was now practicing in Nairobi. Allen was a fine animal photographer and such a lover of wild animals that the authorities had made him an honorary game warden. Allen and Reid were looking for rhinos, and so were we, so we decided to join forces and look together. I felt that this was a lucky break, since I would have to worry less about strict park regulations in the company of an honorary game warden, especially if he took the lead which he did.

After an hour or so of rough riding, we came upon a big cow rhino with two calves, a rare sight that I was delighted to record on film. But the beasts began to move away as we approached, and Dr. Allen took out after them. I knew that we were not supposed to chase animals in the sanctuary, but if an honorary game warden did it, I certainly wanted to tag along behind and get what pictures I could. The rhinos put on steam, and so did we. We were gaining on them when suddenly another car appeared, a car whose driver stopped our chase of the rhinos. He was a game warden—full-fledged, not honorary —from another region, taking a kind of busman's holiday. He informed us rather acidly of the regulation against chasing animals in national parks and seemed unimpressed by the presence of an honorary game warden. We gave up our rhino photography for the day, of course. I knew he would report the incident to headquarters, a black mark against me that might conceivably lessen the amount of cooperation and help I'd always had from game and conservation officials. So I proceeded, as soon as possible, to make a report and explanation myself. I received a friendly but firm "Be careful in the future" warning, and continued to receive the best cooperation from authorities in Kenya and Tanganyika.

Blois and Douglass were delighted by their first day in Africa, in spite of this incident, for they had seen and chased wild rhinos. And they continued to see what they wanted to see. On the second day we came upon an enormous herd of elephants in a swamp. I took them along on our scheduled trip to the Ngorongoro Crater where they saw the largest wild game herds left in the world, to the number of close to one hundred thousand animals. Then on to the Serengeti Plains where they saw some fine lions and were present when the game warden of the area brought in some native poachers. They spent their last two days getting in some shooting with a white hunter and then took off for India by plane, saying that their three weeks in Africa had been the most memorable in their lives.

To get back to rhinos, we filmed one very touching sequence on a rhino hunt with Pellegrini. That expert animal catcher had roped a big cow rhino, which struggled frantically to free herself. But just as he roped the animal, the truck bogged down with one wheel in a deep hole. Pellegrini and his men started to extricate the truck when they were rudely interrupted by a huge and very angry bull rhino, the mate of the cow they had captured. He had obviously come to rescue her, and he was not going to let several men and a big truck stand in his way.

The cow rhino, fastened to the truck with a stout rope, tried desperately to get away, tugging at the rope until it seemed she might tear off the hind leg to which it was tied. The bull rhino stood watching her struggles about ten yards away, then decided the situation called for action. The men all clambered into the doubtful safety of the truck as the big rhino prepared to charge. With lowered head, he quickly picked up speed until he was thundering down on the truck like an express train. If he had struck the side of the truck he might have well tipped it over, but fortunately he aimed for the front and smacked the heavy grillwork with such force that the vehicle was almost shaken out of its pothole. Bewildered and perhaps a little dazed, the rhino backed off and surveyed the situation again, nervously eying his mate and the truck which seemed impervious to his blows. Then he decided to try again, and on he raced once more, crashing against the front of the truck with a savage blow.

When he backed up this time, he looked genuinely bewildered as well as frustrated and angry. All this time, of course, the mate he was trying so hard to save against such great odds was struggling to free herself and join him. But he didn't know what to do. He shifted uneasily on his stubby legs, looked about as if puzzled, plainly trying to figure out what he could possibly do in this dreadful situation. All he could conclude, of course, was the usual answer of a rhino to every problem—

charge. So for the third time he hurled himself against the front of the truck. If I had been in charge of the exploration, I would have been inclined to free the cow rhino. But we were guests of Pellegrini, and he was determined to keep his valuable captive.

He decided that he had better try to get rid of this most persistent and dangerous male. It might change its tactics and charge the truck from the side, possibly knocking it over and spilling out its occupants, who would not stand much of a chance against the furious animal. Pellegrini took a slender pole about fifteen feet long and, standing in the truck, waved it menacingly toward the rhino. I can't understand why a waving pole should intimidate a rhino, but it seemed to. The beast backed away a few yards but then held his ground. Pellegrini had to descend from the truck and advance toward the rhino on foot, slowly and cautiously, all the time waving the pole at him.

The rhino backed away slowly, reluctantly, confused by the approaching man and the strange thing reaching out in the air toward him. He might have become even more angry and charged, of course, but the man knew what he was doing and showed great courage. He advanced steadily, and the rhino retreated steadily. Finally, even after Pellegrini had stopped, the animal kept moving away reluctantly until, just before disappearing in the thick bush, he turned for one last look at the mate he had tried so hard to rescue.

An aroused buffalo is just as vindictive as a rhinoceros, but he is certainly more predictable. With the rhino, we are dealing with stupidity and deficient senses, so many of his actions appear senseless, incomprehensible. The buffalo knows what he's about and you can tell that he does.

When you come upon a herd of buffalo grazing they look from a distance not unlike a herd of domestic cows, peaceful and contented. You can often spot a herd from a distance, even in rather tall grass, from the white egrets flying overhead, then settling on the animals' backs to pick the lice from the hair and hide. When you first see a buffalo close up, you can't help admiring him, for he is a magnificent creature, weighing up to two thousand pounds and all muscle. His sweeping ebony horns are as thick as an arm at the base, and taper to fine sabre points.

Many people have said that the biggest danger from a buffalo herd is a stampede, but they don't commonly attack *en masse*. A lone buffalo usually makes the charge, although others stay close to take up the battle if necessary. My experience tends to verify this. When I approached a herd closely, it was always one buffalo who glowered, lowered his head, and contemplated a charge. The others looked—but made no menacing gesture when they saw that one of their number had the matter in hand.

All Africans have a healthy respect for the buffalo. Occasionally herds get to be great nuisances around *shambas*, especially in areas newly opened to agriculture. They eat and trample down the crops and kill the owners who try to drive them away. In such cases, officials usually send white hunters to clear out the troublesome tribe, but generally buffalo are protected. Natives enjoy buffalo meat, and they used to like the hides for making shields. Nothing was as thick and tough as buffalo hide.

Most animals refrain from tangling with the buffalo, but a lion that is hungry enough and can find no smaller prey will sometimes attack. Here is a battle I'd like to see, for it is just about the evenest match one can imagine. The bones of a lion and a buffalo have been found side by side after a battle in which both of them died.

In East Africa you hear many tales about the buffalo, and each one demonstrates his extreme vindictiveness. The worst I've heard of many verified experiences was told by a hunter who was never the same again. He and a companion were surprised by a charging buffalo and each ran for a tree, dropping his gun in fear and for the sake of speed. One man just barely reached his tree in time, so the buffalo kept his charge going for the other hunter, who was just pulling himself up to the lowest branch when the enraged beast caught him on his horns. He tossed the hunter in the air repeatedly, then trampled on him as if out of his mind. The hunter in the tree could do nothing to help his friend, because his gun was far away on the ground. He could just sit in his tree and watch the obliteration of a human being. For five minutes the buffalo trampled and kicked until there was actually nothing left of the man but small pieces that could not be distinguished from the bloody earth. The animal then kicked some dirt over the spot in a brief and contemptuous burial, and departed.

Elephants give their victims a more thorough burial perhaps because, being less vicious, there is something left to bury. An angry elephant can do a thorough job, of course, goring, stamping and picking it up in the trunk to bang against the earth or a sturdy tree trunk. Unless he is wounded, attacked, or has young to protect, however, an elephant is not really belligerent. He is so big he has few enemies to challenge him, and —most important—he is undoubtedly the most intelligent of all wild animals. Many people think this is because the elephant's brain is so large, but his brain actually occupies only a very small part of that big skull. Many an amateur hunter has found that out to his sorrow, shooting too high and hitting only spongy skull tissue which doesn't even slow down a charging elephant.

Everywhere I've gone in Africa I've seen elephants. Although they like the great plains covered with low bush and elephant grass, they seem equally at home in thick jungle like the Ituri Forest or rocky mountains. I've seen a huge elephant —just about the bulkiest thing you can think of—push through almost impenetrable forest growth silently and without disturbing too many leaves. And I've seen one clamber up a steep mountainside with speed and agility, if not with grace. As a matter of fact, elephant trails are as well engineered as any route could be, as surveyors long ago learned.

There's something deeply moving about watching a herd of elephants grazing or moving across the ground in calm and purposeful fashion. They possess great dignity, in spite of their wrinkled and ill-fitting skins, their baggy Charlie-Chaplin pants, and their ridiculous tails. When you look at a few elephants from the rear, you decide that the pants belong to them but the legs don't. They're entirely too short and squat. Somehow, this makes the big animals even more lovable and tempers their dignity enough to appeal to your sentimentality. Then, of course, it helps to learn that elephants are somewhat sentimental, too. A male will travel miles to visit the grave of his dead mate, where he stands and mourns a while before going on to other feeding grounds or a water hole. How do we know he mourns—and are we once more falling into that fatal trap of attributing human feelings to animals? Well, it is a hard question or set of questions to answer, but I don't think you can put any other interpretation on the verified facts of an elephant traveling with its herd, detouring several miles to the spot where its mate was killed and its bones remained, standing there for several hours, and then hurrying to catch up with the rest of the herd. If you can think of another meaning, go right ahead. I prefer mine.

Another thing—elephants are among the few wild animals that consciously help each other. Some creatures hunt in packs or cooperate in making their kills for the group, but that is not what I am talking about. If one elephant is hurt, others will gather around solicitously and try to help. I have seen a young elephant try to uproot a tree to get at the succulent roots, and when it proved too tough for him, go away to find a friend who would help. Together they uprooted the tree and feasted. If you are ever charged by an elephant and escape by climbing high into the branches of a strong tree, don't feel too safe. *Tembo* will summon a couple of friends to help him knock the tree down.

Some men who know a lot about Africa and animals have expressed doubts about the stories of elephants helping a wounded comrade from the field of battle. But I have seen it and so has Allan Tarlton and so have many others whose word

cannot be doubted. An elephant is wounded and falls to his
knees but does not collapse. Two other elephants come along,
one on either side of him. Pushing against his body they not
only lift him to his feet but support him firmly as they all walk
away seeking safety.

Despite their general non-belligerence, elephants in some
areas have caused much damage to farms and *shambas*. Since
they like the food they find there as much as food found
anywhere else, they may ruin village after village with their
eating and tramping around. Elephants need a tremendous
amount of food to keep their huge hulks going—and the quantity must be extra large since they are vegetarians. They spend
about fourteen to sixteen hours out of every twenty-four eating
—lazily and slowly but still eating—with stomachs rumbling
loudly. I've passed through spots in the forest where a good-
sized herd of elephants has been eating and it looks like
complete devastation. The forest grows again quickly, of course,
but not a farmer's plantings. When herds have been repeatedly
destructive in a neighborhood, the officials send out professional
hunters to kill the beasts—and most white hunters have taken
on this task at one time or another.

About a thousand elephants a year are killed by game
control officers in East Africa—and the chief interest of these
men is to preserve the game. But apparently the elephant population does not diminish appreciably, if at all. The birth rate
seems sufficient to take care of the loss. And this is surprising,
since an elephant can give birth to a young one only about
every four years. The gestation period is almost two years—
probably twenty-two months. But an elephant lives a long time
—from eighty to more than a hundred years normally—so a female may have twenty young ones during her lifetime.

Even with the necessary game control killings and the
increased hunting in Africa—but strictly under license and limited—there are probably fewer elephants killed than in the old
days of unrestricted hunting, and wide-scale ivory hunting. In
those times a good pair of tusks weighed one hundred fifty

pounds each, and some have been recorded at well over two hundred pounds, but the average these days is thirty to forty pounds. The longer an elephant lives the bigger and more valuable his ivory becomes. Right now we're going through a period of slim pickings because of the excessive killing of a few decades ago. In another thirty or forty years, there may be plenty of elephants with the giant tusks of the old days. But poachers are always a problem, and they look for the old fellows with big tusks.

You would think that something as big as an elephant would be easy to spot, but this is not always the case. His gray hide blends with the earth and general background in many regions, and in other places he unconsciously gives himself a disguise. An elephant loves water. He likes to drink it, wallow in it, and squirt it over himself. In most places the water is muddy, so that elephants regularly coat their hides with mud which is the exact color of all the earth nearby.

At Mudanda Rock in Tsavo National Park, for instance, all the elephants look pink or red, because that is the color of the dirt in that area. The water at the rock is muddy, red-colored, and serves as a perfect coating to disguise the big beasts. Incidentally, if you go to East Africa, be sure to visit Mudanda Rock and the new dam they are building at the other end of the Park. There is always water here, even though there may be a drought for many miles around, so all the elephants come from great distances. The herds line up, taking their turns with all good humor, to drink, bathe, squirt and wallow. During a particularly bad drought you can see as many as five hundred elephants in one day there.

With so many elephants congregating in one area, it is not surprising that some of the babies get lost, as at Coney Island and other popular resorts. David Sheldrick, my 1946 lion-hunting guide who succeeded Lionel Hartley as game warden of Tsavo National Park, took in a couple of elephant babies recently. He fed them, escorted them to a feeding ground each day to protect them from lions—they were quite small and helpless—and even gave them a big house to sleep in. They became quite friendly with him and his rangers, but remained suspicious of all other humans. When they are big and strong enough they will go their own way and join their herd—or some herd—again.

For decades the prevalent opinion was that African elephants would not become that tame and friendly. Everyone agreed that they could never be trained like Indian elephants. But the Belgians in the Congo were not convinced. They looked at numerous historical evidences of trained African elephants—notably those of Hannibal's army crossing the Alps to conquer Rome—and decided that it could be done. About 1910 they started an elephant school at Gangala na Bodio in the northeast corner of the Congo, on the Dungu River. Later they converted a huge area across the river into the Gambara National Park, where elephants were completely protected. Right next door, therefore, there was a guaranteed supply of young elephants for the school.

I visited Gangala na Bodio in 1946 and was heartily welcomed by the director of the school, who installed me in a guest pavilion, and showed me everything there was to see. I even witnessed an elephant hunt in the National Park, where young fellows from twelve to twenty years of age are taken for training. At this age they are considered old and strong enough to stand the strains of captivity but not too old to learn new tricks. But it is not an easy task to pick and choose your elephant like that and to get him back to the school without harm and, if possible, without hurting other elephants in the herd from which he is taken. The men who actually catch the elephants by lasso are usually Azande tribesmen, rigorously trained for the dangerous job which they seem to love. They are protected by skilled professional hunters with elephant guns who will shoot to kill when one of the men is in danger. The most important members of the hunting party are probably the trained elephants, or monitors, who go along to calm the captured animals, soothe them and bring them back to school.

When a herd of elephants is located, the commander of the school picks out the animals he wants, points them out to his hunters, and then starts the movement to cut them off from the rest of the herd. Guns are fired in the air to stampede the group of elephants, at which point the hunters rush in to divert the chosen ones. Many get away, of course, but some are lassoed—and that is not an easy job. You can't really get an elephant around the head because his trunk will usually throw the rope off, so the hunters try to entangle one of the hind legs.

An elephant that is caught fights and struggles for all he is worth, of course, and the hunters make every effort to keep from frightening him too much. Some elephants have been known to die of fright, of heart attack, just after capture so everyone tries to keep the capturing as kind and gentle as possible.

Just as soon as a few young elephants are secure, the monitors are called up. They are elephants who have not only gone through the school but have proved themselves particularly reliable. Monitors are never sold to zoos or let out for hard labor but are kept for the express purpose of helping to calm and train new elephants. Each monitor has his *mahout*, or *cornac* as he is called in the Congo, who gives him his orders. A monitor elephant stands on either side of the captured animal while a rope is tied around the young elephant's middle and around each monitor's neck. When the captured animal bucks or holds back, it hurts the monitors, so they punish him, argue with him, or in some way tell him to stop being so stubborn. Meanwhile the *cornacs* are talking soothingly in the way they have learned to talk to elephants and by the time the elephant gets to the school he is no longer belligerent or rebellious—at least in most cases.

Food and plenty of water do a good deal of the job for the next few weeks. The captured elephants come to know the *cornacs* who bring them especially delicious meals each day, hose them off, fill their pools, and so on. Then the training period begins, and a *cornac* does the entire job, with the help of elephant monitors. Elephants are obviously fond of their *cornacs* even when they are still suspicious of other humans, and they certainly listen to the monitor elephants who tell them what a pleasant life this is.

And it certainly is a good life. Elephants in zoos and circuses, even when treated with kindness, must find their quarters very confining. But the elephants at Gangala na Bodio have miles of room to roam around in, the Dungu River to swim and cavort in, and plenty of company. Such a natural life is led, in fact, that I witnessed a copulation scene near the river banks.

Love affairs are encouraged at this coeducational school because elephants born at the school require no catching and grow up with the idea that humans are kind and helpful, even though masters demand a certain amount of work.

There are unfortunate accidents here, of course. A few hunters get killed, and I heard of one *cornac* who fell from the head of a monitor that had been gentle and obedient for years. The elephant impaled him with his tusk; for what reason no one could discern. Another *cornac* fell from his elephant while that animal was bathing, and a crocodile snatched him and ate him before anyone could come to his help.

There is some doubt about how economical elephants are for working purposes. They require so much food, and take such a long time to eat it, that production is small in proportion to consumption. Some people insist that tractors are better, even with the high cost of gasoline in the interior of Africa. Many elephants are doing good work, however, in addition to supplying zoos—and the Belgians have thoroughly disproved the old idea that African elephants could not be trained and tamed.

In the old days they used to capture elephants by shooting the mother and then taking a young one who stayed by her side. But the Belgians at Gangala na Bodio, and a few hunters, elsewhere learned that the job could be done more humanely and at the same time more efficiently. Elephants are shy, timid, and sensitive creatures; they are more likely to live if they are introduced to civilization with a minimum of shock. American cow-boy methods were adapted to the big game of Africa, the idea being to cut the desired animal out of the herd and then lasso it.

We filmed several such hunts with Pellegrini. They were back-breaking experiences, but they packed as much excitement as any of our special photographic missions.

First a base camp had to be established in good elephant country where the animals were not protected—trackless country through which trucks could travel. And that's where the back-breaking part came in, for most people would not have considered the area we covered passable. Pellegrini could take a truck almost anywhere, often at high speed—and he did. He skirted boggy marshland and occasionally stopped at a ten-foot ravine with perpendicular sides, but rocks, stumps, underbrush, potholes, streams and washboard terrain with foot-high corrugations could not even slow him down when he was after elephants. Twice in one week he broke springs on his truck, but he had come equipped for such emergencies and replaced the springs himself, after a full day's chase in the broiling sun.

We usually had Dave Mason in the "catching" truck, driven by one of Pellegrini's men, and another cameraman, Freddie Ford Jr., in a second truck that followed along behind. On the first foray, the second truck was left a mile behind, and Pellegrini had already lassoed one little elephant by the time it caught up. After that, truck number two kept up with the catching truck no matter what happened to the backs and heads of the jouncing, rocking passengers. The cameramen suffered particularly because they could not hold onto anything. They had to protect their precious cameras, clutching them with both hands to keep them from banging against the truck. At the end of a day's hunting, the men were battered and sore. So was everyone else, but Pellegrini was the only one who seemed never to mind. He had only one thought—catch elephants.

When he first spotted a herd in the distance, he examined it carefully. Sometimes he said, "No, we won't go after that one. I don't like it." We could never figure out just how he reached his conclusions about a herd that might cause trouble and one that he could tackle with comparative safety and assurance of success. It was just a feeling he had. Once he had chosen a big herd as satisfactory, he headed toward it in the trucks, keeping the wind right so the animals would not start running away too soon. As he approached, with the truck crashing through the thick low brush, skipping from furrow to furrow in the hard-baked earth, he tried to pick out the elephant he wanted, a youngster he could handle but not quite a baby. While one truck scattered the herd, Pellegrini maneuvered his so that he could cut this one elephant away from the rest, or at least cut it off with only one or two others. And finally, he had to catch up with the racing elephant, come alongside close enough, and throw his rope to catch it. This was only a small part of the job, for Pellegrini and his helpers had to calm the captured elephant enough to get it into the back of his truck. Then, after such a day's work, he had to drive fifty miles to a mission where he had built a paddock to contain his captured elephants. Later, after the hunt was over, he would see about moving his whole catch— five or six young elephants—to Arusha.

There were days when, after miles and miles of this roughest of travel, not an elephant would be seen. Other days a herd would be sighted but, on approach, would turn out to be on the opposite side of an impassable ravine. At other times a herd would head into a marsh where the trucks could not follow. Here was the toughest route of all, for near the edges of the marsh elephant footprints two feet deep, made when the ground was muddy, had dried as hard as rocks.

Twice our cameramen were almost killed. Once after an elephant had been caught, the rope holding it was temporarily tied to the rear of the second truck. There was a hatch in the top of this truck, through which a cameraman could stick his head, arms and camera. Dave Mason was up there, very pleased with shots he had taken of the lassoing of the young elephant. Suddenly the captured animal darted for the front of the truck, scraping the rope across the top of the vehicle. With an elephant tugging on it, the rope might well have decapitated Mason if he had not moved like lightning. And it is not easy to get oneself and a big camera down through a narrow hatch in a hurry. Just as Dave was jerking his head down, the rope caught the back of it, smacked it hard against the front of the hatch, and scraped over the top of his head. He fell down in the bottom of the truck with blood streaming from his nose, but the first thing he looked for was the camera, which had not been damaged.

Another time, Freddie Ford Jr. had lashed himself to the struts at the back of the catching truck so that he could get some pictures with the truck in motion. With both hands on the camera, he had to tie himself to keep from being thrown out. In the midst of the cutting-out operation, one of the big elephants became angry and started chasing the catching truck. The driver, intent on the prey ahead, did not even realize that he was being pursued. But Freddie, tied securely, saw the angry elephant bearing down on him, getting closer and closer. In spite of the danger he kept photographing the pursuing elephant. The men in the second truck, which fortunately was close by, saw what was happening and yelled to the driver of the catching truck. But there was so much noise he could not hear. The elephant was so near, finally, that he started stretching out his trunk for Freddie, and the tip of that trunk was only four feet away from him. Pellegrini, in the cab of the catching truck, suddenly realized what was happening, turned and saw the elephant bearing down on them. With a jerk and a spurt of speed the truck pulled away from the mammoth pursuer, and this was one time that no one minded the terrific pounding and rocketing of the vehicle. Freddie was vastly relieved, but what he talked about most was the unusual shots he must have taken.

Pellegrini was still determined to get another elephant. A fine herd was seen late one afternoon, so everyone camped out near the spot, sleeping in the trucks, with the hope that the elephants could not move away at dawn without being seen and followed. The next morning, however, as the elephant herd

started moving, the trucks followed and were stopped by ground
that even Pellegrini found impassable. But this did not discour-
age him. Some fine open terrain, solid and easy to maneuver
on, lay some distance to the right, and he meant to get the
elephants to move in that direction. So with two helpers he set off
through the tall elephant grass on foot, determined to circle
around the herd and drive it toward the good ground. The others
sat in the trucks and waited. In about two hours Pellegrini came
back, having been caught in a bush fire, completely submerged
in a river he had to cross, but smiling triumphantly. He had
managed to head the elephants toward the good ground.

Soon the herd appeared, ambling along rather reluctantly toward the good ground, and the trucks followed them slowly.
Then the herd stopped. For some reason they did not want to go
ahead. They did not want to turn back where the bush fire was
burning. As if all the elephants in the herd—at least twenty of
them—had thought of the same thing at once, they turned toward the trucks. Why not go in that direction? Only a few men
and a couple of trucks were in the way.

Pellegrini knows his elephants, and he obviously knew what
they were contemplating. He ordered one of his men to start a
bush fire at once, not far from the trucks. The man was afraid
and refused, but Pellegrini knew the seriousness of the situation.

"If we don't start a fire to turn them," he said, "they'll head
this way in a few minutes. And don't think you'll be safe in the
truck. They'll turn it over in a flash."

By the time the dry brush was blazing, the elephants were
moving slowly toward the trucks—eighty yards away, seventy
yards away, sixty yards away. Someone snatched up a piece of
the burning bush and tossed it in a thick patch of dry grass,
which blazed up with a roaring whoosh. The elephants stopped,
stared, and finally turned. At last they moved off toward the
good ground. Pellegrini didn't know what made them so reluctant to go there—it was just the sort of terrain elephants like.

The trucks moved in after the herd and, because the ground
was smoother than ever before, were able to get fairly steady

shots of the entire action of cutting out and catching a young elephant.

Nobody had any food that day, but there was the satisfaction of knowing that something exciting and unusual had been recorded in color. And that was what we had come to Africa for.

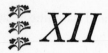# XII

Misses and Near Misses

EVERY time I've gone back to Africa, I have stayed longer, traveled farther, penetrated deeper, and taken more chances in my efforts to get good and unusual pictures. But there were some scenes fairly close to the main towns and roads that kept eluding me. One was Kilimanjaro. With all the glamour that has surrounded this highest of African mountains, I felt that leaving Africa without seeing it would be like leaving Pisa without a view of the leaning tower. But that is not as easy as it sounds. Kilimanjaro is a shy thing that keeps herself clothed in clouds a good deal of the time. The first explorers who saw it could not quite believe their eyes, for it was not there the next day—or the next. Had they seen only a mirage? Eternal snow so near the equator was a hard thing to believe anyway, and people back in Europe thought the explorers had been touched with the fever when they heard about it.

Kilimanjaro has captured men's imagination as have few mountains in the world. Rising slowly and gently from the torrid plains—you can walk up one side of it, so gradual is the ascent, without any real climbing ability—it keeps on mounting to the sky until it has reached almost twenty thousand feet at Kibo Peak. The last few thousand feet, gracefully draped with snow, look like something ethereal, far removed from things of the world. We've all seen photographs in which the forested and barren lower slopes fade mistily from view, blending with the background and leaving the glistening white peaks suspended far above in the heavens. Then it is a ghost mountain, a mysterious presence hovering over puny men below.

You are lucky to be able to see Kilimanjaro like this. During

my 1937 trip I waited and looked in vain for it to emerge from
the clouds. Finally, Cézaire and I decided to walk up, but local
authorities assured us we would find it disappointing. Standing
on it, no one could appreciate its beauty or magnitude—and until passing the forest line at about ten thousand feet nothing but
trees could be seen.

"All right, we'll fly around it," I decided, and chartered a
small plane at the town of Moshi, on the dry steppe near the foot
of the mountain amidst great plantations of coffee and sisal. On
the lower slopes of Kilimanjaro live thousands of the Chagga
tribe—all growing coffee that is almost as good as that found
around Lake Kivu.

From the plane we could see the plantations and the beginning of the forest above them. Then the clouds closed in for a
time while we climbed steadily through them. Suddenly we
broke through them into air so clear and sparkling that it seemed
to emanate from a perfectly cut diamond. Close at hand—or at
least in that air it appeared close—lay the slopes of the mountain showing the end of the forest belt and the beginning of
the fringe of giant lobelia, senecio and tree heather. Above came
green, green grass sprinkled with millions of Alpine flowers. But
what held our eyes was the gleaming, shimmering white of Kibo
Peak which loomed high above us although we were flying at
about fifteen thousand feet. In this world of air, seemingly de-
tached completely from the earth, the mountain was suspended.

We circled around Kilimanjaro and feasted our eyes on it,
then sloped down through the clouds and landed on the prosaic
earth again. I had seen Kilimanjaro and while it was a thrilling
experience, it was not completely satisfying. Seeing it from a
plane, above a blanket of clouds, robbed me of a view of the
mountain entire, from plains to snowy peak. I wanted to look at
it with my feet on the ground and follow the lines of it all the
way up. From a plane is was not quite real.

Again in 1946, although I spent weeks in and around the
country from which magnificent views of Kilimanjaro could be
seen, I didn't get one clear sight of it—and not a single picture.

Finally, in 1954, fortune favored me and the clouds cleared
while I was in Amboseli. For three whole days Kilimanjaro was
revealed. I often found my mind and eyes wandering from the
business at hand—rhinos and elephants usually—toward the
snow-covered mountain. And at the end of a day, it brought
a strange peace and relaxation.

Another African "must" that kept eluding me photographically was, of all things, flamingoes. I saw them by the thousands,
but could get no pictures of them. They feed in huge flocks on
three slightly saline lakes in East Africa—Nakura, Elmenteita
and Hannington. The nature of the water aids the growth of
food upon which flamingoes dote and the lakes are rather shallow, so the long-legged birds can wander over wide stretches
around the shore. As you approach the lakes, you think some
kind of pink water-lilies must have been strewn over thousands
of square yards of shoreline for you can see nothing but a slightly
moving mass of brilliant pink. When you get close enough to
make out a few individual birds on the periphery, they are likely
to take off. A flamingo, like most big birds, requires a runway almost as long as one of our big bombers, so the creatures in the
middle of the feeding flock cannot move immediately. The outer
edges of the pink mass move first, with a great whirring of wings
and splashing of the water. All the others follow in one great
slow wave that becomes airborne as in a slow-motion movie. In
the air they spread out and circle around the lake, making a pink
cloud between you and the sun.

I was particularly eager in 1937 to get moving pictures of
this sight because I was taking the first colored nature picture to
come out of Africa, and the sight is almost breath-taking in full
color. For three days I waited at Lake Nakura, which was supposed to have the largest flamingo colony, while thick gray
clouds hovered overhead. Finally I had to give up, and went on
my way without the pictures. So in 1946 flamingoes were again
on my list of pictures to take. Hearing that Lake Nakura had
receded considerably in the past few years, we went to Lake

Elmenteita, where we found the biggest flocks of pink flamingoes I had ever seen. Having a professional cameraman along, I turned over the photography to him, stationing him in an ideal spot where the light was perfect. Then I approached the flocks of flamingoes to set them into flight. Everything went off just as I planned it—except that my cameraman told me the next day, after we had gone on our way, that his film had been threaded incorrectly and all flamingo footage was ruined! In 1954, we finally obtained good footage of thousands of flamingoes taking to the air, the beat of their countless wings sounding like that of a distant cascade.

Birds are difficult to photograph, unless you set out to be a nature photographer specializing in birds. Otherwise you must confine yourself to the big birds that usually abound in clusters at some spot. Vultures were easy to get, of course, because they congregate wherever there is carrion and are quite courageous in sticking to their meals even though you come close. And marabou storks often accompany the vultures. It is strange how this bird came to be a carrion-eater, for his big bill is not made for tearing and eating flesh. If it weren't for the vultures, he'd starve or have to change his diet. He waits for a vulture to rip off a great chunk of flesh, then tries to snatch if from him. If he gets hold of a piece, it disappears in that gigantic bill, and the vulture must go back to the carcass for more.

Pelicans are big enough to get pictures of, and I particularly enjoyed a group in 1954 in Queen Elizabeth Park, Uganda, which seemed to be hunting in formation. They fly along about ten or fifteen feet above the surface of the water, looking for fish, then fold their wings and swoop like a dive-bomber when they spot one. This is an interesting sight at any time, but when you see ten or twelve pelicans flying like that in a straight line and diving together, all at the same angle, as if on the command of a sergeant—that's the unexpected camera shot that brings joy to one's heart.

Africa is as rich in birds as in animals, and I saw egrets, ducks of different kinds, hornbills, cormorants, darters, terns, gulls, eagles, bustards, francolins, grouse and partridge and quail, humming birds, sun birds, widow birds, blackbirds, cuckoos, doves, warblers, Egyptian geese, plovers, herons, crested and other cranes, snake-hunting secretary birds, and parrots of endless variety. Only a few of these could I capture on film.

The continent really outdoes itself when it comes to insect life of which I got no pictures at all. There are not just thousands of species, but hundreds of thousands—and scientists find a dozen or more new kinds each year. Mosquitoes, flies, ants and termites are the only small creatures that come to the attention of most visitors, but they can kill you or drive you almost crazy. Among the flies, of course, is the tsetse which carries the trypanosome of sleeping sickness. Much of Tanganyika is tsetse country, but authorities are taking area after area to work on, cleaning out the bush, the swamps and the breeding places. This means cleaning out the wild life, too, so there is considerable opposition. In other instances, entire populations have been moved from tsetse country.

Sleeping sickness can be cured, of course, but many natives will not come in to the doctors in time to get rid of it. Malaria can be forestalled by travelers if they will obey orders and take the right number of capsules weekly. Chiggers may bore into the skin between your toes even if you wear good shoes and bathe regularly, but these habits will make it unlikely. I never had to have a chigger cut out during all my three trips to Africa. In fact, I never became sick in Africa although I traveled through every kind of country and was for long stretches away from the benefits of running water.

I encountered snakes but was never bitten by one. There was the black mamba in the Ituri, a cobra in the Ngorongoro crater and many others. But snakes are almost impossible to film unless they are in captivity. The natural habitat of most snakes has insufficient light for photography. Their protective coloration is such that you can scarcely see them until they move, and then they are gone in a flash. I concluded that a python was the only reptile big enough to show up on film, but not until my 1954-55 trip did I find a man who knew enough about snakes to help me. That was Allan Tarlton.

Tarlton is one of those rare humans—a man who likes snakes. Nephew of Leslie Tarlton, the first professional white hunter in East Africa and the man who guided Theodore Roosevelt on his famous hunts there, Allan himself has been one of the best-known white hunters for several decades. This makes his interest in snakes even more striking, for most hunters I've known can't stand the creatures. Carr Hartley, for example, who fears no animal and makes pets of hyenas and rhinos, has such a sickening aversion for snakes that he must turn over to another man any business involving them.

For more than thirty years, however, Allan Tarlton has been fascinated by snakes and has kept every African variety in captivity at one time or another, sometimes having hundreds on hand at one time. Because of the almost universal human aversion for snakes, he feels that we know too little about them. They thrive in captivity, he says, and become quite accustomed to being handled, some even reaching the amiable point of being called tame. This doesn't mean that he abandons all caution when fondling his pets and he has been bitten scores of times—fortunately never by a cobra, mamba or other member of the elapine group for which there is no known antidote.

The cobra is probably the nastiest snake of all, Tarlton says, because its poison is so potent. Anyone getting a full dose of it hasn't a chance. The nerve centers at the base of the brain are immediately paralyzed, but the poison is so powerful a stimulant that the victim's heart keeps beating for almost half an hour.

Tarlton's hobby, which started when he was just a boy, has developed into a business that eventually became more important than his chosen profession of white hunter. In addition to acting as snake adviser to most of the big companies making African movies—and there have been a number in recent years—

he had a snake farm where he produced venom for serums and for research. During the war he was in charge of a serpentarium supplying dehydrated venom to the South African Institute of Medical Research, and managed more than three thousand captive snakes which he personally "milked" regularly. That meant grasping and extracting the venom from about four hundred snakes a day, keeping track of each one so that each snake would produce at each milking the same amount and potency of venom.

Toward the end of such a day, he admits, he used to get pretty tired—and this was always the dangerous time, when muscles were fatigued and alertness dulled. A puff adder might then wrench his head free and drive his poison-bearing teeth into his flesh. Despite his great experience and caution, he was bitten nineteen times during the war years. These, in addition to his other bites, has led to his having a strange kind of ailment —over-immunization. Each time he was bitten, of course, he was given the necessary serum that would serve as an antidote to the poison, and each time he himself built up in his blood stream more and more immunity to the poisons of snakes—like the legendary king who took more and more arsenic each day until he could eat doses that would kill half a dozen normal men. This sounds fine for a snake-handler, but such immunization means a delicate balance within the blood stream. Now what he has to watch out for is the bite of a bee or any other insect injecting formic acid with the bite. The great danger here is a sudden and total breakdown of blood and tissue cells as a result of even mild alteration of the blood balance.

A bee sting could easily kill Tarlton, but he has managed to survive three or four such stings with only a period of unconsciousness. This is because he goes completely prepared at all times with hypodermic syringe, tourniquet, anti-venin and heart stimulants. If he can manage to keep his heart going while the formic acid is being dissipated in the body, he will recover. At the same time, he has to guard more carefully than ever against more snake bites. Seven or eight years ago, doctors told him that his blood was in such precarious balance that one more bite would be fatal. But did he stop handling snakes? No. And he has been bitten four times since then and says he feels as fine as he ever did in his life.

When I met Tarlton in Arusha, I asked if it would be possible to film a genuine, undomesticated python in a scene involving human beings. He said yes, and added that perhaps a python was the only reptile I could use for such a sequence. A python has sharp teeth and powerful jaws, but he injects no poison. His method of killing is to clamp his jaws onto his victim just to hold him, then get his tail wound around a tree trunk or rock so he will have some leverage when he coils his body around his victim to crush it to death. The way to handle a python, Tarlton told me, is never to let it hook that tail onto anything, for without its purchase it cannot squeeze even a lemon. Of course, you try to avoid the bite, too, because it hurts even if it isn't poisonous.

He made it all sound so simple that I decided I could handle a python myself—with Tarlton at hand. He agreed that it should not be too difficult or dangerous, so we decided to set the stage for the capture of a python. There was only one hitch —the python usually lives in thick growth where there is almost no light. We'd have to get ours out into the open so we could photograph it. When I pointed out that I wanted to avoid too much "staging" of any scene, that I insisted on genuineness and accuracy, Tarlton assured me that there would be no staging beyond placing a good big python in a spot with excellent light. He'd go into the bush, capture a python, take it to a nice spreading tree standing alone in the plains, and put it on a low branch. Then he'd let it go and we'd film our discovery and capture of the reptile. If anything, the reptile would be angrier than normal, after that handling.

We found a good spot, set up cameras, and Tarlton and his helpers brought the python and placed it on a low branch of the tree we had selected. Then Tarlton and I moved off some distance. The cameras started turning as we walked toward the tree and saw the python. Close-up of python. Decision to capture same. Tarlton's natives had a gunny-sack, but they hung back as we approached the big snake. As Tarlton came close, the python suddenly shot his massive head forward, aiming a stunning blow at the man, who ducked it like an expert boxer without retreating. The snake coiled its thick body back for another thrust and again missed Tarlton only by inches.

Apparently feeling that it could battle better on the ground, it slithered down the tree trunk and made directly for us with speed and determination. But now Tarlton had the python where he wanted it. This time, as it unleashed a vicious blow at Tarlton's legs, he deftly sidestepped and, with a speed to equal the snake's, dove and grabbed its neck with both hands. A moment later I leaped on the python's body, holding on to its writhing rear end for all I was worth. It was sickeningly cold, twice as thick as my arm and possessed of amazing strength. But I held on despite all its lashing and twisting.

The natives ran up with the gunny-sack and with their help we managed to shove the writhing python inside. The whole incident took only a few minutes, but they were exciting and strenuous minutes. I was glad to get away from the clammy feeling of the reptile, cold like the flesh of a dead creature. But this python had been very much alive.

That one experience with reptiles was enough for me, and I happily returned to the business of photographing wild animals and tribes. I wanted to film another scene I had missed on my first two expeditions—perhaps the most exciting and dramatic hunt in the world—Masai tribesmen killing a lion with their spears.

XIII

Cattlemen with Spears

THE Masai have been much photographed and written about because they are handsome, proud and romantic. Even today, when they have dwindled in numbers, degenerated into considerable loafing, drinking, and venereal disease and been forced to abandon their warlike customs, they are appealing. You can see this appeal most clearly among the British officials of Kenya and Tanganyika, who look upon the Masai as extremely difficult; but at the same time they complain about what headaches the Masai are, they speak with pride in their voices, with admiration for the sometimes overbearing insolence of this tribe. I knew one official, in charge of the Masai Reserve, who always talked of "my Masai," as one would of a talented and likable child who was a holy terror. The British recognize in the Masai another people who, like themselves, are born with the unshakable conviction that they are a superior race. Even the lowliest Masai feels absolutely certain that he occupies a plane far above other human beings. He doesn't have to prove it, to himself or anyone else, for Nature ordered things in that fashion. Some distance below, the Masai places the British but everyone else in the world is out of sight—beneath the reach of the Masai's glance.

In spite of this superiority, the Masai is a friendly person. He doesn't throw his weight around or act obnoxious. He is cooperative in any venture that makes sense, considerate, polite. But I would hate to be on the other side of the fence when he decides that he does not like you. He is a formidable enemy, even in a more or less subject state.

The self-confidence of the Masai is the kind that has been

part of a race's heritage and legend for centuries, but we don't know their history that far back. They are probably a Hamitic race, with some Bantu added and possibly some strains of the Nilotic. Not too long ago—a couple of centuries perhaps—they moved down from the north as conquerors. We do know that in the 19th century they were the top dogs in all of East Africa. They had overcome all of the Bantu tribes in their way, they kept making raids and extending their territory, they scared the slave-trading Arabs so thoroughly that they detoured around the Masai, and no Masai was ever enslaved.

You can still see this era of kingship in the walk and bearing and glance of a Masai *moran*, or warrior. He is tall—around six feet or more—thin, well-proportioned, and walks with a graceful loping stride. He wears a dark cloth loosely thrown over one shoulder—except for lion-hunting, when he strips for action. He glows with a kind of reddish-orange hue, from the ochre mud that he smears on his body and, chiefly, in his hair which is gathered into three or four small pigtails. He doesn't tattoo his body and wears relatively little decoration. Pierced earlobes, however, have been stretched and stretched until they are long loops, from which dangle heavy ornaments of copper or iron.

This is the professional warrior, part of the Masai standing army, which consists of every able-bodied male between the ages of about eighteen and thirty. This was all very well, perhaps, when the Masai were rulers and conquerors, but nowadays it is rather troublesome to have such a large body of professional warriors and no one to fight. Idle soldiers have a tendency to make or get into trouble, and the Masai *moran* is no exception.

As a boy he has been trained for this warrior period of his life, has dreamed of the day he will reach it. At about fourteen he goes through a painful and rigorous circumcision ceremony, remarkably like that of primitive tribes elsewhere in Africa and as far away as South America and Australia. As he approaches his 18th year, he allows his hair to grow—up to that time it has been shaved off, as with all Masai except the warriors.

Finally he goes out on a lion hunt with some of the veteran warriors, and that makes him into *el moran*. Since the old lion-spearing expeditions are now almost nonexistent, I don't know what the occasion is for the introduction of a young man into the warrior band. At any rate, a warrior devotes his life and thoughts to being a warrior and nothing else. He cannot marry. He cannot live with his family, but instead lives at a special *manyatta*, or village, for fighting men. But this doesn't mean any Spartan-like abstinence on his part, for he may have one or more young girls living at the *manyatta*, too.

Girls living with the warriors are usually so young that they have not yet reached puberty and thus there is little chance of their conceiving. When they approach that age, they withdraw from the *moran manyatta*, go through a rigorous circumcision ceremony of their own, and are considered marriageable. And they are supposed to remain more or less chaste until married, faithful afterward, except when, as often happens, the husband gives permission for her to entertain a guest or friend.

For about twelve years the young Masai man is a warrior, with no wars going on any more. At thirty, however, he retires, cuts off his pigtails, and marries. If he has been a good hunter and fighter, if he is smart and respected, he becomes one of the elders of his clan, and may be elected headman by the other elders.

Women don't have much to say among the Masai, but are on the whole rather well treated. They give themselves their own punishment, so far as I could see, by wearing pounds and pounds of decoration, usually thick copper wire formed into rings around arms, legs, and neck. Each limb may carry up to fifteen pounds of copper, and once put on it is never taken off. Some women carry such a load around their necks that they have to support it in a wooden frame when they lie down to sleep. It is colorful, but I didn't find it particularly attractive.

The Masai are cattle herders and blood drinkers. A few groups of this once large tribe, isolated from the others in course of migrations and wars, have turned to agriculture and a settled life, but the vast majority, including those of southern Kenya and Tanganyika, are pastoral folk who consider it degrading to hoe the earth. Like herdsmen the world over, the Masai must lead a more or less nomadic life as they move about seeking good pastures for their cattle, but they keep themselves within a pretty well restricted area and build homes that are at least a little more permanent than tents.

Wealth and prestige depend largely upon a person's cattle, but unlike the Watussi, the Masai count the number of cattle only and pay little attention to the quality. Actually, the Masai cows are generally a small and sorry-looking lot, and their milk production is not very large. But most of the sustenance of these natives must come from the cattle. Milk in its many forms— cheese, smoked milk, butter, clarified butter called *ghee*—form the basis of most food, but the *pièce de resistance* is blood drawn from the jugular vein of one of the cattle. It may be taken straight or mixed with milk into a kind of thin porridge. This high protein diet may account in part for the lean, muscular appearance of most Masai.

Cattle are the central focus of life for all Masai. Even the lion-hunting for which they are famous and through which a young fellow proves his manhood stems from cattle keeping, for the lions go after the cattle. Whatever steals a Masai warrior's cattle is the enemy, and the lion is the arch enemy. These magnificent hunters never hunt anything else, and they do not eat the meat of any game.

Just as cattle are the center of Masai life, so are cattle the source of much Masai crime and deviltry. In the older days of war, the Masai raided neighboring tribes to steal cattle or good pasture-land. In these days of enforced peace, individual Masai *moran* or small groups of restless young men may steal cattle from a neighboring tribe, even of Masai. The government's troubles revolve much of the time around cattle. The Masai are not very cooperative about taking steps to protect their cattle from the rinderpest or the trypanosomiasis given by the tsetse fly. They move their herds onto game preserves or other restricted areas when they are not supposed to. And they resist, actively or passively, the government requirement that they must sell a certain number of their cattle each year. Since the cattle use so much of the land and constitute a primary nutritional resource of the area, they must be used to support the population—even the non-Masai part of the population.

On my 1946 trip, while I was in Uganda and before reaching Kenya or Tanganyika, I read a newspaper report of the killing of a British official, Major Hugh Grant, by a Masai. Feelings ran high over the murder and the subsequent trial of the native. A few weeks later, when I reached Kenya and had gone out to the Narok area—in Masai country—with David Sheldrick and Mark Williams, I got the story from them.

When the government regulation first went into effect, requiring each Masai cattleman to sell a certain percentage of his herd to the government, these wily natives invariably picked out the very worst of their animals. So the government stepped in and said that its officials would select the cows to be purchased. They did not select the best, but a representative group, good, fair and poor—leaning over backwards most of the time to be fair. The system worked all right most of the time, but the British had not taken into account the fact that sometimes a Masai herder will become deeply attached to one or two particular cows. This is often an emotional feeling such as one might have for a devoted dog or other domestic pet. When the government official inadvertently picked out one of these pets to be purchased, the Masai would be desolate and would plead with the official not to take that particular animal. Take any other, even a fatter one, but not this cherished creature.

The officials, at the outset, agreed to a substitution each time this situation arose which was not too common to cause any difficulty. But then the Masai decided they could use this sentimental understanding of the British. Some of them claimed that every fat, sleek and hearty cow was a particular pet. Being excellent actors, like most primitives, the Masai would weep and plead with great urgency—but they carried the stratagem too far. Major Grant had been one of the most gracious in allowing substitutions, so he found himself taken advantage of more than any other official. And he reacted as almost anyone would. No more substitutions!

Then came the time that he chose his cattle from a Masai herd and picked, without knowing it, one of the herdsman's dearest pets. The Masai begged to be allowed to keep this one beast, but Major Grant had made a ruling—no more substitutions—and would not reconsider. When the Masai saw that the Major meant business, he lifted his spear, hurled it at Grant and impaled him against the wall.

The native was tried and convicted, of course, but there was much bad feeling on both sides. Generally, however, the Masai are not actually dangerous as are the Kikuyu, who started the Mau Mau movement. They are troublesome, proud, and insolent, but rarely murderers.

I saw my first Masai in 1937, and felt the same admiration for them that almost everyone does. There's something fine in the sight of two or three Masai *moran* striding across the flat plains, with their very long and thin spears and tough colorful shields. Nowadays, of course, most of the Masai in Kenya and some elsewhere have been deprived of both spears and shields so they cannot war on their neighbors. Some of the men carry staffs instead of the spears, but they are not the same thing, by any means. And something has happened to the Masai soul with this major deprivation. In some areas of Tanganyika, fortunately, the Masai have kept shields and spears and may keep them so long as they are well behaved. But this is almost as soul-wrenching a deprivation as taking away the weapons themselves. A Masai warrior cannot really reconcile himself to the idea of a spear and a shield as nothing but ornaments.

For my 1937 trip into the fabulous Ngorongoro crater, I needed Masai guides. Through the kind offices of British officials in Arusha, I went to a Masai village to make the necessary arrangements, and here my partial disillusionment with the Masai began. I didn't expect beauty in a nomad's temporary settlement, precisely, but after seeing the proud and handsome Masai men I expected something in keeping with the people and their personality. Of course my standards are different, and I can make many allowances for that fact, but filth just does not fit—in my mind—with personal beauty, strength, bravery and pride.

The first view of a Masai *manyatta* is rather striking, for all you can see is a big circle of tangled thornbushes, ten or twelve feet high, designed not just to keep lions out but to keep cattle in. A determined and hungry lion can find his way through or over such a barrier, and the Masai know it, but the thorn wall is a deterrent for any but the hungriest.

Inside the circle, I saw a cluster of flat-roofed huts made of earth and dung—with plenty of odor to confirm the latter. There was more to the smell than just cow manure, however, which was accounted for when I was told that the Masai use cattle urine for washing. They certainly do not waste any product of their herds!

I wanted to look into one of the huts, unprepossessing as it was, so made my way through a cloud of flies that had found a paradise on earth. The Masai do not seem to have a well organized or systematized religion, but they believe that the spirits of their ancestors abide in all living things—except the lion. Even flies are creatures that may bear an ancestor's spirit, so they must not be molested. The Masai will not even shoo them away.

The doors of Masai huts are very low, so I got down on my hands and knees to crawl in and have a look. I could not see much, for there are no windows, but a fire was burning dully, filling the place with thick smoke. A calf tried to moo at me from a far corner, but I did not investigate further. The smoke made my eyes smart, and the smell was ten times as strong inside as it had been outside. The floor of the hut was made of manure, damp and sticky!

I abandoned my investigation at that point, since my curiosity seemed to have evaporated. My first reaction was what yours might be—the feeling that any people who could live that way could not really be admirable. But as I went on my way to Ngorongoro with a group of Masai *moran* who were obviously admirable, my perspective returned. All I could say with assurance was that I would never want to live in such huts or such villages. I might even go so far as to say that anyone in my own civilization who would live that way would have something wrong with him. But the Masai are living as Masai people have lived for centuries. You have to try to look at it inside the Masai framework. All it proved to me was that my standards of town-planning, architecture, sanitation and hygiene did not necessarily have much bearing on the character of a people.

Still, I like to think of the Masai as they are when hunting lions. It is this which has caused explorers and big-game hunters to call them the "bravest of the brave." A few white hunters who in the old days accompanied Masai on a lion hunt have sworn they could never summon the courage that seems a commonplace thing among Masai men, and some have been so frightened that at the crucial moment they fired a gun and spoiled the hunt for the natives.

When a lion has killed a cow—that's the time when the Masai go after the beast. Sometimes only a few take up the trail, but usually ten or more strip themselves for action and track down the killer. They usually locate the lion in a thick growth into which they throw rocks until the beast leaps out in an effort to get away. In a flash the Masai hunters are after it, and in short order the lion turns to attack its pursuers. At this point the hunters encircle the animal, closing in on it step by step, shields held before them, spears poised to strike.

When the men are ten or fifteen feet away, the lion usually chooses one to attack; one that he will kill to escape from the ring closing round him. With three twitches of the tail the big cat leaps, and the hunter facing it drops to one knee and lifts his shield to bear the force of the pounce, at the same time hurling his spear at the lion in mid-air. Even if the spear hits its mark—and it may pass completely through the lion—that does

not stop the animal, by any means. The big body lands on the
shield, the claws raking and scratching for all they're worth.
Even though the other hunters have thrown their spears, and
the lion may look like a pin-cushion, the man who takes the
lion's attack is almost always mauled considerably, and sometimes killed. The other hunters, after flinging their spears, rush
in with their *simis*, double-edged knives about two feet long, and
hack away at the lion until the animal is nothing but hunks of
bone and a mass of bloody fur. They don't care about skins or
trophies—only about dead lions.

The hunters come back home happy and triumphant, proud
of their wounds and their bent spears. The man who took the
charge is a special hero in most instances, but on occasion there
is one who takes precedence even over him. This is the man
who may grab the lion by the tail. If the encircling ring of
hunters gets close enough before the lion springs, one man may
rush forward, snatch the animal's twitching tail, and haul back
on it with all his strength. At this instant, of course, the other
hunters hurl their spears and close in with knives, hoping to
kill the lion before it can whirl and claw the tail-holder. While
this procedure sounds silly, it can acually hamper the footing
and crouch of a lion enough to spoil its pounce—at least for a
very short time. A lion is strong enough, of course, to jerk free
from a tail-hold unless he is killed in that second or two when
thrown off balance and, I would guess, considerably embarrassed.

No one had taken movies of a genuine Masai lion hunt for
years and, so far as I could learn, it had never been shot in color.
So when I went to Africa in 1946, one of my hopes was to film
such a sequence. It would be dangerous, I knew, for when a lion
breaks out of a ring of Masai hunters—as it sometimes does—it
is always wounded, enraged, fast and deadly. If I were close
enough to get good shots of the scene, I would be within easy
reach of the lion. But I figured that I could be covered at such
times by a white hunter with gun.

I did not need to worry, for the authorities would not

give permission for the filming of a Masai lion-spearing. In Kenya few Masai still possessed shields or spears and the authorities were reluctant to put spears in their hands even for a brief period. In Tanganyika, the Masai were armed, but many groups did not even hunt lions any more—they called on the authorities to send hunters with guns to dispose of marauding lions. Some groups still went out in the old fashion after the ancient enemy, Simba, but the officials politely but firmly told me no.

In 1954 I was more hopeful because I was better known: it was clear that I wanted to take accurate, honest pictures without fakery. In addition, I was able to muster considerable friendly influence, if such a thing could have any effect. My good friend, Joan Fontaine, wrote her cousin, Sir Geoffrey De Haviland, whom I met and talked to in England on my way to Africa; Sir Geoffrey then wrote to his good friend, Col. Merwyn Cowie, head of all Kenya Parks and Reserves. Since security might be involved in arming some Masai for a lion hunt, the military aspect was taken care of by General Matthew Ridgway, then Chief of Staff, who had been deeply interested in my travels and films and had aided me greatly on my trip to South America, when he was stationed in Panama. General Ridgway wrote to his good friend and counterpart in the British Army, General Sir Dudley Ward, who took the matter up with the colonial office and East Africa officialdom.

All of this caused the normally friendly and helpful authorities in Kenya and Tanganyika to be even more friendly and helpful. Some of the best footage we obtained would have been impossible without the special consideration we received. But one dispensation I could *not* get was permission to film the Masai hunting lions with spears.

During my entire stay in East Africa in 1954-55, I kept at the project with as much persistence as was consistent with politeness and diplomacy. But I could not even go back to Narok and the region near there, where both Masai and lions abound. I thought of getting some good dance sequences there, but was told quite firmly that Narok was a closed area, because of the increasing infiltration of Mau Mau terrorists.

This was an astonishing development. The Mau Mau sect arose among the Kikuyu, for decades the deadliest enemies of the Masai. How could the fanatic nationalist spirit of the Mau Mau secret society gain adherents among the proud and aristocratic Masai who, though troublesome on occasion, had never shown signs of being revolutionary?

The answer was a strange one. Venereal disease had been spreading rapidly in recent years among the Masai, and as a result many Masai women had become sterile. Masai men had finally begun taking wives from the Kikuyu tribe whose territory adjoined theirs. These wives, some of whose families were ardent Mau Mauists, brought with them the ideas, which found a relatively fertile soil in the thwarted warlike spirit of the Masai.

So I waited for my Masai pictures until I reached Tanganyika. Finally, at Monduli, about fifty miles from Arusha, I took some films that turned out to be more exciting and dangerous than the lion hunt which never did materialize. British District Officer Riley was quite helpful, assigned a Masai interpreter to help me, and sent me to a Masai kraal. From here, word went out to three different Masai headmen to come with some of their warriors for picture taking. From three directions they streamed in—ten times as many as I needed. They were fine looking specimens, and all carried their big shields and long thin spears. My idea was to get footage of Masai dances, some of which I had filmed in 1946 but without shields and with wooden staffs instead of spears. Now I could get the real thing. With two cameramen and more than enough cooperative Masai, things should turn out well.

They had no musical instruments except drums, but these gave out a persistent beat that was hypnotic in its effect. The dancers became more and more ecstatic as the dance progressed, flinging their arms out with great abandon, shouting and throwing their heads back violently. As I saw the rather wild look in

some eyes I recalled stories I had heard about the drastic effect
of the war dance on some Masai *moran*. The resurgence of the
old war spirit occasionally sent a few warriors into uncontrolla-
ble fits like epileptic seizures. I had heard, too, that in Kenya
and other areas where the Masai had been deprived of shields
and swords that even the sight of a shield might send some of
them off into a genuine frenzy.

I had never seen such an incident in a Masai dance, and I
didn't on this occasion, but the jerky gestures and rather wild
looks of some of the men made me credit the tales I had heard.
If this feeling could come across on film, the sequence would
be dramatic and tense, but I was afraid that it would be lost, as
the men were close together and the audience would see only
the rather clumsy dance, without being aware of the feeling
that went with it.

These thoughts gave me an idea, however. If I could select
a few men to keep the scene from becoming cluttered and give
them some action that would arouse their spirits as the dance did,
we might get a good scene. If these out-of-work warriors were
excited by recollections of war, maybe a charge as if against an
enemy in battle would do it. Through the interpreter I spoke to
the three headmen, to find out first of all if such a charge
would be authentic, if the Masai method of battle included a
running attack with spears held high. It did indeed, the headmen assured me with a smile, and the *moran* surrounding us
agreed happily.

So we set up the scene, selecting a low hill for the warriors
to come charging over the crest of, with two cameras set up on
flat ground about fifty yards from the crest. Then I chose
about ten particularly fine specimens from among the warriors,
among them a few I had noticed as displaying special fervor in
the dance. They got the idea readily enough, and seemed to
like it. They were to retire to the other side of the hill, then at a
signal were to charge over the top and race down upon us,
directly for the cameras, whooping and brandishing spears as if
about to slaughter an old enemy. All the other Masai, with the

headmen in the front row, lined up at one side, out of camera range but close to the line of march.

The warriors went over the hill and out of sight. I checked with my cameramen and found everything ready, then gave the signal, which was relayed to the *moran*. Before we saw them we heard wild whoops and the cameras started grinding away. Suddenly the warriors burst over the top of the hill running at breath-taking speed, holding their shields in front of them and brandishing their spears on high. It made a thrilling spectacle and I was delighted. Straight toward us the men raced, two or three in front, the others strung out behind. They were forty yards away, thirty, twenty—and I saw plainly the expressions of ecstatic frenzy on the faces of the leaders, the gleam of joyous ferocity in their eyes. And suddenly I knew that the first man, at least, was no longer acting. He was really going to charge. He was going to pierce me or one of my cameramen with his spear. Perhaps it was the fleck of white foam that appeared on his lips which told me, but the wild look in his eyes was that of a man whose mind has taken flight from reality.

I was too petrified to move, and there wasn't really time, anyway. But the other Masai standing alongside acted with speed and decision, for they obviously saw what was about to happen. When the charging warriors were scarcely ten yards away, several of them hurled themselves at the first two warriors and knocked them to the ground.

"Dave, get it!" I called to Mason, who immediately turned his camera on the scene where the Masai who had saved us were with difficulty holding down the two writhing, kicking warriors, both of whom were frothing at the mouth profusely. One still jerked his arm violently as if to throw his spear. His eyes were turned up so that I could see only the whites—and he was a pitiful if frightening sight. The other warrior recovered from his seizure more quickly, and was soon nursing a deep gash in the calf of his right leg. He had stabbed himself with his own spear as he fell.

Within a few minutes both men were calm. Their frothing

and panting had ceased, as well as their struggles to free themselves. But when they got to their feet, their eyes were vacant, glazed, and both acted somewhat bewildered.

No one seemed to be particularly surprised by the incident, except my cameramen and I, and surprise was hardly the word to describe our feelings. We didn't get over our fright for some time. The headmen knew that this sort of thing happened on occasion, so they were on the lookout for it and, happily, took quick action just in time. They didn't seem to be sorry, and they didn't apologize. They seemed to think that we should understand that Masai warriors cannot always stop being warriors just because some authorities tell them they must not make war any more.

It was some months later, when I was telling someone about this incident, that I learned of a similar occurrence during the filming of "King Solomon's Mines" in Africa. At one point the cameramen on that film had abandoned cameras and everything to run from a surging mock attack of Masai warriors. I strongly recommend that photographers stop putting the poor Masai through actions that will bring back to their minds and hearts their past glories.

About six hundred miles away from the homes of the Masai, I found another group of Africans whose heritage and customs paralleled those of the Masai in many ways. These were the Turkana, tall and thin Hamites, with some infusion of Nilotic and Bantu blood. Their lives revolved around their livestock, and they had a heritage of raiding and war which was even more recently active than that of the Masai.

I took that long and difficult trip to Turkanaland, in the Northern Frontier Province of Kenya, for two reasons. In my old drive to find the genuine primitive, I was forced by expanding civilization to travel farther and farther afield. The Turkana had been visited by relatively few explorers and picture-makers, and they were photogenic. I was not sure—since little had been written about them—how many different varied activities of the

Turkana might make good scenes for "Zanzabuku," but there would be enough to warrant the trip, I hoped.

Second, some Turkana had been involved in scenes with Mike Hartley. It would be a good idea, I decided, to obtain more Turkana shots to serve as background. But I wanted to go to the main body of the Turkana, not to the small offshoot that had migrated south to Isiolo.

It was a long haul, up north through Kenya into the Northern Frontier Province, down a twisting road that wound two thousand feet from the top of the escarpment to the bottom of the Rift, which was quite wide at this point. We had to cross a broad desert—the reason for Turkanaland's being so thoroughly cut off from the rest of Kenya—and go through part of the Suk Closed Area, from which visitors are prohibited except by special permit. The entire trip, in fact, required governmental sanction.

Turkanaland is not much better than desert country itself, arid, rocky, barren of all but scrub growth for most of its area. At the northwest corner where the mountains begin, and along the banks of the two sizable rivers there is more varied vegetation. The trouble is, however, that both rivers are likely to be dried up for seven or eight months out of the year. The natives have learned to dig wells and waterholes along the dried up beds, for there is usually water not too far below the surface at these points.

As always in such country, heavy rains bring bad floods, as the earth won't hold the water suddenly poured down upon it. But rains leave numerous waterholes aside from those at the rivers, and natives use them until they dry up. They also scoop shallow basins in the hard earth, line them with stone, and try to catch a fair amount of water from each rain.

People living in a land like this must be herdsmen, for they cannot grow enough foods to turn to settled agriculture, and wild animals are too scarce to enable men to live chiefly by hunting. So the Turkana are semi-nomadic raisers of livestock. Cows can get enough fodder only in choice areas, such as those near the foothills, but sheep, goats and camels can find enough

to eat almost anywhere, it seems, and manage to thrive in the
lands of the Turkana. They milk all three animals, tap the
arteries of each to obtain blood which they usually mix with
milk for eating purposes. Occasionally they kill an animal and
feast on the meat. Some Turkana women try to cultivate small
garden plots, if they live anywhere near the rivers, where they
may raise a little kaffir corn. Fortunately there are dom palms
in the region, whose nuts give food, and also twenty or more
varieties of berry bushes with edible berries, some of which are
growing the year round. The women make a kind of pounded
and dried berry meal which they can store, later mixing it with
blood or milk or both to cook into cakes.

In spite of the hard life the Turkana people were friendly,
cooperative, and seemed quite happy. I saw little evidence of
their warlike feelings, in spite of the fact that they had been
busy with border raids and wars up until the twenties, when
the British really stepped in to put down the fighting. But each
young man carries a long spear, and often two. He also carries,
slung from his left wrist, a little wooden stool to sit on, said
stool serving also as a headrest to protect his precious coiffure
when lying down to sleep at night. The Turkana have other
weapons, too, knives, clubs, and a device I found fascinating—a
semi-circular knife attached to the right wrist. A devastating
weapon for in-fighting, its razor edge is protected most of the
time by a leather sheath.

We finally reached Lodwar, the administrative center for
Turkanaland, and were warmly greeted by District Commissioner Whitehouse. Lodwar consists of only a few buildings in
the midst of dreary country. The Turkana village near by was
much more colorful, and the men and women so strikingly
photogenic that I knew the long trip would be worth while.
They were tall, strong and graceful—most of the men being well
over six feet. Some were completely naked, while others wore a
kind of toga knotted at the shoulder. Most of the men wore
smooth ivory plugs in their perforated lower lips, objects that
looked from a distance something like brand new golf balls

fixed just below the mouth. Somehow, they were attractive, standing out vividly against the reddish-brown skin. Many men also wore earrings, leg bands, arm bands and necklaces of wire and beads. They carried graceful spears and rectangular shields made of heavy leather, some decorated with big black ostrich-feather balls at the top. I also saw a few wickerwork shields, used in stick fights between one Turkana and another. They supposedly use their spears only on animals or enemies of other tribes, never on each other.

White and orange headdresses, however, were the distinguishing marks of the Turkana—usually made of waving ostrich plumes. They were the crowning glories of elaborate hair-dos which, I learned, were only modest and skimpy versions of the startling coiffures which the Turkana had worn seventy years ago, when first seen by Europeans who discovered Lake Rudolf. Then the hair had grown long and been plastered with mud to form a huge *chignon*, which hung down as far as the waist and was decorated with a kind of snood made of feathers. From the top of this device came other plumes and even wire halos with feather balls suspended over the top of the head.

While the hair-do has shrunk to a good-sized mud-plastered bun on the back of the head, the feathers and waving plumes remain—and on top of a tall man they are striking. The women don't go in for such frippery, merely shaving their heads on the sides and twisting what's left of hair in the center into greased curls that hang down like an old floor mop.

After getting acquainted, we started our camera work. There were a few hunting scenes, involving leopards and hyenas, which go after Turkana livestock and are thus the prime enemies. These tied in nicely with the leopard sequences taken at Hartley's place, where Mike and the Turkana workers there were both involved.

Word went out to other Turkana villages that there were dancing and gifts near Lodwar, and natives began streaming in from all sides, men, women, and children. The District Commissioner had told me that the Turkana were great dancers, but

I had seen plenty of primitive dancers in the previous months and did not expect too much. But I rarely saw any group that loved dancing more than the Turkana. They were always ready and eager to dance before the cameras and once, after we had filmed during the good light for several hours, we knocked off and told them their work was done. But there was no stopping the Turkana. They kept going all that evening and most of the night, and the next day put in another four to six hours dancing.

They had war dances, hunting dances, dances whose character I could not understand, and even an elephant dance—although there was no evidence of elephants having lived anywhere near Turkanaland for centuries if ever. Undoubtedly this tribe, which had probably come to the Rift Valley only a hundred to a hundred fifty years before, had once lived where there were elephants, and the dance had remained a part of their cultural heritage.

No matter what the dance started out to be, it wound up being strongly erotic as night fell and the fires were lit. Because this sort of thing took place in the night I never could get any pictures, but they could not have been shown publicly in any event.

After some time around Lodwar, we decided to go to Lake Rudolf, about forty-five miles to the East. This is one of the least-known large bodies of water in Africa, having been discovered only in 1888 by the Austrian explorer, Count Teleki. It forms the eastern border of Turkanaland, with Ethiopia on the other side and the Sudan to the north, has no known outlet, contains an alkaline water that abounds in fish, crocodiles, and hippos and is beloved of thousands of birds. It is an attractive invitation to aspiring young explorers, for much of it has never been seen by white men and none has ever crossed it.

Commissioner Whitehouse said he thought we'd find the fishing interesting. The Turkana settlements on the shores of the lake were comparatively recent and so was fishing, as an occupation. Although this tribe had a difficult time finding enough food in its arid land, it had never taken to fishing, had not really considered fish edible. Government authorities had finally persuaded some of them to migrate to the lake and eat fish. They brought in nets and other equipment, gave the necessary instructions. And the teaching had borne fruit. There were several Turkana villages on Lake Rudolf, more and more fish were being caught, and people were actually eating the fish.

The lake was so full of fish that they were easy to catch. We took pictures of the men going out in small boats with a long net, then dragging it in to shore loaded with big fish. Tilapia (Nile perch) ranging from forty up to an occasional two hundred pounds, came out of the lake in abundance—and they were delicious eating.

During our stay beside Lake Rudolf, we felt as far removed from the civilized world as if we had been visiting another planet. Looking out across the vast lake we saw no sign of human life, nor was there much on the land around us except for the few Turkana groups, practically untouched by civilization. The remoteness of Turkanaland is indicated by the fact that the Kenya authorities have chosen it for the imprisonment of the most dangerous Mau Mau leaders, including Jomo Kenyatta. In Lodwar, I was the house guest of Commissioner Whitehouse —the type of official that has made the Empire great, in the best sense—and from my window I could look down on the prison compound. Although guarded by vigilant Turkana policemen, I suppose that many of the prisoners could have escaped. But it would have done them no good; on the long trek back home they would have been cut down by their bitter enemies, the Turkana, or would have perished in the almost endless desert.

We sensed this atmosphere of remoteness all the time we were in Turkanaland and it enhanced the enjoyment of our stay there. It was particularly pleasant at Lake Rudolf, where we stayed in thatched huts on a sandy spit jutting out into the lake. After work we sat beneath the palm trees or went swimming in the lake—always keeping a wary eye out for crocs—and watched the magnificent sunsets.

One day when we had stopped filming because of the diminishing light, we were watching the Turkana fishermen haul in a netful of fish. As the net neared the sandy shore we saw a violent thrashing in the water and wondered at the size of the fish that could raise such a commotion. But this was no fish. It was a crocodile that had been netted. It played possum, in its customary fashion, so long as it was some distance from shore but as the net forced it onto the sand in shallow water it started struggling to escape.

Suddenly I understood why the tribesmen carried their spears even when fishing. Two of them ran toward the croc and thrust their spears into him again and again until he was dead.

This would make an unusual and dramatic shot for the film, I decided. We asked the fishermen to signal to us the moment they realized they had netted a croc again and to hold up the final spearing of the creature until our cameraman could run up for a close shot. They willingly agreed, and we posted ourselves on shore every time the men went fishing. The next day, however, there was no croc, nor the day after that. Finally a croc was caught but managed to escape around the end of the net before it was dragged ashore. Finally, our patience was rewarded. There was a violent thrashing in the water, and our cameraman started running for the spot without any signal from the fishermen. But the men forgot our instructions and, in the excitement of the moment, followed their instincts. They had killed the big croc before our cameraman could get set. If they had held off for even thirty seconds, he could have recorded the dramatic scene on film.

That's how close you come, sometimes, to unusual shots when engaging in animal photography. But despite this disappointment, I was pleased with the three-minute sequence that eventually resulted from about three weeks of work in Turkanaland. I had to make three trips to get a film of Kilimanjaro. Why should I expect to catch the spearing of a crocodile in a fishnet with only one expedition?

XIV

Mara Valley

ON my third African trip I kept searching for a truly primitive region with an abundance of wild animals. The heart of the Ituri Forest was still part of the Stone Age, but poor light made animal photography difficult; Turkanaland was certainly isolated and primitive, but so arid and barren that most animals were too smart to live there; the great parks and restricted areas in the Congo, Uganda, Kenya, and Tanganyika offered plenty of animals of great variety, but they were not exactly right for my purposes.

Fortunately, we had been able to work with two of the best animal catchers in East Africa, who took us into unrestricted territory in both Kenya and Tanganyika where we obtained wonderful action footage. But I was not satisfied. I wanted to find still another area so suited to animal life that many creatures lived and loved and fought there; an area that had not been so thoroughly hunted as to thin out the herds or cause them to panic at the first scent of man; an area not yet encircled by farms or cleared in an effort to kill out the tsetse flies; a region more naturally primitive than the parks in that some natives still hunted or trapped the wild animals there; a place far enough away from approaching civilization and hordes of tourist-hunters to have escaped the multitude of regulations set up for the protection of wild life. I had to be able to kill bait for lions, provoke a rhino into a charge, startle a herd of impala into hasty flight, frighten buffalo or zebra into a stampede—in other words, annoy or scare some animals enough to provide action for my cameras.

There are still many such regions in Africa, of course. In

1937, for example, there was the Ngorongoro Crater, a paradise for the largest game herds in the world. The first white man discovered it in 1892, but it was not until after World War I that T. Alexander Barns wrote the first thorough description of it. Since that time someone had built what was euphemistically called a road up the outer slope to the crater's ridge, but beyond that all the going was on foot. Not many people had gone down to the floor of the crater.

Until we reached the twisting road ascending the former volcano we enjoyed a lovely drive, with the western wall of the great Rift Valley dimly visible on our right, plenty of game in the valley through which we traveled, and the still active volcano, Oldonyo-lengai, displaying its almost perfect symmetrical form for a good part of the journey. The Masai look on this mountain as sacred, the source of all that is good and bad in their lives. We saw thousands of flamingoes and pelicans on Lake Manyara, passed through the tiny farming village of Oldeani, and then plunged into thick forests on the slope of Ngorongoro. On the way up, you cannot see much because the jungle is so dense. You realize that you are climbing a mountain only because of the steep grades and many turns, which continue for most of the nine miles or so of the ascent, which leads you to the lip of the crater, eight thousand feet above sea level.

We found a small rest house there, of logs and thatch, built by the government for its game wardens and district officials but also available to travelers passing that way. It was so late by that time that we really could not make out the view, but I was delighted that with dawn there *would* be a view to see. I was worried for fear that even on the edge of the crater we would stand in the midst of forest that would cut off all vision for any distance. There isn't much growth along the rocky edge, however, and where the rest house sits there was none at all.

Writers of more lush prose than mine have tried and failed to describe Ngorongoro Crater. In such cases I usually fall back on colored pictures to do the job for me. But you cannot even take a proper picture of the crater. It is too long, too broad, too deep to catch in one small square of film. And that is one point, I feel, that should be emphasized about the wonderful place. The word *crater* is apt to mislead, because volcanic craters are usually a quarter of a mile, a half mile, even a mile or two across. And down in the bottom of the fair-sized dish is a lake or a mass of black and hardened lava with a little scrub growth. Even when we know in advance that Ngorongoro is the largest crater in the world, we still conjure up in our minds all old associations with the word *crater* and they just don't fit.

Ngorongoro must have been a very big mountain when it was all there—not only in height but in breadth. And when it blew its top on some dateless yesterday, it really blew a top of mighty magnitude—a top that was a good-sized mountain in itself. The crater left behind was twelve miles across, between thirty-five and forty miles in circumference! The floor of the crater lies a full two thousand feet below the rim—a generally flat area of close to a hundred square miles, with a soil rich enough to satisfy even the most delicate and finicky plant.

Even though I knew all this, my first view of Ngorongoro the next morning was breathtaking. In the early morning brightness, I suppose, distances looked even greater than they were, and it seemed to me as if the opposite rim, just catching the first rays of the sun, must be fifty miles away. I've seen many deeper and wider valleys in the mountains, of course, but here the distant mountain rim circles right around on both sides till it reaches the spot on which you stand. Seeing all of the edge of the crater, you realize fully that it *is* a crater rather than a valley, that it is a gigantic saucer filled with a luxuriant growth.

At dawn, the growth is not clearly visible, for it may be obscured by fog or mist. In a short time under the bright sun, the vivid green shows through in larger and larger patches but the mists give the impression that the whole scene is a mirage, something just conjured up by some enchantment. This atmosphere remains, to some degree, during the day for low clouds of white often hover over the rim of the crater.

At first glance, the floor of the crater looks like a huge

smooth green carpet. But then you notice that, although the
floor is essentially flat, there are a few small hills and un-
dulations in the land. And you see darker and taller patches of
green that represent forest rather than grassland. And you can
see the two good-sized lakes, the occasional flash of sun on a
winding river. On my first trip, I saw, through my binoculars,
herds of many thousands of animals moving over the grassy plains.
They appeared so small that I could not make out what they
were, but their numbers amazed me. On my most recent trip I
saw some animal herds, and I also saw herds of Masai cattle
moving not far from them.

In 1937, three Masai guides led Cézaire and me down into
the crater. Shortly after leaving the rim of the crater we plunged
into thick underbrush and then trees, so that our view was cut
off. We followed a path which our guides said was a rhinoceros
trail, with warnings to head for the nearest tree if they shouted
"Faru!" He is one beast that even the Masai want no encounters with. But we met no animals at all on our descent,
probably because we made so much noise ploughing through
the thick growth. Then suddenly the sloping ground leveled
out, we emerged from the bush, and saw the vast level floor
stretching before us.

We stepped out onto a thick green lawn of clover that
bounced resiliently as we walked across it. It was close-cropped
and as even as a fairway—and soon thereafter I saw why. Off to
the right was a herd of several hundred zebra, quietly eating
clover. Just ahead of them a herd of wildebeest—so often found
along with zebra—and they were busy cutting the grass, too.
They looked up at us but, since we did not walk closer, were
not really disturbed. I stopped to take a few pictures and they
went back to their eating. When we started on again, one of
the wildebeests nearest us took offense and trotted away, not
in too big a hurry, and the others followed him. The zebra, seeing this, decided to tag along. For several minutes the crater
resounded with the muted drum of hoofbeats on the grass.

We walked through an acacia forest and then into fields of

white and red clover that came up above our ankles. Its growth
was so rich that even all the animals in the crater could not
keep it cropped. And the crater literally seethed with animals.
Estimates at that time ranged between seventy-five thousand
and one hundred thousand head in the crater, most of them
locked within it and never leaving. Why should they leave? They
had everything an animal wants—food, shelter, shade, sun,
water. There are zebra, eland, giraffe, topi, waterbuck, reedbuck,
bushbuck, steinbok, impala, Thomson's gazelles, Grant's gazelles, duiker, dik-dik, wildebeest, oribi, ostrich, jackals, hyenas,
leopard, elephants, rhinos, hippos, buffalo, cheetah, baboons,
guinea fowl, bustard, quail and the largest lions in Africa with
the most beautiful manes.

We approached Lake Magad, where I hoped to get pictures
of cranes and other waterfowl, and perhaps some animals coming to drink. But the lake was on such flat land that it was surrounded by a half-mile of slimy ooze in which I could hardly
keep my footing and on which there was no cover to hide me
from birds and animals. On one side of the lake I saw the clear
waters of the Lemunge River, which flowed into it, and I wondered how on earth a river came flowing over the side of the
mountain and down into a crater. The answer lay in one of the
two volcanoes which lay at opposite sides of the rim—Oldeani
and Ololmoti. Ololmoti is about ten thousand feet high, well
above the rim of Ngorongoro. The river rises near its summit,
probably from some subterranean stream, flows down its side
and over the edge of Ngorongoro in some lovely waterfalls.

I had come equipped for only a short stay, but I might have
obtained some wonderful pictures if I had remained in the
crater. That's what I was thinking of on later trips, but Ngorongoro had become restricted and full of cattle. The Masai
had three hundred thousand head grazing there—against all
regulations but there, nevertheless. Ngorongoro is still a thrilling
place to visit, but not the spot for the kind of pictures I had to
take. So I went on looking.

Finally I found the Mara Valley, almost by accident. I

knew about the Mara River, but from the Kenya side, where it
started not far from Narok. I had not realized that it cut down
into northern Tanganyika to travel through some really wild
country before emptying into Lake Victoria. When I first went
there in 1954 I did not go because of the river or the country
but because of a nearby tribe I had heard about, the Kuria, who
lived atop the Utimbaro Escarpment, at the bottom of which
flowed the Mara River.

It was F. G. Reid, the American missionary I met in Amboseli Park, who mentioned the Kuria as a tribe that few travelers had visited. He urged me to film them, and wrote a letter
to the Reverend J. A. Schoeman, head of the Seventh Day Adventist Mission at Tarime, in the heart of the Kuria tribal territory. And he told me that I could get there quickly by hiring
a small plane to fly me to a tiny airstrip near an old gold mine
at the foot of the escarpment.

While some of my cameramen were busy with other routine
matters, I took one of them and flew to the airstrip, where a
truck met us and took us to the mission. We were warmly welcomed, hospitably housed, and helped in our contacts with the
natives. I also visited two other missions while I was there—Dr.
Eshelman and his Mennonite Mission, with which a leper
colony is connected, and the Rosana Mission of the Catholic
Church. I was delighted to find that this mission was associated
with Maryknoll, on the Hudson River, which I had often visited,
and that Father Reinhart, Father Smith, and Brother Damien
were all friends of Father Nevins of Maryknoll, whom I knew
well. The District Commissioner at Tarime, Col. Eric Wilson,
V.C., was also most helpful.

I was somewhat disappointed in the Kuria, of whom there
are about one hundred fifty thousand living in that general area.
They were interesting, but not particularly dramatic from a
photographic point of view. We did get an excellent dance sequence on film, but my best shot was connected with the head
medicine man, named Noziburo. His most interesting features
were his ears. The Kuria, like the Masai and many other tribes,

pierce the ears and gradually enlarge the opening by the insertion of larger and larger wooden blocks. I had seen Masai earlobes hanging to the shoulders but never anything like Noziburo's. His came almost to his waist. I examined them, because I could not believe that the small amount of skin of the earlobe could be stretched that far. It was all genuine flesh and fairly ropey at that, good and strong without a break or mended spot. While all the Kuria had long loopy earlobes, none compared favorably with Noziburo's, which was as it should be since he was the witch doctor. And among his most potent magic assets were those earlobes. We filmed a woman with a newborn baby passing the baby through the opening in the earlobe of Noziburo to bring it good health and good luck for the rest of its life. It was, I suppose, the equivalent of a christening ceremony, the most unusual one I had ever seen.

I learned of other interesting customs of the Kuria, but nothing we could film. Both girls and boys went through rigorous circumcision rites. In the old days when any girl became pregnant before circumcision, she was killed, but with the ameliorating effects of civilization, they now only banish her from the tribe. If in the short period between circumcision and marriage a girl became pregnant, no man would marry her—all of which was evidence of a much stricter sexual code, at least for girls, than existed in many tribes. The wayward girl who found herself without a husband had a way to live her life, however. She might be purchased from her father for the customary marriage price of a certain number of cattle—by an older woman, perhaps a widow. The older woman would then set the girl up in a recognized form of prostitution through which men in the tribe could enjoy the young lady. Any children born to her, however, did not belong to her but to the older woman who also owned her. They took the older woman's name, so she was always hoping for male children to carry on the name.

I also became rather interested in the Luo tribe, who lived not far away, because they seemed so different in many ways from their neighbors, the Kuria. The Kuria girl banished for her

waywardness, for instance, could always go and live with the
Luo, where no one had to be circumcised and moral standards
were quite different. We took some good footage of Luo dances
because their colorful shields and fancy headdresses were quite
attractive.

When we finished our work among the Kuria and Luo, only
fairly well pleased with the results, we returned to the airstrip
near the gold mine to meet the little plane that came to pick us
up. I was standing near the craft while the pilot warmed it up
when a man walked up and introduced himself to me. He was
Uys (pronounced Ace) DuPreez. I have mentioned him before,
chiefly in connection with hippo sequences. Actually, however,
this was our first meeting, and at that time I had never heard of
him, knew nothing about his amazing knack with wild animals.
On many occasions I had traveled hundreds of miles to meet
someone who really understood animals, but this time such a
man walked up and introduced himself. A husky, baldish blond
just under forty, he had been born in Kenya of a French Hugue-
not family that had originally gone from France to Holland,
then to South Africa, finally to Kenya.

While the pilot readied the plane, DuPreez and I talked
briefly. He had heard about someone visiting the Kuria to take
pictures and wondered if I were interested in wild animal pictures, too. If so, why hadn't I visited his Mara Valley? It was a
relatively small area, but completely wild, and full of all kinds of
animals.

"Lions?" I asked.

"Plenty of lions," he said.

"Rhinos?"

"Lots of rhinos. There's even a place in the valley we call
Rhino Swamp."

"Antelopes?"

"What species do you want? We have forest roan, impala,
wildebeest, eland, Tommies, hartebeest, topi, and some others."

"Well, well," I said, not knowing what to think of all this.

"And in addition there are hippos, buffalo, zebra, elephants, giraffe, leopard, crocodiles, and, of course, hyenas, jackals and wild dogs. For birds we have ostrich, guinea fowl, spurfowl, partridge, quail, ducks and geese. Plus many varieties of snakes, all in abundance."

"It sounds like animal heaven, the sort of place I've been looking for."

"Well, there are twenty-nine kinds of animals in an area of thirty square miles. And every kind of terrain and growth, too, with the river running through the middle of it, thick forest, rocky plain, swamps, hills, and valleys. Plenty of shelter for animals and for you. Plenty of open areas with good light. You can make our mine your base," DuPreez said. "My brother and I run it with the help of natives. It's at the western end of Mara Valley. There are good places to set up camps in the valley. There are no roads, but I know my way around and I would be happy to help you."

When I learned that DuPreez was the Honorary Game Warden of the area, which was called "controlled" but not "restricted," I felt that he knew what he was talking about. The word "honorary" doesn't mean the same thing in East Africa that it means in America, where a person may receive a title as some kind of recognition or honor. An Honorary Game Warden there is a man who does not officially devote his full time and efforts to the job of protecting the game but takes on this work in addition to private affairs through his love of animals and his knowledge of a particular area and at no pay.

In a "controlled" area like Mara Valley there were no rigid rules or restrictions as to the hunting or filming of animals, or the conduct of people visiting the region. But anyone going into the valley was supposed to obtain the permission of the game warden in charge and conduct himself according to that person's directions. Some animals could be hunted at some times when they were abundant or inclined to wipe out other animals in the area. Native poachers had to be kept out, animal diseases noted, and so on. The purpose in a controlled area is just what the name implies—to exercise control over man's activities

in it so as to preserve the wild life. DuPreez reported to the
Head Game Warden in Arusha and worked in collaboration
with the District Officer at Tarime.

I made a sudden shift in plans as I talked to DuPreez there
on the little airstrip. I said I'd fly back to Nairobi, get some of
my other men and the Power Wagon, which he said was
absolutely necessary. Since DuPreez said we could get all the
animal pictures we might want in four or five days, I decided to
stay a week. We were there six weeks—six wonderful and productive weeks. We camped at four widely separated spots—once
on the edge of the Mara River near a pool beloved of hippos,
once on the edge of a forest that served as home for many lions,
another time along a regularly traveled rhino trail, and again near
a narrow pass through a rocky ridge, called Lion's Pass. Although it was a relatively small area enclosed by the Mara
River on one side and the high escarpment on the other, we
would have become lost in it many times if we had not been
guided by Ace DuPreez.

Ace knew animals not as Mafuta, the gun-bearer, did, whose
knowledge was specially useful to the hunter. He knew them in
a different way from Kuenzler and Pellegrini, who were spec-
tacularly smart in capturing them alive and unharmed. Ace
knew them by living with them. He did not hunt or capture
them, except when such actions were made necessary by his job
as game warden. He lived in Mara Valley with them, and he
knew how they lived their day-to-day lives.

Ace's knowledge inspired such confidence in me that I took
many chances in the Mara Valley that I would have avoided
otherwise. There was the day we saw a singularly large herd of
buffalo on the other side of the river, and I wanted to get close
for pictures. But the trucks could not cross the river at this point
—the water was fairly deep—and Ace said we could wade across
if we didn't mind getting wet. Wet clothes meant nothing to
me when it came to getting good pictures, but I glanced with a
worried expression at the pool of hippos not one hundred feet
from the point where Ace said we should cross.

"I think it will be all right," Ace said, "if we take it slowly." But I noticed that he did not order his helpers to cross. He asked for volunteers, and only three were willing to wade so near the hippos. The others refused. Johnny Coquillon, who never failed any such test, said he would go. Before starting into the stream, whose current was quite rapid, Ace and the rest of us found stout poles with which to brace ourselves. Then we stepped into the water. The hippos nearest us stirred, stared, and submerged themselves. The water was so muddy that we could not tell whether they headed for us or away from us. Ace went steadily ahead, and I followed, with the others close behind me. The water came up to our waists, up to our shoulders, with the current tugging hard at us. Our footing was slippery and none too secure, so we moved quite slowly. Completely occupied with maintaining our balance in those circumstances, we were at the mercy of any animal in the water that felt like attacking us. And we had seen crocs in that river the previous day! We got across the river without incident and shot the buffalo pictures we wanted.

On another occasion our Power Wagon got stuck in the Mara River because it was so heavily loaded with our equipment and three big drums of gasoline. Ace had previously crossed at this point but this time we managed to drop one wheel into a muddy hole and there we sat, churning up the water but getting nowhere. We had to get out and wade around, fix a cable to the winch at the front of the truck, hook it to a tree stump on the other side, and pull ourselves out. Without this wonderful modern equipment we could never have made it. Without Ace I would have been thoroughly scared of the herd of hippos near by.

Ace's biggest contribution to our film came during the rhino sequences—the sort of thing I had always dreamed of getting. Ace had an open jeep he had bought from a nearby mission, and a battered old five-ton truck with four-wheel drive. We often used both in addition to my Power Wagon when we went scouting for animals.

One day Ace was driving the jeep, with cameraman Johnny
Coquillon beside him and the rest of us following in the
Power Wagon, when three or four big rhinos charged out of the
bush at the jeep. Johnny got the charge in his camera, and from
the truck we got the whole scene—rhinos charging jeep, Johnny
manning his camera, Ace maneuvering the jeep to evade the
charges. His handling of the car was magnificent.

One by one the rhinos gave up the chase, but one fellow
was more determined than the rest. Again and again he charged,
missing the jeep only by inches. I could hardly breathe as I
watched the scene, because Johnny had absolutely no protection
from the big horn that came tearing at him. The jeep was low,
putting Johnny at just the right height for a horn thrust, and it
had no sides to deflect or diminish the blow. But Johnny kept
photographing throughout, getting some magnificent shots.

Finally the rhino succeeded—his horn caught the rear of
the jeep about a foot behind Johnny. Ace and Johnny tumbled
out on the other side, Johnny clutching his precious camera,
and we speeded up the truck to close in on the furious rhino,
who was busy poking holes in the jeep and one rear tire. He
charged us and we pulled away. He followed us a short distance
then turned back toward the jeep. Johnny and Ace had gotten
away, meanwhile, so we breathed easier and stopped the truck.
The rhino began pounding away at his first enemy, the jeep, so
I got out of the truck and approached him on foot, taking pictures as I went.

I was about forty feet away when the rhino saw me. He
didn't hesitate, but lowered his head and raced for me, puffing
with that sound which everyone has described, accurately, as like
a steam locomotive. I ran for all I was worth, slipped once,
scrambled to my feet, and leaped into the truck about five feet
ahead of the rhino, who struck the vehicle a glancing blow which
did little harm. The truck took off fast enough to make the exhausted rhino give up the chase. We picked up Johnny and Ace,
caught our breaths, and congratulated each other on the action
pictures we had managed to take without harm to anyone.

Rhinos? I've had them. And I prefer lions.

Ace was full of lion lore. He said that all other animals were apparently fascinated by lions, curious about them, as well as respectful of them. In the daytime, all animals would stare at any lion that showed himself—at a safe distance or after the lion had eaten. They would watch every move the lion made with expressions that clearly showed no fear but only intense curiosity. If the lion moved away, the other animals would often follow him just to watch and see what he did.

Lions seem to have a greater respect for white men than for Africans, Ace insisted, and told a story to illustrate his point. One day he was in his truck with a helper when he came upon the tracks of a zebra that was traveling alone rather than with its herd. From the tracks, the animal was obviously wounded or sick, so Ace decided to follow and see what was wrong, put the zebra out of his misery if need be. After traveling along for a short distance over open country, he saw the zebra ahead, standing about fifty yards from a clump of trees. The zebra was afraid of the truck and wanted to run away, but was equally frightened of something ahead of him at the edge of the forest. Then Ace saw the lion which stood there, looking eagerly toward the zebra. It was a hungry lion, but the approach of the truck had prevented his charging the zebra.

Ace decided at this point to gain a little more information about lions. He had seen very few actual kills made by a lion and wanted to learn how the beast would attack and kill the zebra, who was a goner anyway. Ace stopped the truck and told the worker to get out and walk toward the zebra, thereby forcing it closer to the lion, who might in time make his attack. The man walked a short distance toward the zebra, which moved only a few steps, then stopped. The lion did not move away at all, and the man was afraid to go any closer.

The helper then sat in the truck and Ace climbed out, walking slowly toward the zebra. The lion at once retreated into the bush at the edge of the forest. Ace carried no gun at the time—he had left it in the truck—so he was certain that there was no scent or awareness of a weapon that caused the lion to retreat. The animal had held its ground at the advance of the African, retreated at the advance of a white man—and up to the same point.

Ace went back to the truck, and the lion reappeared. At Ace's orders, the tribesman once more approached the same distance, and the lion held its ground. Ace advanced, lion retreated. There was no doubt in Ace's mind now. Then he took pity on the zebra, which had obviously been seriously wounded by an attack from another lion or a leopard. Ace got his gun from the truck and shot the zebra. The lion disappeared at the sound of the shot, of course, but soon reappeared. At this point, the helper was busy cutting up the zebra's carcass to get some meat to take back home. Ace was sitting in the truck waiting.

The lion, smelling the blood, was obviously aroused. He decided to go after the carcass, even with the African there, and approached. The man ran toward the truck, and the lion came on toward the dead zebra, keeping his eye on the truck all the time. Ace stepped from the truck, walked toward the animals, and the lion retreated.

"It's the same with all wild animals," Ace said. "They fear white men more than natives. The reason? Because the white man is usually not filled with fear, as the African is likely to be. There must be something glandular about it, some odor which a wild animal can smell when a man's guts are filled with fear. That lion knew the man was more scared of him than he of the man. And he knew, also, that I wasn't a bit afraid of him."

Ace told me another fact about lions that I had never heard before. He said that they sometimes stalked game in the presence of rhinos. Antelopes and other natural prey of the lion did not fear rhinos at all, nor did the rhino fear the lion. A lion might use a rhino as a kind of shield or cover when the big stupid creature went wandering toward herds of antelope or zebra.

One of the most interesting lion scenes I witnessed in the Mara Valley would have made a magnificent and humorous sequence for the picture I was producing had circumstances made it possible to get much of it on film. A swift and graceful impala was taunting a lioness until that poor cat was almost crazy. The wind was just right, and we had good cover, so neither animal was aware of the presence of man.

The lioness had some cubs, apparently very young ones, in the bush at the edge of a grove of trees. She was hungry herself and wanted food for them, but she obviously did not want to stray too far from them. In most circumstances, she might have found the father or another lioness to baby-sit while she went after the impala, but no helper was near by. The impala obviously knew it, and knew the lioness was hesitant about leaving the cubs for a long chase. The impala also knew that there was a deep, steep-sided donga not fifty feet away, with a good stream of water flowing at the bottom of it.

The impala danced gaily up toward the lioness. She crept forward, tail beginning to twitch. At the last moment before the spring, the impala turned and darted away, looking back over its shoulder as if laughing at the lioness. The angry cat returned to her cubs, obviously very annoyed. Then the impala came back again, circling about closer and closer to entice the lioness out of the bush again and into another futile charge. Finally the little antelope circled between the lioness and the edge of the donga, and the lioness felt she had her meal this time for sure. The donga was a place she would avoid, finding it difficult to cross, so she apparently assumed the impala would find it a barrier. Confidently the lioness started her charge, but the impala turned, fled gracefully down the steep bank of the donga, swam swiftly over the stream, and clambered up the other side, quite near to us.

There the impala stood, staring insolently back at the lioness who had stopped at the other side of the donga. With a switch of the little tail and a kick of the heels, the lovely creature very plainly thumbed her nose at the lioness and ambled away happily.

At another time I saw two roan antelopes that were far

from happy. This is the sort of scene you just chance upon if you are lucky and stay long enough in an animal paradise like Mara Valley. We were walking along a faint animal path through tall grass and thick bush. We heard a kind of bleating noise, of great distress, heard a rustle of leaves, and then saw a leopard flash across the path directly ahead of us. There was a small animal in its mouth.

The leopard disappeared in a fraction of a second but right on its heels came two roan antelopes, male and female. Then we knew that the leopard had snatched a baby roan and the mother and father were pursuing it to try to save their little one. At this exciting moment, of course, all the animals were oblivious of our presence, so we crashed our way through the bush trying to follow them and see what happened. In a short time we found the father and mother antelopes. They had given up the chase, and were just wandering about forlornly. They were in obvious distress, looking without hope for something they had lost which was very dear to them.

During our travels around the area we came upon three different camps of poachers, who had obviously fled a little before our arrival. Fires still burned, and meat hung in the smoke above them.

Ace was increasingly worried about poaching in the valley. The population up on the escarpment had been growing rapidly in recent years, and villages had been started along the river not far above the controlled area. With food becoming more and more scarce, African hunters came into the valley after animals. They went after every edible creature they could catch, and by any method. Ace had a difficult time catching them and enforcing regulations.

Ace told me about the dead elephant he had come upon shortly before we came to the valley. At first, he had felt that poachers were responsible for the big animal's death and that he had approached before they had a chance to remove the ivory or cut up the carcass for meat. But closer examination showed no signs of violence on the old fellow. Ace then found that both tusks were broken in the sockets and one was badly decayed, so he concluded that old age and tusk-ache had been responsible for death. Later he was able to examine the skull more carefully and found a serious fracture, between the tusks, about a foot long. It must have been very old, for new bone growth had covered the broken area. The socket of one tusk, however, was almost twice the size of the other, and contained numerous fracture marks. Inside there were indications of an old abscess which had caused the expansion of the bones of the skull. The old elephant had been in a serious battle many years before, and had suffered untold agonies from the abscessed tusk. Ace was glad he had never encountered the beast while it was alive, for this would have been a truly vicious rogue.

Before leaving Mara Valley I wanted to get one scene that would convey some sense of the richness and variety and beauty of animal life in Africa. I could, of course, accomplish this by good editing of my film later—placing together, one after another, scenes of zebras, elephants, lions, hippos, rhinos, antelopes and many other animals. But I wanted to take one scene with as many of these as possible in the camera's vision. I wanted a dozen species caught in that small frame of my 35-mm moving picture cameras. And I wanted them moving. This meant a stampede.

I talked the idea over with Ace several times. He was not adverse to the idea of a stampede. The animals would merely run away, temporarily frightened, and would not suffer at all. The problem was to photograph them close enough without endangering myself or my cameramen. Animals that are never dangerous alone may kill you easily when a herd stampedes in fright.

There were plenty of animals in the Mara Valley for the most spectacular stampede in the world, but getting it on film was the big problem. I wanted not only big herds, but herds of many different species at the same time. The area had to be open and the light good. Our cameras had to be placed in the right positions. And finally, the animals had to run past the cameras when they stampeded.

Such a task required many men, so Ace went up to the villages on top of the escarpment and came back with about fifty tribesmen, who were to serve more or less as beaters. This added a commissary problem for the men had to be fed, meat had to be obtained for them—and that meant hunting. When all this was properly organized, we loaded the men into all the available vehicles and went reconnoitering, visiting one after the other all the open plains areas in the valley where Ace thought we might find good herds of animals. And we saw plenty of animals—a herd of zebra here, some eland at another spot a few miles away and so on.

Finally we found what we were looking for, in an open area near the foot of the escarpment. It was a wide plain, and there were many widely scattered herds grazing—zebra, wildebeest, impala, Tommies, topi, an imposing number of eland, and even roan antelope and waterbuck. Ace quickly surveyed the lay of the land to figure out where the animals might run when frightened. The escarpment rose behind them and thick forest bordered two sides of the plain. Obviously they would race toward the open space between the forests.

First we picked the best locations for our cameramen, one in a tree on a hastily built platform, another on a rocky ledge. Then we drove the men to their posts in a wide semicircle around the herds of animals, which took almost an hour of rough driving in the truck and Power Wagon. The men posted themselves all along the sides of the forested areas, looking out onto the broad plain. Then Ace and I returned to the middle of the semicircle and prepared ourselves for the final movements. He was in the jeep at one point, I in the Power Wagon at another a few hundred yards away. At his signal—the waving of his ever-present miner's cap—we started driving very slowly onto the plain. The helpers who saw the signal stepped from the cover of the trees, motioning to the others to follow their lead.

Some of the animals in the herds nearest the approaching men looked up uneasily and began to walk away from them. All the action at this point was slow and calm, although I was tense inwardly. We did not want the animals to panic and run until the various herds were much closer together, for only in this way could we record on film the full impact of the stampede.

Ace and I edged slowly forward in the trucks, and the Africans stepped along at about the same pace. The herd of topi trotted over closer to the zebra and wildebeest. The huge elands stalked closer to the impala and Tommies, who had already shifted next to each other. Everything was going just as planned, with the animals nervously moving away from the tightening circle into a more compact grouping. Then suddenly the shy roan antelopes became frightened and took to their heels in a burst of speed. The Tommies followed at once, and in a few seconds each herd had decided that it must escape quickly. The sight of these animals racing over the plain was so breath-taking that I almost forgot about speeding up the Power Wagon to keep the stampede moving in the right direction. Five or six thousand animals dashed along only a hundred yards ahead of me, the impala leaping like ballet dancers, the eland beating the earth with their hooves until it rumbled, and the Tommies flicking their tails more and more rapidly. Waterbuck, topi, wildebeest and zebra flashed ahead of me, and I tried to imagine that my eye was a camera trained on this inspiringly beautiful scene. If we could put on film only a fraction of it, we'd have something rare!

And for a time it looked as if we would succeed. The thousands of animals had not only come closer together, but they were heading in the right direction, toward our cameras. But then something diverted the impala. I have no idea what it was, but they veered to one side, racing up a hill at the end of the forest, a hill that we never dreamed they would climb in the panic of a stampede. Many of the gazelles followed, although some kept straight ahead. The huge herd of eland split, about three quarters of them taking the route over the hill, the others continuing toward the open country that we had thought would be the only natural way for them to go.

My heart sank as I saw the herds split, and I was particularly chagrined to note that most of the animals ran up the hill and out of sight over its crest. It was out of range for our cameramen, who managed to film the watered-down stampede which finally streamed past them.

We were all terribly disappointed, but thrilled at the magnificent sight we had witnessed. The stampede exhilarated me so much that I felt confident we could succeed another time. If we had found so many animals once, we could do it again, and the next time they certainly would run in the direction we planned.

So the next day we went out again with all cameramen, Africans, trucks, and equipment. We found nothing that day, but the next we came upon a fine group of animals, although there were not so many different species. Once more we laid our plans, built platforms in trees, stationed our men and started our stampede. And once more the stubborn creatures took a totally unexpected direction, *away* from our cameras. It was almost as if the animals knew we wanted to film them and were camera-shy.

Five times we organized animal stampedes and four times we failed to film them satisfactorily. Finally we succeeded, although the film can never quite match what I saw on our first attempt. There were not five thousand animals, and there were not as many different species, but hundreds of zebra and wildebeest and impala streamed past our cameras, the impala leaping gracefully as if defying the law of gravity. It is that scene which opens the film, "Zanzabuku."

I hope there will always be a Mara Valley where African animals live as they have for centuries. But even if civilization continues to push the lost valleys and the animal havens further and further until they are obliterated, I will keep that picture of the stampede—and a thousand others—in my mind, giving thanks that I was able to visit Africa in time to see and know the primitive world.

 *XV*

White Men in a Dark Land

I DON'T think it does much good to talk about what might have been. The white men are in Africa, and they are going to stay—in some places and in some capacity. To talk about the injustices of nineteenth-century colonialism helps no one to solve any problem. Whether right or wrong, it was inevitable that the nations of Europe would scramble for possession of rich Africa. And it is apparently just as inevitable that colonialism is on its way out. The question is—will it go out with bloodshed or a handshake? In the process, will Africans become so embittered that they cast out not only whites but all the good they have done and can do? In an effort to stem the tide, will some white authorities undo all the good they have done and kill the best qualities of the Africans? There is so much that African culture can contribute to the world that I hate to see it erased just because of some unpleasant features. Western civilization has plenty of unpleasant features, too, along with its good ones.

On my first trip to Africa, I saw hundreds of Africans with the raw and gaping sores of yaws. On my last trip I saw relatively few. Doctors with penicillin had done the job. Millions of cattle have been saved from rinderpest by governmental and United Nations teams who will, in time, wipe this plague from the entire continent. Thousands of square miles have been cleared of the tsetse fly, and thousands of Africans removed from areas not yet cleared. Maybe they did not understand or like the forcible removal but many lives were saved as a result. In other words, the medical arm of Western civilization has performed wonders for the people of Africa and can do much more in the future. But I can't help wondering if there is any point in removing their diseases and replacing them with our own, especially venereal disease, which has made many women of some tribes sterile.

In many areas, European authorities have ended age-old tribal warfare, but does that help the African much if we proceed to bring him within civilization's orbit, with its more devastating wars? We are teaching hundreds of thousands to read and write, but are we giving them anything to do with their increased knowledge?

In some colonies, yes—the Africans are definitely given greater power, greater scope, and greater rewards in the wake of education and training, as in Britain's Gold Coast and Nigeria, which are nearing independent status. Uganda is still far from that point, but it is administered primarily for the benefit of the Africans, and no white man may own land. In spite of this enlightened administration, the British have in recent years encountered unrest in Uganda, resulting in their exile of the Kabaka, or king. However, after his return in 1955 it was hoped that bad feelings would subside. There are serious problems in Tanganyika, but even here the fundamental goal of the British authorities is native welfare—and since the Territory is a United Nations mandate, there is regular inspection to see that this goal is maintained. As a matter of fact, a great deal of Africa is now under some kind of jurisdiction of the United Nations, and it is to this organization that more and more Africans look for justice, with a reasonable hope of getting it.

Even in the Belgian Congo, political development of the African is now beginning to be part of the goal of the authorities, who used to feel that economic betterment could fully satisfy native desires and aspirations—at least for some time. Big business methods, development of rich resources, more and more industrialization—these ideas dominate the administration of the Congo, where Africans can get schooling, training, good homes, good jobs, good medical attention—and real material progress, European style. In areas removed from industrial regions, the ordinary African is the subject of a chief or king backed by the Belgian authorities, but he is producing more and varied agricultural products, getting some medical care and perhaps some education. In the Congo there is order, there is peace, there is increased productivity, there is steady improvement in the health and material comforts of many. The question is, how long will that be enough for men who see their brothers in other colonies gaining control of their own affairs?

The Congo proves—to me, at least—that much of the agitation of Africans for political independence stems from economic exploitation. There is less trouble in the Congo because of the economic benefits available. In Kenya, the Kikuyu have been fighting partly because they see white farmers on the best lands. In South Africa, mine-workers get only twenty-eight cents a day plus sustenance, and are considered well paid by other Africans.

Even in Kenya, however, where the Mau Mau movement has struck terror to so many hearts, the ultimate aim of British authorities; if not of all the white settlers, is to find some way in which whites and blacks can get along together, with the Africans gaining an increasing voice in running their affairs.

Only in South Africa have white authorities definitely decided to set the clock back, to reverse the trend not only of the rest of the continent but of the rest of the world, where all native majorities have set their feet firmly on the road to independence, in some form and to some degree. I don't think South Africa *can* make the clock move backwards. It may have more whites in proportion to blacks than many African countries or colonies, but still, two and a half million people cannot permanently enslave and degrade ten million. Not in the world of today and tomorrow.

Everywhere there will be tension and some violence, I'm afraid. There are troubles between different tribes within an area, troubles between Africans and whites, troubles between Africans and the East African Indians, troubles between whites and Indians, troubles between haves and have-nots in all groups.

And the tensions will often erupt in strange ways, of which the
Mau Mau terror is one example.

Terror, secrecy, mumbo-jumbo rituals—they are a part of
African heritage. Almost every tribe has believed in witchcraft, with incantations, the casting of spells, the use of amulets and magic preparations from rhino horns or insects or snake
fangs. Medicine men have wielded great power. The physical
fact of the attainment of puberty has been surrounded in most
tribes with elaborate and usually secret circumcision rites. Sacri-
fices, live and often human, have been made to evil spirits. Warring, hunting, planting, migrating, and other activities have
been preceded and attended by dances, rites, spells, invocations
of spirits.

This way of doing things is not something of the dim past
but of the present. The newspapers this past year told of a wave
of witch killings in Uganda. In the Congo there is still an occasional flare-up of killings by the Anyoto, the Leopardmen—although Belgian authorities have just about succeeded in wiping
out this ancient terror.

During my first trip to Africa, in 1937, I visited a jail in
Irumu, the administrative center for the Ituri District and saw
seven members of the Anyoto in a cell, awaiting trial. I had read
and heard a great deal about the Leopardmen, never quite be-
lieving it because it was such sensational Sunday-supplement
stuff. But even the most hair-raising tales about the secret society were no doubt true. My friend, Dr. James P. Chapin, of
the American Museum of Natural History, had first visited
the Ituri region in 1909 and seen a number of Leopardmen
jailed at Avakubi. The Belgian judge there had vowed to wipe
the secret order out of existence, but all others laughed at him
and said it could never be done. He even went so far as to have a
village surrounded and then searched for Leopardmen, who
were caught and hanged. But the killings did not stop. When
the implements of the society—leopard skin and sharp metal
knives shaped like a leopard's claws—were found, the evidence
was pretty conclusive against a suspect. But before all the Leop-

ardmen could be rounded up, someone had to talk, to point out
the leaders. And no one would talk. Members of the society took
a fearful oath which meant more to them than anything the
authorities might do to them.

In 1934, just three years before my first visit, the town of
Beni went through a reign of terror caused by the Leopardmen,
when forty-two Africans were killed in the course of three
months. Since leopards infested the forests in that vicinity, it
was some time before the deaths were ascribed to the secret society. But leopards just don't go on a concentrated campaign—
the way humans do. By great good luck, the authorities in Beni
unearthed a chapter of the society and discovered that a single
witch doctor had organized and instigated twenty-three murders.
The chief of a nearby tribe had been the actual head of the
chapter.

Nobody has ever really been able to figure out the purpose
behind the Anyoto. At one time or another it has no doubt been
used by a chief or witch doctor to gain his own personal ends of
power or vengeance, but that is just a case of using a weapon at
hand, not explaining the existence of the weapon. Apparently it
is very old indeed, perhaps centuries old. While the Wamba section of the Belgian Congo has been its apparent center during
the last few decades, it has also cropped up sporadically in
Nigeria, Sierra Leone, Angola, Kenya and other parts of Africa
that have no easy and obvious means of communication with
each other—except for the white man's means of communication. Drums are powerful, but not that powerful.

There is a fascination in weird and terrible secret societies
for most humans, it seems. The Ku Klux Klan in our own country kept cropping up time after time over a period of sixty or
seventy years and was difficult to root out. And this in a country
that has supposedly rid itself of superstitions and mumbo-jumbo,
a country that lives by the law instead of by terror. So it should
not be surprising that in the continent of superstitions, among
tribesmen without a universal law, a terroristic secret society
keeps alive for several centuries. The Ku Klux Klan had an os-

tensible goal—white supremacy—but its main appeal was building up the ego of members who might otherwise be Milquetoasts.
Perhaps the same psychological truth holds in Africa. But the
Anyoto has never directed its horrible work toward the end of
black supremacy, as might be expected. In the main, the victims of the Leopardmen have been other Africans.

What did the Leopardmen do? They killed other human
beings, and killed them in such fashion so as to make it look as if
a leopard had done the job. But there were often telltale clues
that obviously showed the work was not that of a wild animal.
The killer wore a leopard skin, an exaggerated leopard mask.
He wore an iron bracelet from which four sharp curved knives
extended so that they lay concealed against the palm when the
hand was extended, but stuck out like four claws when the fist
was clenched. Some even carried a piece of wood carved at the
end to simulate a leopard's paw, which they pressed into the
ground around the bodies of their victims. In some cases it was
an actual paw fixed to the end of a stick.

Leopardmen leaped upon solitary victims in the jungle,
slashing at throat and chest savagely, to kill and leave the marks
of the leopard. Others crept into a village at night, entered a
hut and silently killed their victims. They were smart to choose
the leopard as their symbol, of course, since only the leopard
kills for the pleasure of killing, and leaves its prey lying there
without being eaten. But many Leopardmen followed a practice that clearly gave them away. The female breast had a pecul-
iar fascination for them, and some cut off the breasts of a
woman victim before leaving. No leopard could leave such a
mark, of course. So all the leopard slashes and leopard pawmarks
were futile as cover-ups. As a matter of fact, there was always a
question as to just how seriously the members of the Anyoto
wanted to be taken for leopards. The appeal of the order was
probably dependent in part on the paraphernalia, on the method
of killing as well as the killing itself.

In some instances, the amputated breasts were carried to
the leader of the local Leopardmen as proof of killing, in others

they were eaten—even though the killers might not otherwise be cannibals. I heard that in some areas the eyes of victims were taken and later boiled along with the claw-knives to give them vision in the dark and unerring aim for the throat of the next prey. Despite the minor variations, the society of the Leopard-men was essentially the same wherever it cropped up.

During the day, members of the Anyoto might be normal, respected members of their communities whom no one would suspect—another reason the movement was so hard to put down. Nor was there any significant pattern to most of the killings, which might have given a clue to the killers. In most cases, the Leopardmen just killed the handiest victim, although a large proportion seemed to be women. At initiation into the society, perhaps, a most difficult killing was demanded of the new member—his own father, or someone in his own village, whom he had to kill without leaving a clue or causing any suspicion to be directed toward him.

During a rash of Anyoto killings, the tribesmen of the afflicted area are terror-stricken, convinced that the Leopardmen possess superhuman powers. Even when they strongly suspect certain individuals, they will utter not one word to the authorities. Members of a Leopardman's family cannot help knowing, in time, that he has joined the society, but they will not speak. Usually members will willingly die before naming another.

In spite of the almost insuperable difficulties, Belgian authorities have probably been ninety per cent successful in stamping out the Anyoto after close to half a century of unremitting efforts. It occasionally crops up in the Wamba area—apparently the original home of the society. Bill Spees told me within the past two years of a waterman at the mission—a man who seemed mild and well-behaved ordinarily—who was arrested as a Leopardman killer. The Belgians keep a watchful eye out at all times for the first sign that the terroristic group has revived.

With such an organization as the Anyoto living through centuries as a part of African tradition, it is not surprising that such a group as the Mau Mau in Kenya should arise. But there are two significant differences between Mau Mau and Anyoto killings. First, the Mau Mau have no costume such as the leopard skin, no claw-knives to simulate a wild animal. Second, there was a definite purpose behind Mau Mau killings—to drive the white man out of Africa.

This does not mean that only whites are killed. As a matter of fact, far more Kikuyus than whites have been massacred; in one raid only about twenty-five miles from Nairobi, in 1953, more than three hundred African men, women, and children were slaughtered and their huts burned. The total death list of whites, since the Mau Mau terror began, is still under a hundred.

Africans were killed by the Mau Mau in order to intimidate those who cooperate with white settlers, in order to gain—forcibly if necessary—recruits for the Mau Mau sect, and as a general measure for creating fear and gaining power. The fact that some have been forced to take Mau Mau oaths does not make it less effective. One Kikuyu man, who had worked faithfully and happily on a white settler's farm for many years, came to his employer and told him he was leaving. He had been forced to take the Mau Mau oath and might in time be ordered to kill his master which he would then have to do. If he moved to another region, he might have to kill, but not the man toward whom he felt a deep loyalty. He left. He did not want to become a Mau Mau, but once having taken the oath he would obey it and kill when ordered to kill. Obviously in his mind the consequences of failing to abide by the oath would be too great to consider.

Actually there are numerous Mau Mau oaths and variants of these in different localities, where local leaders have added their own embellishments. But essentially they are of two basic types—one for the general run of members and a more stringent oath for the leaders, active terrorists, the shock troops of the sect. The first is strongly nationalist and aims above all to preserve the secrecy and discipline of the organization. The new member swears never to reveal any information about the group or

inform on anyone, to report known enemies to his leader, to follow orders blindly, to steal and even kill if required.

The oath for active terrorists and leaders is bloodthirsty
and blood-curdling, since it demands killing even one's father
or brother if so ordered, the burning of white farmers' crops,
killing of their cattle, and a gory ritual to be performed with
each murdered victim; the Mau Mau must cut off his head, ex-
tract the eyeballs, and drink the liquid from them. This requirement is subject to several variations, each one more gruesome
than the other.

The oath-taking ceremony has always been a revolting ritual designed to impress the new member, appeal to his superstitions and enforce its domination of his thoughts and actions
from that time on. As the movement grew, these rituals reached
new heights of bestiality, as detailed in confessions of numerous
Mau Mau members. When you get thousands of people in an
organization, some are bound to talk, of course, no matter how
dreadful the oath of secrecy. The oath-taking rituals vary considerably but most involve acts with the viscera and genitals of
animals and the drinking of blood. In the sexual aspects of the
ceremonies, menstruating women usually play a prominent role.

The generally unprintable details of these rituals make the
Kikuyu sound like the most depraved and stupid of primitives.
But Dr. J. C. Carothers, a British physician who spent many
years in Kenya and recently made an exhaustive study of the
psychological aspects of Mau Mau, said in his official government
report that the Kikuyu were people of intelligence comparable
with that of other groups anywhere, white or black; that with
training and education they could become capable of the same
work any of us might perform. He concluded, moreover, that the
oaths were originally devised by a highly intelligent and "so-
phisticated" person, and that they appealed strongly to some almost universal human instincts.

The Mau Mau killings, however, didn't seem to make much
sense, at first, since many of the whites slaughtered were farmers

who trusted and helped the Africans the most. Apparently it was because they wanted to eliminate any possibility of reconciliation and thus bring together one extreme group against the other. Men who are highest on the Mau Mau list are continually on the alert against attack, go armed at all times, and are suspicious of even apparently loyal Kikuyu workers. Such men are difficult to murder, so the Mau Mau have confined most of their attacks to the friendly whites, women, old folks and others who offered good targets. The point of the Mau Mau campaign is not so much to kill leaders but to terrorize the entire white community so that whites will leave the country in fear.

Since the native population outnumbers the whites in Kenya more than a hundred to one, the blacks could obviously kill or drive out every European in a concerted attack, if they were willing to sacrifice enough of their own in the battle. Fortunately, the leaders of the Mau Mau movement have not adopted the tactics of the Jivaro Indians against the Spanish back in 1599, about which I learned on my South American expeditions. Spaniards had established three towns on the eastern slope of the Andes and were encroaching on Jivaro territory, taking some Indians as slaves. The Jivaro tribes, which had spent most of their time warring on each other, buried the hatchet and planned a surprise attack. They didn't go in for halfway measures, either. They burned the three towns to the ground, massacred every inhabitant—between twenty and thirty thousand men, women, and children—and poured molten gold down the throat of the Spanish governor because he seemed to love it so much.

Perhaps one reason the Mau Mau have adopted the hit-and-run method designed to terrorize everyone is that they lack firearms. They have tried to raid some small arsenals and have stolen guns from individuals, resulting in the government law imposing severe fines on anyone who loses a gun or allows it to be stolen.

Although I lived for weeks in the Mau Mau country at Hartley's farm, the incident which affected me most deeply did not involve me personally. You'll recall my mention of Lionel Hartley, Carr Hartley's younger brother and one of the finest white hunters in Kenya. Lionel was later killed in a plane crash, but his wife, Diane, continued to live in Kenya, and I saw her at the outset of my 1954-55 trip.

In October, Diane went to visit her mother and her step-father, who owned a farm at Kibereri, in the neighborhood of Nyeri—strong Mau Mau country. Her stepfather, seventy-year-old G. A. Leakey, was not really afraid, however. He had always trusted the Kikuyu and had even been made a blood brother of the tribe. He could not believe that harm could come to him who had always befriended them, so he did not barricade his farm or keep a gun always at hand. On government instructions, he did have in one bedroom a battery-operated rocket signaling system but he never really expected to use it.

The day after Diane arrived for her visit, she and Mr. Leakey and her mother sat down at the table for dinner. Suddenly about thirty Kikuyu, armed with long knives called *pangas*, burst out of the scrub growth behind the house. They slashed to death a Kikuyu cook outside the door and rushed inside. Diane and her mother ran to the bathroom, which had a removable section in the ceiling for gaining entrance to a kind of attic. Diane's mother pushed her up, but before she could climb to safety the Mau Mau found her. They snatched Mrs. Leakey—without seeing Diane in the attic. Since she had just arrived there the day before, it is likely that the raiders did not even suspect that she might be around. In any event, they strangled Mrs. Leakey on the spot, dragged the body outside, and hacked it with their *pangas* until it lay in a pool of blood. They did not kill Mr. Leakey, but carried him off with them.

It was all over in a few minutes, and Diane rushed to the bedroom where she sent up signal flares from the apparatus there. The flares were seen from a government station a few miles away, but meanwhile Diane raced to the next farm to make sure help came. It was there in short order, but it was too late for Diane's mother or for the cook who had been killed. There was no trace of Mr. Leakey. Of five servants, three had vanished. One was held for questioning, but said nothing of value.

An intensive hunt for Mr. Leakey was begun at once, and at one time two thousand members of the security forces were combing the woods and hills for miles around the farm. They finally found some of his clothing in a cave, where they also captured a Mau Mau who was believed to be a leader of the raiding gang. They learned that the old gentleman had probably died in a sacrificial ritual—the reason for his being abducted rather than killed at his farm. A woman in the area had gained great influence over one part of the Mau Mau group, convincing them that she was a kind of prophetess. She had said that if a prominent Englishman could be captured and buried alive in a sacrifice, Mau Mau fortunes would increase and prosper. Mr. Leakey, along with several goats, had apparently been buried alive in this primitive ritual. The authorities were sure enough of this story to give up the search for him.

I saw Diane in Nairobi a few days after this horrible ordeal. She told me that her two children had been expected to visit at the farm the next day. If the Mau Mau raid had come just one day later, she felt sure they both would have been killed. So in spite of her great loss and the shock of the dreadful experience, she found something to be thankful for.

It is easy to see what happens to the ideas and emotions of other Britishers after such a ferocious and senseless killing as this. Patience, understanding and reason fly out the window, and nothing but hatred takes their place. It is difficult for anyone to see any good in any African, after this, so it is greatly to the credit of the British officials and many Kenya leaders that they are trying to meet the threat with decisiveness and yet with understanding. They know that most Kikuyu are not members of the Mau Mau, but they feel that temporarily no Kikuyu can be trusted because it is so difficult to learn who is Mau Mau and who is not. At the outset, the other tribes in Kenya did not succumb to the Mau Mau appeal, but before long the ideas began to find adherents in some groups, including the Masai of the Narok area which was consequently closed at the time of my visit. This was surprising, as the Masai had always been contemptuous of the Kikuyu, whom they drove from the plains to the hills long ago. At the beginning of the Mau Mau terror, the Masai herdsmen offered to recruit three thousand spears for the British to use against the secret society. The authorities declined, sensing the danger that might come if three thousand Masai warriors went on the rampage again.

If the Mau Mau aim was intimidation of the white settlers, it has not worked. In spite of the danger, few Europeans left the country permanently although quite a few sent their wives and children away. While the influx of new white settlers has ceased, most of the whites in Kenya are more determined than ever to stick it out.

But at what cost and with what result? Where does the blame lie in all this mess? If you go back far enough, to the time when the first white colonizers came to Kenya, you might say the blame rests on Europeans who took land away from native Africans to whom it belonged. But that almost takes us into the realm of metaphysics, for the British, for instance, negotiated in good faith with the Kikuyu for occupation of this land —which was comparatively unoccupied—but there was a fundamental misunderstanding which no one realized at the time: the British thought they were acquiring perpetual rights to the land but the Kikuyu conception of land rights was that the inalienable title rested in the tribe. Most of Africa was taken over by European powers, and much of it was cruelly exploited. In the past decades, at least, a new concept of the role of the colonizer has developed, and world opinion asks of colonial powers that they treat indigenous peoples fairly—that they educate and train them to assume eventual control of their territories, or in some instances to share control. In those regions in which whites in good numbers have settled on the land and made it fruitful, they are not likely to leave. They have invested money and years of labor under the protection of a long-established government, just as settlers came to America and were encouraged to pioneer on lands taken from the American Indians.

From one point of view, the white farmer in Kenya is right. But what about the Kikuyu point of view? Well, they sold the land to the white settlers, even if some of them were forced into the transactions. Some Africans continued to live on white farms, more or less as share-croppers. They contributed some labor and produce in exchange for the right to live on the land, keep some cattle, grow food for themselves and families. In time—this began in the thirties—the white farmers were able to take over for cultivation or pasture more and more of the land they had bought. They told the Kikuyu "squatters" to leave. The tribesmen could not understand. Some of them had been born on these farms, had thought of them as *their* pieces of land for decades—or at least had considered that they had some kind of vested right in it. Then they were evicted.

Legally, the farmers were correct, but many Kikuyu do not comprehend European laws or legal processes. Their very concept of ownership is different. They were moved to reserves, land that had been set aside for the Kikuyu by the government. Some of this was beautiful and fertile land, but it was usually forty or fifty miles away from the places where they had always lived and farther from the market for their goods—Nairobi. They were thus handicapped in competing with white farmers and they did not like any of it. Later, when the Mau Mau terror began, most of the remaining squatters were evicted because farmers did not want any Kikuyu living on their land.

For some years the reserves have been bursting at the seams with more people than the land can support. While the white population has for some time remained comparatively stable, the native population has been increasing at a high rate. When I first visited Kenya in 1937 there were approximately three million Africans and about thirty-eight thousand white Europeans there. Today the African population is five million five hundred thousand while the whites number only forty-three thousand. In addition, there are one hundred sixty-five thousand Indians to complicate the political and social situation with a third dissatisfied and potent factor which must be considered in any settlement of Kenya's problems.

If the population continues to increase as it has in the recent past, another decade or two will bring unbearable overcrowding and poverty for the blacks. The whites will be overwhelmed by sheer numbers, and their position will be untenable. Some solution must be found long before such a crisis is reached.

The government has sent agricultural experts into the reserves to help the Kikuyu farmers increase productivity, stop erosion and learn improved methods. Generally the tribesmen have cooperated, but even greater efforts along this line can do no more than scratch the surface of the problem.

Although it is a bitter pill for the diehard white-supremacy settlers to swallow, they must find some way to share the country and its management with the Africans. If they fail, they will eventually have to go—and probably with much bloodshed.

An all-race council now exists in Kenya, consisting of six white Europeans, two Asians, and one African. A more equitable representation seems inevitable if a true multi-racial government is to be inaugurated that will come anywhere near satisfying the Africans. The increase in participation must be gradual, however. From my observation, the Africans of Kenya will for many years need political and economic guidance, for not enough of them are educated to allow for more active participation now. It may well be the fault of the British that the education of the Africans has been so badly neglected, but the fact remains that the vast majority are incapable of self-government today. If the Mau Mau uprising had been successful, it would have been a calamity not only for the one million two hundred thousand Kikuyu but also for the other native tribes of Kenya.

For their own self-protection if for no other reason, the whites in Kenya must set about the urgent task of bringing the Africans to a level of education, security and self-respect that will make them capable partners in the government of the colony.

My lugubrious guess is that the government will perhaps take too-small steps too late, and that impatient, stupid, or selfish nationalist leaders will not give the present multi-racial council a chance to evolve into a true multi-racial government.

I hold in high regard the white settlers. They have worked terribly hard for what they have. Few are rich. They have had to contend with heartbreaking problems, including drought, rinderpest and locusts which have put most of them in debt to the banks. But perhaps their most difficult task lies ahead—helping the African to the point at which he will merit partnership in running a beautiful and productive country.

Will they do it? Judging by the past, it looks unlikely, for there were many plain warnings that a bloody explosion would eventually come. Back in 1922, almost eight thousand Kikuyu marched to government house in Nairobi to protest the arrest of their most prominent leader, Harry Thuku. Police fired into the crowd, killing and wounding many men and women—casualties were estimated at around two hundred. Certainly this did not encourage them to believe that they could get anything from the authorities by mere talk and negotiation. It is significant, too, that the secretary of the organization of which Thuku was the leader was Jomo Kenyatta, who became the head of Mau Mau. He had an early demonstration of the effectiveness of armed force.

During my 1937 trip I saw Kikuyu families being forcibly moved, lock, stock and barrel, from areas in which their ancestors had lived for generations. They didn't like it. On my 1946 trip the pot was definitely boiling, but many Kenya farmers concentrated their attention on berating the British Colonial office for being soft-hearted. Then in the fall of 1952, the pot boiled over with massacre, murder and terror. It should not have surprised the whites of Kenya.

At this writing the Mau Mau killings have subsided. Since the start of the uprising, the Mau Mau have lost approximately

fifteen thousand killed or hanged, while unknown numbers have
been eliminated in internecine struggles and by air bombard-
ment of the Aberdare Mountains and other known hideouts.
There are approximately sixty-five thousand Mau Mau members, sympathizers, or suspects in jails or detention camps, including all the important leaders. But the authorities can't keep
all of them there forever. One may well grant that when they
are released many of the originally lukewarm sympathizers will
have become fanatic and will join a hard core of irreconcilable,
embittered and vindictive terrorists.

It is not a pretty picture, but it will get worse unless the
British take immediate and decisive steps to prove that the
Africans will gain security and eventual, but not too long delayed, partnership. And incidentally, in the process they should
pay more attention to the Kikuyu women, who are high-spirited
and vigorous, and to the youngsters who are being thoroughly
indoctrinated with deep nationalistic fervor.

As in the case of tensions between nations everywhere, and
between one organized group and another, everything would be
fine if you consulted the people concerned *as people* rather than
as members of a group or nation. Ordinary Germans didn't want
to fight ordinary Frenchmen or Englishmen, just as I'm sure
ordinary Russians don't want to fight anyone. Similarly, ordinary Kikuyu natives—even some who are members of Mau Mau
—don't thirst to kill white people. The majority of white settlers
in Kenya want to give adequate good land and a good living—
yes, even a good voice in running their affairs—to the Africans,
even if a bit more education and training are necessary for the
last.

I have come to know hundreds of Africans pretty well, and
I know that they are generally kind, cooperative, helpful. Their
fundamental instincts are good, and they are no more bloodthirsty or cruel than I am. I also know hundreds of whites in
Africa, including officials, settlers, and hunters in Kenya. Except
for some red-necked blusterers of the old school who still want
to live in the last century, they are decent, kind, helpful, coopera-

tive. Their instincts are good and they would like to see other
people, white or black, get fair treatment and lead happy lives.

The white settlers in Kenya lead closer to normal lives than
most Europeans in Africa—except for South Africa which is a
thoroughgoing white civilization. In the Belgian Congo, for instance, there are not many Belgians who settle down and intend
to remain in the Congo for the rest of their lives. Most of them
come out for definitely limited periods, whether they are government officials, missionaries, doctors or supervisory executives in
the many big corporations operating in the Congo. They plan to
go back home some time, although a few find that Africa grows
on them so much that they return to it when they no longer have
to.

Europeans in much of Central Africa are in the same category—temporary rather than permanent residents. These men,
in the main, lead somewhat abnormal lives. Some take African
mistresses, who run their households, bear their children and
develop close attachments. Others find the loneliness and strange-
ness of the life a strain, especially if they must be isolated
from the good-sized cities filled with other Europeans, and take
to drink as if it were a duty.

European women probably find the going rougher than
European men. Wives of officials, et cetera, find that servants are
so easy to obtain that they have nothing whatsoever to do. They
are bored, they feel cut off from their world and the standards
that go with it. Affairs are quite common, and there's an old saying in Kenya that "no one even has an opinion on matters connected with sex."

It is easy to exaggerate such tales, because they make good
copy for short stories, articles and the yellow press. But on the
other hand, there is no use denying that many white men and
women do not lead in Africa the kind of moral lives they would
lead at home. This is particularly true of the men and women
of what might be the middle classes in Africa. The men at the
top are usually too busy and too devoted to their work to have
much time for play of any kind.

I never met a cynical or brutal government official in the Congo, Uganda, Kenya, or Tanganyika. M. Ryckmanns, who was Governor General of the Congo during my first visit and was later Belgium's delegate to the United Nations, is one of the finest men I have ever met, intelligent, dedicated to his task of improving the lot and the futures of the natives of the Congo. His successor, M. Jungers, was Vice-Governor General on my first trips, in charge of Ruanda-Urundi, and a man of the same stripe—strong, kind, intelligent and conscientious.

The same was true of government officials on a lower level, as well as their counterparts in Uganda, Tanganyika and even in troubled Kenya. But, you may say, even good men may be used as the tools of a bad plan. Perhaps, but not in the case of these men. They had great power in determining the plan, for one thing, and were as dedicated to helping the African as are missionaries. There are exceptions, to be sure, but I never encountered any at the highest levels and mighty few at any level.

Among the missionaries and missionary doctors, there are no exceptions at all. Every one of them is thoroughly and completely devoted—and most of them on a practical plane. While the ultimate goal of missionareis may be the improvement of the morals and souls of Africans, they spend most of their time and efforts improving their health and education. The way to save a soul is to save a life first, obviously, and one way to make a man like your God is to make him like you and your way of life.

The old-fashioned missionary was often so shocked at the nakedness of natives that his first idea was to put clothing on them—which may have helped the missionary's soul but had little effect on the Africans. While many of today's missionaries do try to inculcate in their African charges a sense of modesty and decency, most of them I met feel that such things can come later. After spending decades among naked primitives, they themselves are not very upset at the sight of unclothed bodies. They have vigorously combated cannibalism where they found it—one of the methods being to help the African find other sources for meat. They do not encourage polygamy, naturally, but they know better than to fight ancient customs at the outset of their attempted conversions.

Health and education—these are the routes by which the missionaries hope to bring the superstitious into the Christian fold. With some peoples the method seems to work; in others, such as among Pygmies, it has made scarcely a dent even after twenty or thirty years of hard labor. Meanwhile, however, many are being helped. I have visited Catholic, Seventh Day Adventist, Mennonite and other missions in many sections of Central and East Africa and have found in each of them truly dedicated men curing hundreds and thousands of people of dread disease, teaching thousands to write, read, weave, farm, build—and think more clearly. Incidentally, I have been warmly welcomed in all these missions—given food, shelter, invaluable advice about the local tribesmen, and all kinds of help in meeting and photographing them. Without Bill Deans and William Spees, for instance, I could never have penetrated the Ituri Forest as I did. And without the suggestions and help of F. G. Reid and Dr. George W. Allen I probably would never have gone to the fabulous Mara Valley.

Of all these fine men, those who impress me most are the missionary doctors. I have met many in the course of my African trips, but I shall never forget Dr. Roy C. Woodhams. It was in 1937 in the Congo that I visited him and his small "hospital." A mere shack with a wooden operating table and shelves for instruments and drugs, it had been the scene of many life-saving operations and treatments.

Dr. Woodhams told me that medical knowledge alone was not enough to effect cures in the heart of Africa. Before he could conquer sickness he had to conquer superstition and fear. A man bitten by a poisonous snake, for example, was often convinced that death was inevitable. A bite of that snake had killed his tribesmen for generations—why shouldn't it kill him? No medicine man had found a cure, so how could the white medicine man? The difficulty was to get him to believe enough so that he would come in for serum after having been bitten. Even then, he would attribute the saving of his life to magic rather than medicine. On many occasions Dr. Woodhams used the modern equivalent of magic—psychology. Knowing the African's fears and superstitions, he found that many men died just because they were convinced they were going to die, above all if their own medicine men had told them this would happen. Dr. Woodhams was in constant competition with medicine men, but he had devised some effective psychological weapons in that war against witchcraft. The most useful was the hypodermic needle, which his patients concluded was a far more potent gadget than any owned by medicine men. It hurt, for one thing, which proved its power. And it usually cleared up yaws, even before the advent of penicillin. It had also been used on many occasions to cure, with nothing but water, ailments induced or aggravated by fear or superstition. Dr. Woodhams also kept on hand a vile-flavored concoction of no medicinal value but great psychological potency. It tasted so horrible that it instilled great faith in those who drank it. Anything so foul, they knew, was certain to work wonders.

So Dr. Woodhams used not only the knowledge of modern medical science in bringing health to the Africans but diplomacy, understanding and psychology. Above all, he brought love and devotion to his work, which kept him isolated year after year in the heart of a continent of heat, insects, bad smells and loneliness. When I talked to him, he had no desire to leave.

Of all the white men in Africa, one very small and highly special group stands out—the professional white hunters. They have for years received publicity far beyond that of any other class, yet there are probably never more than forty or fifty men earning their livelihoods as hunters. They have no appreciable effect on the course of events in Africa, since they are not concerned in governmental affairs or race relations or economic development. They may carry some weight in matters of game conservation, although they carry out rather than determine broad policies in this field.

Despite their small numbers and their even smaller weight
in important African affairs, they spring to people's minds when
anyone mentions the white man in Africa. Most Americans are
not, never will be, and don't want to be big-game hunters, but
their picture of the white man in Africa is the intrepid white
hunter. He has been glamorized in fiction, fact and movies as
have few characters anywhere.

And here is the odd part of it—the white hunter is, in plain
truth, just about as glamorous and admirable a character as
even the movies portray him. I've met and talked to, and spent
many weeks with, several different hunters and they were probably pretty representative of them all. Lionel Hartley, David Sheldrick, Mark Williams and Russell Douglass were the men I came
to know best among professional hunters, and they even looked
the part—lean, virile, good-looking, courageous. There is about
all white hunters I've known an aura of excitement in reserve.
They spell adventure in their walk, attitude, expressions and
manner.

There are several explanations for this, I think. In the first
place, the job of white hunter attracts a certain kind of man—
one who loves excitement, danger and the outdoors. Of those attracted to the profession, only the best make good—men who
keep calm in the midst of excitement, brave in the face of danger,
and strong enough to withstand the most punishing rigors which
the outdoors can offer—and in Africa they are plenty. Finally,
the life they lead accentuates and strengthens these qualities,
creating in time that aura in which every white hunter moves.

The white hunter has to be much more than just a good
man with a gun. When he goes out on safari with a client, he is
in absolute authority—even if he is a staff hunter on the payroll
of one of the big outfitting companies in Nairobi or Arusha.
Once the hunting expedition goes out from civilization, the
white hunter is boss—not only of his helpers but of the hunting
clients. So he has an air of authority about him, which he must
exercise firmly but with discretion. In the old days before cars
and trucks were widely used, he might be in charge of fifty to

several hundred porters on a safari. This meant he had to know how to handle Africans. He had to know their language, their ways, their foibles. A safari can be ruined by grumbling helpers and worse than ruined by a rebellious group.

The white hunter has to outfit any hunting trip complete —and within the means of the client. The necessary guns, ammunition, tents, food, trucks, gasoline, medicines, and so on are ordered by him. On the really fancy safaris of rich men and rajahs, this means bringing along kerosene-burning refrigerators, tent bathrooms and perhaps carpets; and he must arrange to have plenty of clean, safe water, to have special foods flown to the campsite or dropped by parachute. There are not many such safaris, of course, but each trip has its problems and each one is different.

The white hunter must then find a good campsite, and finally find the game which his client wants to shoot. And that client may turn out to be an expert marksman, a fearful amateur, a bloodthirsty killer of all game in sight, an alcoholic, an amorous woman with or without jealous husband. The professional hunter must keep them all happy, keep out of all embarrassing entanglements, make his clients obey all game laws and see that they get the trophies they want—with appropriate photographs. In the course of the hunt, if the client wounds an animal, no white hunter can leave until he has tracked the wounded animal into bush or jungle and killed it. In doing this, every hunter takes his life in his hands with a regularity that might breed contempt but doesn't.

During the long evenings, on days when it pours rain, on days when no game can be found, the white hunter must try to keep his clients entertained and amused. So he becomes a fine teller of tales, a gracious host, a concocter of amusements varied and suitable. The client must go home happy, because the white hunter has no method of advertising other than satisfied clients. Above all, he must come home alive—and on this score the white hunters of East Africa have a remarkable record.

Without wishing to detract a jot from the admiring picture

I have drawn of the white hunter, I must add that many a hunter is *made* by his African gun-bearer. The hunters themselves will all admit this truth, insisting that a good gun-bearer is the most valuable asset a hunter can have. On my trips I have met several, all good, but none who could compare with Mafuta, whom I've mentioned as gun-bearer for David Sheldrick when he and Mark Williams took me to the Narok area in 1946 in search of lions. I admired him not only for his uncanny knowledge of animals and the country, but for his personality, character and wonderful story-telling. From the Wakamba tribe, Mafuta had been a gun-bearer most of his life. He had worked with Martin Johnson, had been gun-bearer when James Clark obtained his wonderful lion group for the Museum of Natural History. He knew intimately every game area in Kenya and Tanganyika, and could find his way through them easily where no one else could catch a clue as to his whereabouts. When he was with us, I noticed that his alert eyes seemed to be everywhere at once, noting rocks, trees, tracks and all features on the terrain. He would never forget them, either, once he had marked them down on the big and accurate map in his mind.

Mafuta had originally been trained by the great hunter who was called by many other hunters the best of all, Al Klein, who was born in New Jersey and died in Kenya in 1947. But no one could have trained into him the uncanny understanding of animals which he possessed. It sounds rather far-fetched, I know, but Mafuta could and did put himself in the place of animals so that he felt what they felt. Some human beings can do this rather well with other human beings; they are *simpático* in a way that all of us cannot understand. Well, Mafuta was that way with wild animals. He could look at a lion or elephant or rhino and tell me at once if that beast were *kali*, irritable and likely to charge with or without provocation. At other times he would tell me it was safe to approach quite close. And he was always right. Over and over again I saw Sheldrick and Williams depend absolutely upon Mafuta's words about an animal's mood and intentions. When a lion was wounded and disappeared into the bush—always the most dangerous time for a hunter going after him—Mafuta knew where that bloodthirsty creature was hiding, waiting to spring on his pursuers. If you asked him how he knew, he would smile, shrug, and say, "Well, that's where I would hide if I were a wounded lion."

On the 1946 trip we had wandered in our trucks far from Narok, and Sheldrick decided it would be shorter, on our return, to cut across country rather than follow the route we had taken out. Mafuta said that there would be six dongas, or dried out river beds, to cross but that we ought to be able to make it all right. They can be almost impassable at times, with thick thorn-bushes along the banks, rocks and potholes, plus the steep sides. We made three of them all right. When we came to the fourth, it seemed impassable, so the trucks rode along parallel while we looked for an opening. It was Mafuta who found the spot to cross, a spot not even the experienced Sheldrick and Williams noticed. The fifth presented no difficulties, but the sixth was the worst of all. For two hours we rode along beside it, and once again it was Mafuta who found the safe way across it. By that time we had traveled so far off our direct route that Sheldrick and Williams didn't know where we were. But Mafuta knew, gave careful directions, and we arrived back in Narok safely. We all knew that it was Mafuta who had brought us there.

Whenever I think of the increasing difficulties between white and black men in Africa, I think of Sheldrick, Williams and Mafuta. Somehow I wish all racial problems could be solved the way these white men and this black man had solved theirs, working together in harmony and achieving the goal set, a goal helpful to both, in ways that were fair to both. Mafuta was being helped by the knowledge and mechanical equipment of the whites, and the whites were being helped—perhaps their lives saved sometimes—by the special knowledge and abilities of Mafuta. Each partner here retained his individuality, his personality, his own traditions, and yet each helped a common enterprise by contributing what he himself could do better than anyone else.

Making Africa a happy and productive home for millions of blacks and whites is probably one of the most difficult tasks human society has faced, and there is not much time left to meet the challenge—twenty years at most, perhaps only five. Can whites and blacks find the way to cooperate in that short space? If not, the explosion of a continent is sure to spread its devastation over the entire world.

Index

Chevrolet, 13, 25, 146, 208, 243
chiggers, 8, 15, 127, 282
chimpanzees, 21, 59, 61, 207
Chinese, 163
Chrysler Corporation, 128, 186
Chui, 193ff.
cinchona, 33, 140
Clark, Dr. James L., 10, 350
cobra, 117, 282, 283
cobra, spitting, 117
cobs, 50
Coco, 202-03, 204
coffee, 15, 19, 140, 142, 279
Congo, Belgian, 11, 12 13, 14, 22, 23, 26, 44, 48, 50, 82, 101, 145, 164,
    166, 167, 168, 169, 170, 175, 181, 182, 183, 241, 270, 271, 272, 307,
    328, 329, 330, 331, 344, 345, 346
Congo River, 8, 137, 170, 171, 172
"Cook's Pygmies," 59
Coquillon, Johnny, 185, 261, 317, 318
cormorants, 281
cornac, 271ff.
cotton, 15
Cowie, Col. Merwyn, 296
crane, crested, 148, 157, 282
cranes, 282, 311
crocodile, 47, 139, 237ff., 242, 243, 244, 245, 246, 272, 304, 306,
    315, 317
cuckoos, 282

daisies, 21
dance
  elephant, 78ff.
  Masai, 277ff.
  Pygmy, 76ff.
  Watussi, 155
Danish, 163
Damien, Brother, 312
darters, 281
Darwin, Mr., 207
Daudi Chiva, 239
Dead Sea, 20
Deans, Bill, 61, 82, 83, 88, 94, 95, 98, 115, 116, 346